SOMEONE to WATCH OVER ME

SOMEONE to WATCH OVER ME

OVER ME

A PORTRAIT OF ELEANOR ROOSEVELT AND THE TORTURED FATHER WHO SHAPED HER LIFE

ERIC BURNS

PEGASUS BOOKS

NEW YORK LONDON

SOMEONE TO WATCH OVER ME

Pegasus Books Ltd.
148 W 37th Street, 13th Floor
New York, NY 10018

First Pegasus Books cloth edition March 2017

Interior design by Maria Fernandez

Library of Congress Cataloging-in-Publication Data is available.

ISBN: 978-1-68177-328-5

10 9 8 7 6 5 4 3 2 1

Printed in the United States of America
Distributed by W. W. Norton & Company

For
Lorraine Battipaglia,
il mio miracolo,
sempre, sempre

*Elliott Roosevelt and his beloved daughter, Eleanor, his little Nell, whom
he treated like no one else, and thus made all the difference.*

Elliott, after having returned from India, in his dashing younger days that fooled everyone

"The First Lady of the World"

CONTENTS

SOMEONE to WATCH OVER ME

THE PROBLEMS OF THE STORY

ELLIOTT BULLOCH ROOSEVELT, ONE OF the two costars of this book, was the brother of Theodore Roosevelt and the father of Eleanor. Which means he was the sibling of one president of the United States and the father-in-law of another. It is a claim no other American can make.

Yet to historians and biographers, he has had very little relationship at all. The former often ignore Elliott in their volumes, or perhaps toss him a handful of lines, something in the manner of an aside when they are writing about Eleanor; for the most part, though, he is an insignificant figure in a significant era. Biographers might give him more attention—a few paragraphs, a few pages, perhaps even a chapter's worth of information scattered throughout their more-thorough tales of his daughter's life. But nowhere is Elliott examined in detail; he remains a shadowy figure, a man of puzzling behavior and unclear motives in a family of more illustrious men and women. Yet it is these very shadows that make him worth knowing. Or worth trying to know—for his was not a life that lends itself to easy entrance, a clear interpretation.

According to my research, and that of others who have assisted me, no one has ever written a book about Elliott Roosevelt, and I have managed to turn up only two magazine articles about him, both of them helpful but limited, and both in publications of which you have likely never heard: *The Freeholder* and *The Hudson Valley Regional Review*. Fortunately, the magazines provide bits and pieces of information not available elsewhere.

I also found a feature story about Elliott's exile from his family, which will be explained later, in a long-ago edition of the *Richmond Times-Dispatch*. As far as I know, no one else who has written about this particular Roosevelt has utilized these sources.

However, the FDR Presidential Museum and Library in Hyde Park, New York, has a complete, or nearly complete, collection of Elliott's letters, especially to his daughter, and they were indispensable to the writing of this book. For the most part, they cover only a two-year period, but they gave me not only a sense of the man's character but also an understanding of the tribulations that he both suffered and inflicted on others. Further, they revealed the strength of will he exerted to hide these tribulations from his beloved daughter. He loved Eleanor more than anyone else ever did, certainly including her husband. And he influenced her character more than anyone else ever did, both profoundly and beneficially, despite himself. It seems impossible, but truth sometimes appears in disguise.

It is this influence that prompted me to write *Someone to Watch Over Me*, so intriguing is it to contemplate how a father like Elliott could have produced a daughter like Eleanor. Especially considering the hostility—or, less harshly, the lack of rapport—between Eleanor and her mother.

The letters, then, both to and from Elliott Roosevelt, have enabled me to acquaint myself with the man as much as any author has yet been acquainted with him, or so I like to think. And they have enabled me to provide him with the most prominent role he has yet known in a book, even though it is not a book of great heft.

But although the letters were a solution to the problem of the man's relative anonymity, they raised another problem the moment I opened the first of several boxes that contained them. Most of the letters are undated. How was I to know where to place them in the narrative, to learn where an individual letter fit into the order of events?

The answer proved to be simpler than I had initially thought; already familiar with the events about which I was writing, I now had to become just as familiar with the correspondence. I read it diligently, much of it more than once, and as I found out more and more about my two principals, I became more and more able to determine the dates upon which they wrote or received mail from each other. It is upon these deductions, and occasional certainties, that I have relied. Any mistakes I have made . . . well, I can do no more than apologize for them in advance. Regardless, I am certain that they are few in number and, more to the point, that they do no harm. The essential truths, so compelling about this most unusual of fathers, are captured on the pages.

As for the letters that *are* dated, it should go without saying that I have been able to incorporate them into the text without difficulty.

In a sense, *Someone to Watch Over Me: A Portrait of Eleanor Roosevelt and the Tortured Father Who Shaped Her Life* is a sequel to my previous volume, *The Golden Lad: The Haunting Story of Quentin and Theodore Roosevelt*. In both books, what I have done is ignore much about the public lives of this famous family in favor of the personal. And in both cases, I mean "personal" to refer to the bond between parent and child, how and why it was formed, and what the consequences of the bond proved to be for both individuals.

In this book, however, I have found a very different kind of parental love for a child than I did with Theodore and Quentin, a love that could easily have been destructive for the little girl. Perhaps *should* have been destructive. Yet, somehow, it contributed more than any other factor to her unlikely rise to eminence, and to her becoming the most esteemed woman of the twentieth century. This particular story has never been told before, at least not in something close to its entirety.

It was a painful ascent from childhood for Eleanor Roosevelt. I trust I have been both accurate and properly analytical in describing its steepness and the extraordinary, and in many ways mysterious, role that was played by her father, Elliott.

PROLOGUE

HUMAN RIGHTS

The date: December 10, 1948.

The time: 3:00 A.M.

The place: Paris, France.

The occasion: A meeting of the United
Nations General Assembly, running late.

SUDDENLY, ACCORDING TO *NEW YORK TIMES* correspondent Richard
N. Gardner, "something happened that never happened in the
United Nations before or since. The Delegates [*sic*] rose to give
a standing ovation to a single delegate, a shy, elderly lady with a
rather formal demeanor but a very warm smile."

The lady had spoken to the general assembly about her topic many times before, both in Paris and elsewhere, as well as to other groups at other venues. But tonight was different. Tonight she was not urging that the document about which she would speak be passed by the UN. For the document, finally, *had* been passed. Tonight the title of her address was "On the Adoption of the Universal Declaration of Human Rights."

She was restrained, but could not have been more pleased.

"Mr. President, fellow delegates," she began. "The long and meticulous study and debate of which this Universal Declaration of Human Rights is the product means that it reflects the composite views of the many men and governments who have contributed to its formulation. Not every man nor every government can have what he wants in a document of this kind. There are of course particular provisions in the Declaration before us with which we [the United States delegation] are not fully satisfied. I have no doubt this is true of other delegations, and it would still be true if we continued our labors over many years."

There must have been some among the men who listened to her, if not a majority, who sat in wonder—not so much at the words to which they were listening but at the person who spoke them. For it was she, more than any other single member of the United Nations, who was responsible for the Declaration's passage. A tall woman but of unprepossessing appearance. A woman of iron will, yet with a voice now gentled by age. And a *woman*. It was 1948, remember, and there were no more females working under the aegis of the United Nations than there were in any of the world's other prestigious organizations.

"I should like to comment briefly on the amendments proposed by the Soviet delegation. The language of these amendments has been dressed up somewhat, but the substance is the same as the amendments which were offered by the Soviet delegation in committee and rejected after exhaustive discussion. We in the United States admire those who fight for their convictions, and the Soviet delegation has fought for their convictions. But in the older democracies we have learned that sometimes we bow to the will of the majority. . . . I feel bound to say that I think perhaps it is somewhat of an imposition on this Assembly to have these amendments offered again here, and I am confident that they will be rejected without debate."

Rejected they were. "'The Russians seem to have met their match in Mrs. Roosevelt,'" the *New York Times* observed.

And it was not surprising. The woman at the podium was no one to cross, as she had proven in steering the Universal Declaration of Human Rights to passage in the first place. "Determined to press the Declaration to completion, Mrs. Roosevelt drove her colleagues mercilessly," it had been stated in the piece. "There were fourteen-, sixteen-hour days and some delegates may have secretly whispered the prayer ascribed to President Roosevelt: 'O Lord, make Eleanor tired!' A delegate from Panama begged Mrs. Roosevelt to remember that United Nations delegates have human rights, too."

"The Soviet amendment to article 20," Eleanor continued, in the first hours of December 10, 1948, "is obviously a very restrictive statement of the right to freedom of opinion and expression. It sets up standards which would enable any state practically to deny all freedom of opinion and expression without violating the article. . . ."

Outside the auditorium, the darkness remained at its predawn blackest. Inside, Eleanor Roosevelt, whom the Lord had not seen fit to tire, still had more to say. . . .

PART ONE

ELLIOTT

❖

A S A CHILD, SHE ADORED him. She was Daddy's little girl and could not have been prouder. He was the only security that Eleanor Roosevelt would know for most of her childhood, the only constant source of encouragement and, when necessary, forgiveness. She found him "charming, good-looking, loved by all who came in contact with him." She, of course, loved him more than anyone. The feeling was mutual.

Elliott Roosevelt, tenderhearted and exuberantly affectionate toward his only daughter, had perhaps practiced such feelings by reacting similarly toward his parents. At thirteen, he wrote, "Oh! My darling Sweetest of Fathers I wish I could kiss you." In another missive, he referred to his father as:

Dear old Govenor—for I *will* call you that not in Publick
but in private for it does seem to suit you, you splendid

3

Man just my ideal, made to govern & doing it so light
and affectionately that I can call you by the name as a
pet one . . .

He longed for his father's daily return from work and was saddened when his work took him away from home for a few days.

As for his mother, she was to Elliott "little Motherling," or "his
sweet little China Dresden," and it was said that "Elliott had a
special claim on her affections." When she died of typhoid fever,
her twenty-four-year-old son found himself suddenly adrift, for "[s]
he had been his anchor." In the wake of her passing, Elliott's pain
was physical as well as emotional. He was revisited by a fever that
had beset him when traveling through the Himalayas three or four
years earlier, although it seemed worse the second time around;
for relief, he turned not to medicine but to alcoholic beverages. He
could not imagine life without Martha Bulloch Roosevelt. None of
his three siblings, including his older brother, Theodore, would miss
her as much as he did. It might have been the trauma that started,
or at least was the first sign of, the decline that would eventually
seem inevitable.

But worse was to come. His father, whom Elliott worshipped even
more than his mother, had yet to pass away.

❖

To HIS AUNT, MRS. JAMES Bulloch, the child was her "Ellie boy," or
sometimes just Ellie, and to a few other members of the family he
was little Nell, sharing the nickname with the angelic but terribly
mistreated little girl in Charles Dickens's *The Old Curiosity Shop*.
It was, of course, an unusual nickname for a male, but all who saw
Elliott found it appropriate. He was, after all, "decidedly pretty."

Which is not to say that there was anything soft about him, anything effeminate. To the contrary, he was what we would today refer to as a man's man: "dashing, outgoing, volatile and sensual." He was, in other words, an unusual combination of traits.

The example he set for others was sometimes a fearless one. "As a youth he exhibited leadership, athletic prowess, intellectual potential, poetic introspection, a curious mind." He demonstrated his athletic prowess by rowing, running, sailing, wrestling, boxing, and, when he reached his early twenties, by mastering polo and hunting big game—a remarkable range of physical talents that he would try extending, much to his regret, to circus performing.

A "blessedly robust" fellow, Elliott was also a weight lifter, often in competition with Theodore, his older brother by a year and a half. But, after conquering the asthma that plagued his earliest years, Theodore always outdid Elliott—lifting more pounds, accumulating more reps, and many times ending his exertions with a hearty, self-congratulatory laugh. Laughing at *me*? Elliott might have wondered. But he didn't; it was not his style. He believed Theodore was entitled to think highly of himself. *He* thought highly of Theodore. Theodore would influence his life in so many ways, would in time take the place of his father—although in circumstances so different from those of childhood, so much more troubling.

⊰◇⊱

ELLIOTT FELT "PROTECTIVE OF HIS elder brother" when he was battling asthma, and prided himself on keeping the bullies away if necessary. But it was not necessary for long, as Theodore conquered his affliction with a punishing physical regimen, of which weight lifting was only one part.

When Theodore's asthma was no longer a problem, when Elliott was no longer needed as bodyguard, the boy lost a sense of purpose. As a result, the dynamic between the brothers changed. Theodore began urging Elliott to join him in the boxing ring and on the wrestling mats. Although reluctant, the younger boy complied. Now the elder had more about which to laugh—landing punch after punch, pinning Elliott's shoulders time after time. "By showing Elliott up," writes one of Theodore's scores of biographers, he "proved to himself that he was the better man. He relished beating Ellie as often as he could . . . in contests of strength and intellect."

Ellie, however, ignored Theodore's "aggressive egotism." As far as anyone could tell, it did not affect his feelings for "Thee," a pet name for the boys' father that had been passed down to his first-born child. He answered to it, however, only in his youth and only to his family. He also answered, for a few years, to "Tede," properly spelled "Teedie." Regardless of what he was called, though, as Theodore surpassed Elliott in athleticism and outshone him in academic pursuits, he began to suspect that Elliott's feelings, rather than turning resentful, began to approach idol worship. He was right.

> Oh, Father, [Elliott wrote] will you ever think *me* a "noble boy" you are right about he is one & no mistake a boy I would give a good deal to be like in many respects.
>
> If you ever see me not stand by Thee you may know I am entirely changed, no Father I am not likly [*sic*] to desert a fellow I love as I do my Brother even you don't know what a good noble boy he is & what a splendid man he is going to be as I do. No, I love him. I love him very *very* dearly & will never desert him and if I know him he will *never* desert me.

On a later occasion, Elliott learned that his brother had triumphed on some issue or another as an assemblyman in the New York State legislature. "Has not our dear Thee done well," he wrote to his younger sister. Notice no question mark; Elliott was telling, not asking.

Later still, as a young adult traveling in Europe and Asia, Elliott heard that Theodore had purchased land upon which he and his wife could "build their dream house." Elliott wrote to his brother immediately. "It delights me beyond all bounds, to see the way you have 'gone in' for everything as a son of the dear old father should, and I will come back ready and eager to put my shoulder by yours at the wheel, Thee."

Thee enjoyed getting the message, and others like them. Actually, he enjoyed most of his communications and time spent with Elliott. Despite finding his brother insufficiently competitive anymore and too starry-eyed, Theodore held on to a regard for him. In fact, in at least one activity, he was willing to admit that Elliott outperformed him. "He had always envied the ease with which Elliott rode and shot . . ." and was never capable of it himself. When Theodore wrote *Hunting Trips of a Ranchman*, a book about his adventures in the Badlands of South Dakota, he dedicated the volume "to that keenest of sportsmen and truest of friends, Elliott Roosevelt."

But relationships between brothers, especially when they are close in age, are often complicated matters, and "the long competition still smoldered." Eventually, when the boys were no longer boys but men in their thirties, it would become destructive, with Theodore forced into a decision that would hurt both men in different ways. He believed he had no choice. Somewhere inside, Elliott might even have agreed. But he would find that Theodore's words at the time were as punitive as his actions, and, thus, hurtful, so very hurtful. From that point on, the relationship between the two men would be severed, until Elliott's death. Only then would Theodore relent. And by then, it would be too late.

But this sundering was still in the future for the two brothers, and no one could have seen it coming when both were children.

⬥

To MOST PEOPLE, THEODORE WAS the most admirable of the family's four youngsters. But not to all. As was observed in the *Hudson Valley Regional Review* story on Elliott, he "was not self-righteous, as was his brother Theodore, nor had he much of Theodore's combativeness and pomposity. He was immensely well liked everywhere he went for his generosity, his tenderness, and his unaffected way of talking to people. What the other person had to say in a conversation was all that mattered to him."

John S. Wise, an author, attorney, and, for a term, the governor of Virginia, was a friend of the extended Roosevelt clan, and spoke one day of Theodore. Then he changed the subject to his brother. Elliott was "the Roosevelt he liked best," he said, "about whom the general public knew little or nothing." A shame, Wise thought, as the young man was "the most lovable Roosevelt I ever knew."

> He was one of my earliest acquaintances in New York and our attachment grew from the moment of our first meeting until his death. Perhaps he was nothing like so aggressive or so forceful a man as Theodore, but if personal popularity could have bestowed public honors on any man there was nothing beyond the reach of Elliott Roosevelt.

Even one of the boys' two sisters, a year and a half younger than Elliott, had reason to prefer him to the future president. "How different people are," Corinne Roosevelt opined once when all were adolescents, noting that "there is Teddy, for instance, he is devoted to me . . . but if I were to do something that he thought very weak or wrong, he would never forgive me, whereas Elliott no matter how much he might despise the sin, would forgive the sinner . . ."

It was a perceptive comment for Corinne to have made at so young an age.

⊰◈⊱

REACHING HIS EARLY TWENTIES, ELLIOTT lived grandly in New York, a fixture in the society columns, a fixture at the events that the society columns found so fascinating. He was seen as "a remarkable combination of grace, beauty, and talent." He went to all the right places with all the right people. In fact, the sight of his carriage parked outside of a home or restaurant or theater often indicated that it *was* the right place, at least for the night. He ate the finest of foods and drank the most expensive of champagnes and was always quick to toast someone else. He was, by acclimation, "one of the most popular and attractive men in late Victorian New York society."

More than that, he was regarded as "one of society's great gallants. His haunts were the Knickerbocker Club and Meadow Brook [a private establishment where the principal activities were hunting, polo, and self-aggrandizement]. . . . 'A young lady's cup flowed over,' said Daisy Harriman, 'when she was asked down to Meadow Brook,' especially by Elliott Roosevelt." And in the words of Joseph Lash, one of Eleanor's two most comprehensive biographers, her father's "appeal to women of his Victorian day was undeniable; it went beyond his effortless humor, good looks, and flawless manners. 'If he noticed me at all, I had received an accolade,' one of his many female admirers said."

In the end, though, there would be only two female admirers who mattered to Elliott. One of them, whom he had yet to meet, was his wife, a woman with so splendid a pedigree that she could trace her ancestors back to eminence at the time of our nation's founding; "one signed the Declaration of Independence and another administered the oath of office to George Washington." Two other relatives of long ago served as secretary of state.

The other female, who would come to matter most of all to Elliott, was the daughter his wife would bear him.

⬥

WHEN SHE WAS FIVE OR SIX, says Eleanor, her father introduced her to his charity work, impressing upon her the need for such service from people as fortunate as they. It might have been his pleasure to frequent the Knickerbocker Club and Meadow Brook, but it was his duty, he told Eleanor, to attend places far less glamorous. He "took me to help serve Thanksgiving dinner in one of the newsboys' clubs," she would write in her autobiography, a club that had been founded by Elliott's father, Theodore Sr. And Eleanor would write that Elliott "was also a trustee of the Children's Aid Society for many years. My father explained that many of these ragged little boys had no home and lived in little wooden shanties in empty lots, or slept in vestibules of houses or public buildings or any place where they could be moderately warm, yet they were independent and earned their own livings." Elliott was proud of them, of their grit, their perseverance in daunting circumstances. Not believing he had such strength himself, he enjoyed his association with those who did. They might have been boys on the outside, but they were men on the inside, and Elliott wanted Eleanor to appreciate their fortitude as much as he did.

In fact, there was something in her father's voice that might have suggested he was jealous of the boys.

Odd, Eleanor could easily have thought, why would a man of her father's pedigree envy those of lesser years with no pedigree at all? Did he question his pedigree? Did he believe it did not provide all it seemed to provide? And if something was missing, what might it be?

It was her auntie Gracie who continued the girl's education in philanthropy by taking her to the New York Orthopedic Hospital, where Elliott also volunteered, and of which his father had again been one of the founders. Elliott helped out in whatever ways he could, often doing tasks that other volunteers found too demanding or unpleasant. Sometimes, when staff physicians and nurses were otherwise engaged, he assisted in amputations, although he did nothing that required specific medical knowledge. As for Eleanor, who sometimes wandered freely around the hospital, she recalled seeing "innumerable little children in casts and splints. Some of them lay patiently for months in strange and curious positions."

It was a curiously poignant sight for Eleanor, meaningful to her not just because of Theodore Sr.'s and Elliott's connection to the institution.

Although not as seriously injured or deformed as the patients she visited, Eleanor was herself the victim of an orthopedic mal-formation, a curvature of the spine. As a result, she spent several of her childhood years wearing "a steel brace which was vastly uncomfortable and prevented my bending over." But the sight of so many other children who had greater woes than she, forced to spend so much time "in strange and curious positions," made Eleanor more patient with her own difficulties than she might otherwise have been.

It seems to have been precisely what her father had in mind.

The brace, however, was visible through her clothes, an abnormal protrusion, and would prove to be yet one more reason for the sorrows inflicted on her early years.

◆

AT ELLIOTT'S REQUEST, ELEANOR'S MATERNAL grandmother, Mary Livingston Ludlow Hall, took her to help decorate the Christmas tree in the babies' ward at yet another hospital. And as the holiday approached during Eleanor's seventh year, she witnessed what she would believe to be the greatest act of kindness she had witnessed in her life.

One night, Elliott left the family house for a walk in the brisk, winter air. When he returned, more than an hour later, his daughter noticed, he was hugging himself, shivering, no longer wearing his overcoat. He had acquired the coat only a few weeks earlier, an expensive purchase that he considered the highlight of his wardrobe, and he had been wearing it as he left the house. When Eleanor asked her father what happened to it, he casually told her that he had given it away, having encountered "a small and ragged urchin who looked cold." Elliott explained to his daughter that he had other coats. The boy on the street did not.

On occasions like this, it is no wonder that Eleanor's admiration of her father knew no bounds. "He was the one great love of my life as a child," she said, and would remain so long after she learned why the rest of the family felt otherwise.

◆

IN 1880, AT THE AGE of twenty, Theodore married, and Elliott served as his best man. He was, Theodore would later state, the only person

12

he ever considered to stand at his side. When the ceremony ended, Elliott and the groom exchanged handshakes, back slaps, and best wishes, and then the younger brother bid his family adieu and sailed for London, the first stop on a round-the-world trip that would mark the apogee of his career as a hunter.

But not his apogee of reckless spending.

Theodore Sr., known simply as "Senior" to some and "Greatheart" to others, had long been a successful New York businessman. He had died at the age of forty-six, two years before Theodore's wedding and Elliott's journey, and the last days of his struggle with cancer of the bowels were excruciating.

As the illness worsened, consuming him, Elliott did everything he could to ease the suffering and alter the outcome. He laid a cold washcloth across his head, gave him sips of water, held his hand as if the boy could squeeze out the man's anguish. "He was so mad with pain," Elliott said, "that beyond groans and horrible writhes and twists he could do nothing." At one point, his children had to hold him down on the bed so he would not tumble off. "Oh my God my Father," Elliott cried, "what agonies you suffered." Historian David McCullough tells us that Elliott's "devotion to his father over the last week or so of his father's life had been heroic. He had hardly taken time to eat or sleep. He was ill, close to a complete collapse, his 'young strength . . . poured out,' as [his sister Corinne] remembered even before the day began."

All of New York took notice of Greatheart's passing. "He was extolled from a half-dozen pulpits and by the editorial pages of nearly every newspaper in the city . . . praised for his 'high moral purpose' . . . 'his singular public spirit' [and] for preserving the honor of a great family name."

As for Elliott, he could not think in such lofty terms. His loss was personal, not civic. He "seemed demolished by the loss of his father; certainly he felt confused and lonely." His recovery was so slow as to be unnoticeable to some, and in the view of his siblings, never complete. They believed that, if something had changed in him after his mother died, the change was exacerbated with both parents now gone. It might have been subtle at first, but eventually it became all too noticeable to all too many people.

Upon resuming his life, which at the time meant a return to classes at Harvard, Elliott was still emotionally raw. He took to his diary more than his schoolbooks, and among other things recorded his father's last words, whispered in his ear. It was as close as he could come to consolation. His father assured him that "I had never caused him a moment's pain . . . that after all I was the dearest of his children to him." Not Theodore, who would go on to be the most famous of the brood. No, the dearest was Elliott, and he held on to the thought with the tightest grip.

♦

ELLIOTT'S SORROW WAS EASED SOMEWHAT by the inheritance that Senior had provided to his four children. Theodore and his sisters, Corinne and Anna (known as Bamie), handled their money responsibly. Elliott, at times, seemed to be scattering it to the wind or, more accurately, to New York's most elegant vendors of nightlife. Theodore was now a married man, while Elliott was scattering even more of his father's posthumous largesse to those who provided ocean vessels and foreign travel; his trek abroad was first-class in all ways possible. As was his reception upon arrival.

Blanche Wiesen Cook, who has written the other comprehensive biographies of Eleanor, summarizes Elliott's journey. "From the beginning, he was treated like royalty by countless friends who dedicated themselves to his care." The Roosevelt name opened doors even on the other side of the world.

❖

DEPARTING FROM LONDON, HE JOURNEYED overland to Italy, where he and his party rested for a few days before moving on to India, his principal destination. Elliott's first impression was not the exotic landscape, the palatial architecture, or the majesty of the animals he sought to slay; it was, rather, the opposite—the "ocean of misery and degradation" around him: "paupers, beggars, children whose ribs showed through their chests." The sight, he found, was horrifying, like nothing he had ever seen. It "might teach our 'lovers of men' to know new horrors and sadness that the mortal frames and still more the Immortal Souls of Beings in God's image made, should be brought so low. The number and existence of these some millions of poor wretches has upset many preconceived notions of mine."

But there was none of this misery for Elliott. He was greeted in India as warmly as he had been in London. "Arriving in Bombay in mid January he was put up at the Byculla Club and provided with a full-time servant who slept outside his door. There were lunches ('tiffins') in his honor, a round of elaborate dinners." He was made to feel like "a grand prince," he wrote to his family, confessing, "I would not trust myself to live here. There is no temptation to do anything but what you please." Elliott seems to have resisted temptation—most of it, at any rate—but could not make himself feel at ease, finding his accommodations and experiences "all too Arabian night–like."

His ruminations aside, however, there was the sporting life to lead, and from this he took much satisfaction. Elliott's greatest triumph in India was shooting and killing one of the largest tigers ever seen by any of the men accompanying him, measuring more than nine feet in length and standing three and a half feet tall. But he would stand no more. Elliott fired several shots into the animal, the final blow being expelled from a weapon called the Bone Crusher. "By George," he exclaimed, "what a hole that gun makes." He wished that Theodore could have been with him. He would certainly show him a photograph that would be taken of man and beast. Elliott believed his brother would be impressed by the feat.

Perhaps so. More likely, he would have scoffed. Having already brought down a bear with his own rifle, Theodore would probably have pointed out "that a grizzly's size and ferocity would certainly enable it to make short work even of the largest tiger."

Although Elliott seems still to have been regarded as the preeminent hunter in the family, he was about to give up the mantle. Theodore would eventually surpass him—and by a multitude of kills. The younger brother and his slain prey would fill but a few picture frames. By the time the elder brother had yielded the White House and completed a year's safari in Africa, his carcasses would fill several museums, including yet another institution that his late father had helped found, the American Museum of Natural History in New York. Theodore's safari would also result in shipments of animals and animal parts to the Smithsonian Institution, and the two showcases would find themselves so overwhelmed by contributions that they would distribute many of them to other museums across the country.

Once again, Elliott could not compete.

At least his father, he felt sure, would have enjoyed the picture of him by the tiger.

❖

His social life in India, shepherded by friends from New York, was at times frantic. They were "all of them hard-drinking, fast-living, dedicated sportsmen accustomed to luxury and service." It was because of his companions that his pangs of conscience began to ease and he accustomed himself to the luxury forced upon him. "In fact, he rather swooned over the manners of 'the quiet service—no sound of boots, for the boys go without them, and the clothes make no noise. They are certainly wonderful servants. . . .'" On one of his last nights in India, Elliott was escorted to dinner "through long lines of motionless blacks holding flaming torches." He smiled through the procession, but although his conscience was troubling him less now, it was not dormant. Silently cursing British colonialism for imposing such conditions on India's poor and disenfranchised, he also cursed himself for taking advantage of them and began to wish he were a man of greater character, or at least one who could make sense of his contradictory feelings. He would later confess that he could not understand the fuss people were making over him, "for if ever there was a man of few resources and moderate talents, I am he, yet all events and people seem to give me the best of times on my holiday visit."

Theodore, Elliott knew, would have had no such misgivings. He would have strutted through the corridor of torches as if it were his due, perhaps expecting even more illumination, contrasted with more black lackeys providing it. Theodore would probably have written a book about his experiences in India, although surely not one as introspective as the volume Elliott was now longing to produce. And, in fact, started to produce.

Later, he would be "'working up' his travel notes, compiling his letters and journal entries, with the thought of doing a book on big-game hunting." But he never put a word on paper. He did not have it in him, and was disappointed in himself.

For Theodore, on the other hand, *Hunting Trips of a Ranchman* was not a fluke. Man of action though he was, he produced more than thirty volumes of history and adventure in his fifty-nine years of life.

❖

ELLIOTT MADE HIS WAY HOME by stopping first to Ceylon, today's Sri Lanka. There he killed two elephants—one of which, particularly stubborn, required sixteen shots to be sent to his eternal rest. Next it was on to Singapore, Saigon, and Hong Kong, among other, briefer stops, before crossing the Pacific and making port weeks later in San Francisco. Then came a long, wearying and filthy train trip cross-country before finally arriving, messier than his family had ever seen him, at the Roosevelt home in New York. His big brother did not care about his appearance, bear-hugging him in welcome, exclaiming "What a fellow that is." Elliott had been abroad for a year and four months. He settled back in America just in time to be named one of two godfathers to a new infant in the family, Franklin Delano Roosevelt. His journey was, thus, bookended by prominent ceremonial roles in the lives of the extended family's two presidents of the United States.

Elliott was relieved to be back on familiar turf, and deeply satisfied with his exploits. Several years later, he would relive them, telling exaggerated versions to Eleanor.* The little girl would bounce on her father's knee as she learned that he was a man of derring-do, a fearsome gamesman, a world traveler venerated wherever he went. Eleanor beamed at every word.

What she would *not* learn, not until later in life, was that, although the journey had started out grandly for Elliott, it did not end the same way. "In his travels to reach the high Himalayas," author Mason White reports, "he came down with a fever that made him so weak

---

* Theodore would do the same thing with his adventures as a Rough Rider during the Spanish-American War, sanitizing them and converting them into bedtime stories to which his children, four of them boys, listened avidly.

he had to give up the expedition without having bagged the ibex and markhor he had so eagerly sought." The damage to his health in the long term, certainly including his mental health, would prove more severe than the damage to his ego.

But, as White continues about Elliott in the short term, "he made a triumphant return to New York society. That he had hunted and traveled in a country where very few Americans had gone before him made him seem more glamorous than ever."

Especially, as it turned out, to a lovely woman, if distant and self-engaged, named Anna Rebecca Ludlow Hall. She was a creature of a totally different sort from those he had been stalking abroad, although, as would later become apparent, possessed of her own dangers for the successful stalker.

ANNA

I N THE YEARS AFTER THE Civil War, there was a reconstruction of sorts in the North just as there was, or was supposed to have been, in the South. The latter, in many places, had to rebuild itself from ashes and scorched farmland, and the task was as long as it was arduous. But in time, new homes and commercial establishments rose on land where the old ones had been razed by battle, new industries claimed their own ground, fields became fertile again with fruits and vegetables, and institutions and traditions were either renewed or substituted for those no longer viable.

Under pressure from the federal government, the South discovered a new basis, actually bases, for a healthy economy, one that would take the place of the society whose foundation had long been the forced labor of enslaved African-Americans. Not that the latter was eradicated; its presence, however, now became less pervasive, and as decade succeeded decade, African-Americans gradually began to assume more prominent positions in the South, as it enjoyed boom times such as it had never known in the days when cotton was king and plantations, more than cities, were centers of culture.

"In the economic renaissance of the South," writes Harold Whitman Bradley, of a part of the country that was becoming unrecognizable from its former self,

> lumber vied with iron and textiles for preeminence. . . . At the turn of the century, southern forest provided 40 per cent of the lumber in the nation. . . . Textiles were, more than any other industry, the symbol of the new South. . . . The mill owners recruited their labor force from the farms. Men and women accustomed to the insecurity of tenant farming flocked to the mill towns to work sixty hours a week . . .

The pay was terrible, but those who earned it had found a better life nonetheless, one not subject to the vagaries of nature and the receptiveness of soil to seed.

If the South reconstructed its society, the North, on the other hand, began the reconstruction of its *high* society. Especially in New York and Boston, where men in top hats and women in layered gowns and jewelry-by-the-pound began to populate the night again, stepping out of carriages and gliding through the murky, otherworldly glow of gaslight. They were on their way to parties and banquets and entertainment of the most elite nature—if not the most purposeful. At evening, they were dining in elegance with friends of similar social rank. During the daylight hours, they were dressing elegantly as they made themselves as visible as possible, with strolls through Central

Park, ending their procession "with dinner at the [Hotel] Brunswick, its dining room festooned with whips, whiffletrees, and coach horns."

The war was over. Life resumed as it was once known by the upper classes—or, as they were known to some, the "Swells."

Calling cards were once more left on trays inside grand foyers; tea was served promptly at four; the utensils laid out for dinner were not just silver but, in many cases grand baroque, polished to a squint-inducing sheen by the kitchen help, slaves of the North. Private clubs admitted only the richest and most comically dignified of men to their precincts, and did not permit women at all. For these people, "the New York of the eighteen eighties was gracious and society a self-contained little island of brownstones that stretched from Washington Square to Central Park along Fifth and Madison Avenues."

Stylish residences these were, but it was perpetual twilight within. Heavy curtains were almost always drawn, one flap over the other, not a sliver of sunshine visible. Rooms were overly furnished, overly decorated, overly somber, smelling at once sweet and musty. Paintings that could have been—and eventually would be—museum pieces hung on the walls in ridiculously scrolled golden frames. Thick carpeting covered floors and stairways and helped, with the curtains, to mute the unsavory sounds of humbler life outside.

The families who lived in these city homes often had a country place or two, and occasionally sailed to Paris for further variety in dwelling. The humble ones sometimes gathered at the docks to watch their betters board their ships, responding to the Swells with awe more than resentment. They waved and wished a bon voyage to people they didn't know. The people in the first-class cabins, who did not wave back, were as much a separate species as a distinct class.

⊸◆⊸

A DECADE OR SO AFTER the war ended, the reconstruction in the North gave way to the Gilded Age. The term was Mark Twain's, from his book of the same title, his first, full-length work of fiction. For some reason, the Swells found the term acceptable, even though to Twain and his coauthor, Charles Dudley Warner, *The Gilded Age* was a satire of its snobbish citizenry. But it is "a serious satirical book," writes Fred Kaplan, one of two Kaplans who produced biographies of Twain.

From Justin Kaplan comes a description not of the book, but of the era.

> *The Gilded Age* echoes the sounds of its times—the rustle of greenbacks and the hiss of steam, pigs grunting in the village mud, the clang of railroad iron and the boom of blasting charges, the quiet talk of men in committee rooms and bankers' offices. Its raw materials are disaster, poverty, blighted hopes, bribery, hypocrisy, seduction, betrayal, blackmail, murder, and mob violence.

But the Swells were impervious to criticism; it always came from people beneath them and thus was just more of their clatter. Besides, what was there to criticize? Just as the South was climbing back to prosperity, so was the North leading the entire country in that direction.

Refrigerator cars became common on freight trains, carrying meat from stockyards in Chicago to consumers in the east and changing the eating patterns of a nation. Electric trolleys and street railways sped people through the great urban centers, soon followed by elevated railways and subways.

Automobiles powered by electricity and gasoline were built in the same year, 1892.

Between 1865 and 1908, the output of wheat in America increased 256 percent, corn 222 percent, coal 800 percent, and miles of railway track by 567 percent.

By the start of the twentieth century, the United States led the world in per capita income and the production of manufactured goods.

In 1901, the frustrated British journalist W. T. Stead would ask, "What is the secret of American success?" It was a plaint, however, more than a question, and he might have been speaking for the whole industrial world.

But under the industrial and agricultural gilding, as Twain and Warner pointed out, were statistics that were more appalling than impressive. These were numbers that told of poverty, hunger, malnutrition, greed, shoddy housing, degrading employment, rampant illness, and the stripping of rights from African-Americans, who had so recently been "freed." It was the underbelly of the United States, as horrid in its own way as what Elliott had experienced in India.

To their credit, and as Elliott demonstrated, some of the upper classes felt a responsibility to improve the hardships that others faced. But only some of them. Further, that was only part of the story. In her adult years, Eleanor Roosevelt would write about the extremes of priority that her caste heeded. *Some* of her caste.

> In that society you were kind to the poor, you did not neglect your philanthropic duties, you assisted the hospitals and did something for the needy. You accepted invitations to dine and to dance with the right people only, you lived where you would be in their midst. You thought seriously about your children's education, you read the books that everybody read, you were familiar with good literature. In short, you conformed to the conventional pattern.

Observing her mother, though, Eleanor found someone quite different, a member of "that New York Society which thought itself all-important. Old Mr. Peter Marié, who gave choice parties and whose approval stamped young girls and young matrons a success, called my mother a queen, and bowed before her charm and beauty, and to her this was all important." Anna was a much-envied young denizen of society, a member in good standing of democracy's royalty. She did not neglect her philanthropic duties so much as dismiss them as the burden of others.

In terms of her appearance, however, Eleanor could not help but agree with the consensus. Her mother was "one of the most beautiful women I have ever seen." In the "season" of 1881–82, when the public eye first focused on Anna, she was "acclaimed as one of society's most glamorous women." David McCullough describes her as "stunning, regal, with a magnificent figure and large, haunting blue eyes," framed by hair that was golden more than blond.

In the early 1880s, Anna Rebecca Ludlow Hall's life was the stuff of Henry James's fiction: "polo and tennis matches, the evenings at the opera, the cotillions, the midnight suppers, the horse-shows, and everything else that was a fixture in society." For exercise, she enjoyed a weekly dancing class and a gentle jog of three miles with friends for afternoon tea at a favorite restaurant. Anna might have been inserted into almost any of James's novels—a secondary character, granted, but a perfect fit.

She and her friends were among those who "set the fashion in dress and manners," according to Joseph Lash, "and the anxious ones knocked at their doors. Anna's graceful beauty and charming manners were everywhere [the subject of adulation]. 'Fair, frail and fragile, and therefore a good illustration of beauty in American women,' a society columnist rhapsodized. . . . 'The proud set of the head on the shoulders was the distinctive look of the Halls,' recalled Mrs. Lucius Wilmerding, whose mother was a close friend of Anna."

But all was not as it seemed for the stunning Ms. Hall. She would soon discover "that she lacked the stamina—and probably the enthusiasm—for such a dizzying whirl" of activity as her fellow Swells felt mandatory. Despite her practiced smile and hard-learned manners, there seemed at times to be something about Anna that was amiss, something not quite in keeping with the other young lovelies of Swelldom. It would eventually show itself in the desperation brought on by her relationship with Elliott Roosevelt.

❖

By virtue of lineage, if lineage may be called a "virtue," the Hall family was among the so-called "Four Hundred." Supposedly, although not in fact, this was the number of people who could fit with comfort and dance gracefully in the ballroom of Mrs. William B. Astor Jr. The actual number, someone once pointlessly calculated, was a precise 297, meaning that one poor soul either sat alone in a corner or waltzed by himself.

Regardless, to be invited to one of Mrs. Astor's galas was a form of anointment, the tap of a sword upon the shoulder of those who knelt at the altar of the beau monde. Anna was so tapped, and when it came time for her to be "presented"—which is to say, for a gala to be held to celebrate her "coming out" as a blue-blooded debutante, now officially an object of affection for suitors of similar stock—she seemed eager to bask in the attention.

Perhaps no one was more attentive to her than the poet Robert Browning, who once asked permission to "sit and gaze" as her portrait was being painted. That's all—he just wanted a chair, just a look, although a long one. He hadn't the skill to create a portrait of her himself; he wanted only to be in the same room and stare into her face as she sat in repose for someone who did have the skill.

It is possible that the result of Browning's immersion was his own version of Anna Hall's portrait, verbal rather than visual. She seems to have contributed greatly to one of his most romantic poems, "A Pretty Woman":

X.

Why, with beauty, needs there money be,
Love with liking?
Crush the fly-king
In his gauze, because no honey bee?

XI.

May not liking be so simple-sweet,
If love grew there
'Twould under there
All that breaks the cheek to dimples sweet?

XII.

Is the creature too imperfect?
Would you mend it?
And so end it?
Since not all addition perfects aye?

XIII.

Or is it of its kind, perhaps,
Just perfection
Whence, rejection—
Of a grace not to its mind, perhaps.

◈

ANNA WAS THE OLDEST OF four Hall girls and two brothers and was set apart from them not just by age but by temperament. The girls were said to be "slightly but attractively mad"—all except Anna, more properly described as "prim and cool." She could be friendly on occasion, standoffish on more occasions. She was eager for a husband, perhaps more so than for love, but, as was the way with young ladies of her class, showed a veneer of indifference in the company of men. It was, after all, unseemly for one to appear too eager. To Browning, for example, she feigned a total indifference.

It could be difficult for people to make up their minds about Anna Hall, but her daughter would not be among them. As a child, Eleanor was firm in her view of Anna's loveliness, and would never change her mind. She would, however, expand her mind, developing a less flattering view of her mother's character, and her sometimes ruthless behavior toward her only daughter.

Elliott would, in time, become equally unyielding. So moved was he by her appearance that he would reveal his feelings in an attempt at a short story; like his safari memoir, it was never published. But it has found a place in the family archives. Its grimness is stunning and inexplicable for a man on the eve of courtship.

Elliott created a beautiful Manhattan society belle named Sophie Vedder. She is living overseas in the tale but clearly patterned after Anna. As the story begins, Sophie believes she has "so many friends, so many good and lovable qualities." An apparently courageous sort, she claims she does not fear death; she will have Strauss waltzes played at her funeral. "My life has been a gamble. I have lived for pleasure only. I have never done anything I disliked when I could possibly avoid it. . . . I hoped against hope that something would turn up and pull me through."

But nothing ever does. And, once achieved, the pleasure for which Sophie lives turns out to be not as pleasurable as she had always believed it would be. She has never married, having dismissed one suitor as the "same colorless thing" he had always been, and rejecting another, a wealthy man who could have saved her from poverty, as a "little fat figure of fun." Eventually, Elliott's protagonist is driven to talk to herself in the most horrid of circumstances. "Poor Sophie," she says aloud, a couple of hours after dismissing the fat little rich man and therefore consigning herself to poverty, "what a frivolous, useless thing you are." She is standing in front of a mirror as she speaks, which will be the final act of her life, for, as she commiserates with herself, her finger pulls the trigger of a gun with the barrel pushed into her head.

It is fiction, though. Only fiction.

❖

ANNA'S PARENTS WERE AS HIGHLY stratified as their daughters, members of the "Hudson River gentry." As such, they raised their girls "in a household that demanded discipline and viewed playfulness as an affront to God"—a household, according to Theodore's biographer Nathan Miller, "out of a gothic novel," through which "religious fanaticism" spread like mildew in a damp basement.

Had Elliott ever tried his hand at a gothic novel, Anna's father, Valentine, would have been perfect for the paterfamilias. A man who believed his family owed its status to the Almighty, he further insisted that the family was in turn indebted to him. Religion, in its strictest forms, was an important part of Hall life. As was appearance, which Valentine somehow determined would make Anna and her sisters worthy of divine attention. The old man devised an exercise for them. "In the country," wrote Eleanor in her autobiography, "they walked several times a day from the manse to the main road with a stick across their backs in the crook of their elbows to improve their carriage. [The girls' father] was a severe judge of what they read and wrote and how they expressed themselves, and held them to the highest standards of conduct." The result, or at least one of them, was not just a rigid posture, but "a certain rigidity in conforming to a conventional pattern, which had been put before them as the only proper existence for a lady." Other than this, and her religious training, Anna took lessons in etiquette—nothing else. No intellectual passions were ever stirred in her; she developed no outside interests. There are not even any indications that she became as familiar with the Bible as Valentine had wished.

Taken all together, the young woman's upbringing made for someone who looked like a work of art and conversed like a shopgirl.

COURTSHIP

HER SEVENTEENTH AND EIGHTEENTH YEARS were difficult ones for Anna. Her father had passed away and her mother sank into a state of ennui and depression. On some days she remained in her bedclothes and would often not even leave her chamber, seeming oblivious to all that was around her. Once meticulous about her household, Mary Livingston Ludlow Hall became indifferent; if it were up to her, the Hall manse would approach the disarray of one of those downtown tenements. But she remained, after all, Hudson River gentry; there were maids to do the cleaning, even without m'lady's instructions.

Among other things, Mrs. Hall's withdrawal from life left her oldest child to discipline her untamed younger brothers, aged twelve and nine. Her efforts were a failure; the boys ran wild and incorrigible, sometimes leaving Anna in tears. In addition, she had those three "slightly but attractively mad" sisters with whom to deal, girls who were almost as averse to self-restraint as the family's boys and, in their own ways, needier. It was one versus five: unconquerable odds.

There were aunts and uncles in the family who offered Anna what help they could, and it sometimes proved substantial. Still, the quotidian was too much for her. As Joseph Lash describes Anna, unkindly but accurately, she was "completely helpless when faced with the smallest everyday tasks. She was habitually, almost compulsively, tardy, and household accounts were a mystery to her." She tried her best to bring order to the Hall brood, but her "efforts at control were exhausting and futile. It was not at all the sort of life a belle was meant to lead." Especially one who had been kept from school, or even a governess, by her late father, who was wealthy, righteous, and misguided. One day, Anna was to have received a substantial sum of money from her parents' estate. Genetically, however, her inheritance was more of a curse than a beneficence.

⊰◈⊱

FOR SOME REASON, ANNA'S PROBLEMS did not dissuade swainish Elliott. Still riding the crest of popular renown bestowed by his adventures in India and elsewhere, and still able to have his choice of women from New York's highest classes, he met Anna at the peak of her young life's crisis. But he didn't know that. He only knew what he saw at various social events, and that was a young woman of breathtaking looks and apparent good breeding. As for the turmoil beneath, Anna hid it at social events with her natural imperiousness. To a friend, Elliott described her as a "tall, slender, fair-haired little beauty." She would be *his* beauty, he decided; it was something like love at first sight.

As for Anna, she was equally struck by her fiancé-to-be, although less effusive in describing him as "the dashing, well-traveled, if somewhat eccentric Elliott Roosevelt."

⊰◈⊱

ELLIOTT WAS ADORED BY ALL women, but especially by those who were kin. His mother used to call him her "only comfort," and to his two sisters he was virtually an idol, a young man to whom they dedicated "our interests, our lives." And the son and brother was similarly affected by the three females.

But:

> Elliott's reverence for the women of his family was complicated by his fear, disdain, distrust, and hatred for "the life and character of the generality of women that I have met." Over time, in his travels, he had been hurt and disappointed by, and "learned a contempt" for, "thoughtless" women and "really bad women."

One might ask whether Elliott was overreacting, or perhaps comporting himself in the wrong neighborhoods. Nevertheless, his emotions about the opposite sex were, at best, mixed. It was not an ideal quality to bring to a marriage.

⊰◈⊱

WHEN HE FIRST MET ANNA Hall, however, he forgot "thoughtless" women, "really bad women." He forgot *all* women—and, as the following example demonstrates, many of the rules of coherent expression—save for Anna, who was "a Sweet Hearted, a true, loving

Earnest Woman who lives the life she professed. Womanly in all purity, holiness and beauty an angel in tolerance, in forgiveness and in faith—My Love Thank God our Father—And in her true promise to be my wife I find the peace and happiness which God has taken from me for so long."

That promise to be his wife had not yet been given; Elliott was rambling. But he and Anna did seem to have something in common beside being members of the same elite social class. Anna had been "taught that success in life is the result of self-discipline built upon a strong foundation of trust in God. Self-indulgence and weakness insulted all that was holy. It was ironic but understandable, that Anna, who was brought up to be high-minded and self-controlled, was drawn to a man of passion and daring." Elliott had been raised with a similar regard for self-discipline, as well as a similar disdain for self-indulgence and weakness. That his lessons were more secular in foundation than religious was not of consequence for the young lovers; that Elliott would not be able to heed the lessons *would* be of consequence, but not yet, not until they were apparent—in a few more years it would be.

So Anna was drawn to him heedlessly, and in retrospect recklessly. As a result, "The two young people soon fell deeply in love, providing strong evidence that opposites attract."

Nonetheless, it could not be called a match made in heaven. More like a match made in Mrs. Astor's ballroom, and that was not as auspicious as it sounded.

❖

It was the spring of 1883 when Elliott and Anna became a couple, not officially, but their names were now linked by other Swells nevertheless. On Memorial Day, at a gathering on the grounds of Algonac, the estate of the Delano family, where Franklin Roosevelt, then just a year old, and his ever-intrusive mother, Sara, lived, Elliott asked Anna to marry him. Expecting the question, she answered with well-practiced restraint. She said she was flattered by Elliott's interest but needed time to think. Expecting the answer, Elliott felt confident about her eventual reply. Friends of theirs, who had arranged the gathering to bring the two closer together, were also encouraged. Anna, they knew, was simply adhering to ritual by not accepting a beau's first proposal.

From that point on, Elliott also followed custom. He stepped up the pace of his wooing. "He sent flowers, took her driving in the park," and whispered to her sweetly about the kind of life that would one day be theirs, which was actually a continuation of the life they were already living—a life that could, after all, hardly be improved upon. "There were morning walks down by the Hudson, tennis in the afternoon, and evening picnics in the hemlock grove. As the chill of fall began to descend, they would hold hands by the fire and exchange words of undying love." According to David McCullough, they "were seen at parties. They knew the same people; their families, of course, knew one another and all about one another."

But I take issue here with McCullough. Anna and Elliott did *not* know "all about one another," and the process of learning turned into an unexpected trial. "The summer of '83 became a time of tremendous highs and lows for Elliott Roosevelt. He spent most of his weekdays at Meadow Brook, on Long Island, where he played polo with reckless abandon and was injured repeatedly. On weekends, he rushed to catch the Hudson River train to see his fiancée at Oak Terrace, her family estate far upriver at Tivoli, New York," which had finally been brought under some semblance of control.

Theodore watched his brother from afar. He was troubled by the frenetic pace at which Elliott spent his days, writing to sister Bamie: "I don't know whether he could get along without the excitement now, but it is certainly unhealthy, and leads to nothing."

Anna also fretted. She wanted Elliott to spend more of his weekdays with her; neither, after all, had to stoop to employment, both of them able to live on money handed down through the generations.

And she had other concerns about her intense young gallant, as did he about her. Elliott was said to be temperamental after unofficially winning Anna's hand in the summer of 1883, on some occasions even "gloomy"; the former was a frequent, although not constant, condition of his, the latter a term that had not previously been associated with him. In addition, she "feared his sudden explosions of jealousy. She was concerned about his morose and mercurial moods, which caused him to disappear for days, behind the locked door of his room, writing, drawing, smoking. Was he drinking as well? She did not ask, and the possibility was not mentioned."

So it was that Anna had reasons other than ritual for not having accepted Elliott's offer of marriage immediately. She needed time to think; the problem was that she could find so little. A constant din of urging from her fluttery companions intruded on any reflective time for which she might have hoped. Elliott was too much the man about town, they told her, too much of a prize for society's debs to be kept waiting too long or, perish the thought, rejected. And Anna's mother seemed to regain her health, even her sparkle, when she learned that her daughter had caught Elliott's eye. She believed it was an omen. Anna had no choice but to be Mr. Roosevelt's wife, and why, for heaven's sake, would she even deliberate?

But before the day of her acceptance finally came, she wrote him a letter.

> All my love and ambition are now centered in you. . . . I . . . shall not be happy unless I feel that all your troubles, joys, sins and misfortunes are to be mine too. Please never keep anything from me for fear of giving me pain or say to yourself "there can be no possible use of my telling her." Believe me, I am quite strong enough to face, with you, the storms of this life and I shall always be so happy when I know that you have told and will tell me every thought, and I can perhaps sometimes be of use to you. . . .
>
> I think for the future as far as I am concerned, you will have to bury [your] fierce doubts. . . .

Elliott replied with a variety of missives both apologetic and pleading. In one, he confessed: "I know I am blue and disagreeable often, but please[,] darling, bear with me and I will come out all right in the end, and it really is an honest effort to do the right that makes me so often quiet and thoughtful about it all."

Anna allowed herself to be placated. Not long afterward, she formally accepted the proposal of New York's most eligible bachelor.

❖

As if they were on opposite ends of a seesaw, the renewed vigor of Anna's mother coincided with a surprising decline in Elliott's health. He began to suffer occasional illnesses, some of them surely the lingering effects of his Himalayan fever. But there were others of an unspecified nature, although we do not know how many nor how long they lasted. In addition, he wrote to a largely unsympathetic Anna, he had his many polo injuries with which to contend.

> Darling Baby
> You will have to hurry up and marry me if you expect to have anything left to marry—It seems some of it from one bad scrape into another. That beastly leg gave me so much pain that I went to the Doctor and I'm in for it this time, I'm afraid, not to get on a horse for a week and not to walk about more than is absolutely necessary. Oh! my! *Poultices! Ointment!*
> And three evenings alone by myself at 57th St. [his residence] with my leg on a chair.

But he concluded the missive in far better spirits.

> My beautiful Sweet Heart I could write you now a love letter but fear that after this long business note it would tire you, I . . . love and long for you every hour more than more. Good bye Darling, My own little Baby dear.
> Your lover
> Ellie

Anna was not sure of the extent to which he loved and longed for her. Perhaps, she sometimes thought, it would be more accurate to say that he idealized her, found her an example of perfection in the female form rather than the object of a deeply felt personal affection. "Womanly," he had declared she was, "in all purity, holiness and beauty." But with such a statement, and others like it, she wondered whether Elliott was going too far. Could she possibly live up to such a vision? It was something more for her to fret about, and she could only hope that Elliott's exaggeration, if indeed he was overstating, was the result of love's initial bloom, and would in time settle into a more manageable state.

❖

WHEN DOUGLAS ROBINSON JR., CORINNE Roosevelt's husband, heard the news of Anna's engagement, he wrote to the future bride ecstatically.

> My dear Miss Hall,
>   I cannot tell you how delighted I was to hear the news from Elliott on Sunday . . . for the truest friend & best hearted man I have ever known has asked you to be his wife & I am sure that he will be all to you that a husband should be: all his friends will tell you that he is a "good fellow" & that with me includes everything . . .

Another of Anna's friends, Constance Spencer, expressed the surprise of many intimates.

> My dear Anna,
>   I write—and tell me whether the report—that you are engaged is really true—I cannot believe that it—is really so. . . .

The future bride also heard from Sarah Steward, who was less surprised, more enthusiastic. She communicated all the way from Leamington, England.

> Dearest Anna,
>   The news of your engagement has only just reached me and I hasten to congratulate you. Need I say that I

wish you every possible happiness! I think you are a very
lucky girl as although I have never met Mr. Roosevelt, I
have heard that he was very nice, in fact charming.

Letters like the preceding came almost daily to one or the other
of the couple. Glasses were raised in their honor at parties and
dinners. Good wishes were expressed by friends who knew them
both and were certain that their future would bring success, happiness, and an increasingly solidified position in their Manhattan's
world of the upper crust.

Anna could not have been more pleased by the reaction to her
coming nuptials. Elliott, too, was delighted, but occasionally vexed as
well. He was a member in good standing of New York's high society,
and he knew it; he lived the life, accepted the values. Or thought he
did. But just as Anna occasionally felt ill at ease with her position,
so did her intended. He could not say what bothered him, not yet.
But deep inside, where a man's reasons and motives are the murkiest
yet their infrastructure is laid, he felt at times that he was neither
Swell nor swell.

It was about to get worse.

MARRIAGE

Elliott Bulloch Roosevelt, twenty-three years old, and Anna Rebecca Ludlow Hall, nineteen, were married on December 1, 1883, at the Calvary Church in downtown New York, two blocks from Elliott's birthplace. It was, according to the *New York Herald*, "one of the most brilliant social events of the season." The *New York Times* was almost identical in its language, calling the ceremony, "One of the most brilliant weddings of the season." The event proved such an attraction that, according to a few reports, the crowd was standing room only, with latecomers squeezed against the church's back doors.

The groom's attire was not mentioned, but the bridal gown "was of white satin, covered with point lace: the point lace veil fastened with a diamond crescent and caught at the shoulder cut orange blossoms."

The bridesmaids' dresses were also described in detail, one of which was that the sleeves "were in the Catherine de Medici style."

Standing at an altar covered with tropical flowers, the couple "pledged a life together to be filled with the sunshine of their happiness."

Valentine Hall was not mentioned in any accounts of the ceremony, and no one to commented on his daughter's posture.

After the church service, the bride's mother hosted a reception for family and close friends at her Manhattan residence.

The following day, the newlyweds headed south. Stopping in Philadelphia, Elliott wrote to Anna's mother. "Dear Lady," he said, "do not fear about trusting your daughter to me. It shall be my great object all my life to comfort and care for her." Prior to the ceremony, the widowed Mrs. Hall had pleaded with the bride and groom "to enter their union with their hearts turned to God." They assured her they would.

❖

FOLLOWING THE HONEYMOON, ELLIOTT WENT to work for Anna's family, which managed what was perhaps New York's leading real estate firm at the time. He had never had any experience in real estate, and was certainly not qualified for a top position in the field, but such was the property boom in the early 1880s that the company almost ran itself, something of a perpetual motion machine. All Elliott had to do was go along for the ride and observe carefully. He did not need the money, of course, but accepted the job because its purpose, at least as far as the Ludlows were concerned, was to help embed him among New York's most powerful men of commerce. Elliott was appreciative. He persuaded himself that there was nothing wrong with working. A lot of Swells worked, and even J. P. Morgan had a job, didn't he?

As for Anna, she became one of New York's youngest society matrons, the position preordained for her and one that she thought, most of the time, would suit her to perfection.

The newlyweds moved into a brownstone in the Thirties, which was uptown at the time. They entertained as much as they could, but there were some people they could not invite, some who would consider a request for their company from the Roosevelts a presumption. "Their income," it was noted, "although comfortable, did not permit them to receive on the scale of such friends as the Cornelius Vanderbilts. Nevertheless, they were prominent members of New York society and were invited to dinners, dances, or theater parties nearly every night." The dinners were sumptuous, the dances often lasted into the early hours of the morning, and the theater parties were almost always followed by indulgence in the kind of conviviality that flows from bottle to glass to brain.

YES, ELLIOTT AND ANNA WERE leading the life they had expected to live, the one they had already known. Yet after their marriage, it all became too much for the groom. He could no longer meet his social responsibilities, did not *want* to meet them. Nor was he able to meet his responsibilities, limited though they were, at work. He might have moved in exalted circles, but he was beginning to wonder whether he was living the life he had expected to live, or if he had been forced into the life he was doomed to live. The question haunted him. After a time, and a remarkably short one postnuptially, he could bear it no longer. He decided to leave not only society and his vocation behind but, for the time being, his country as well.

In the spring of 1887, Elliott, nervous, moody, and worn out from a ceaseless round of games and dissipation, quit the Ludlow firm and sailed to Europe with Anna and her sister, Tissie. Anna had pleaded for the trip, believing that time away from Elliott's Long Island cronies would make him healthy enough to resume his rightful place as head of a household in one of New York's most respectable families. . . . Elliott's moods switched on and off between depression, delight, self-disgust, and enthusiasm.

They continued switching when he returned.

❖

ELLIOTT FOUND ANOTHER JOB, ESCAPING from real estate and the Ludlows and becoming a banker and investment counselor for his uncle, James King Gracie. Once again, a position about which he knew little or less, and for which he cared little or less. And, once again, a position whose purpose had more to do with gaining status than achieving vocational goals. More and more, Elliott spent his spare moments at Meadow Brook, riding to the hounds as well as playing polo. But, as had been the case during their courtship, Anna was beginning to feel bored and abandoned, with physical distress the inevitable result. She was reluctant to discuss the matter with anyone in her family except the man who was causing it; with him, she could not have been more blunt. "My dear Elliott," she wrote during one of his absences, "I have just come in from playing tennis and my hand is shaking so that I can hardly form a letter. Do you know that I think your influence on me must be a very weak living one. I used to be able to play tennis all day, & now before I am through with one set I am *perfectly exhausted*. All I seem to be capable of is sitting still." In another message she complained to him that "I am really not the same strong girl I used to be. . . . All I can do is sleep & yet I feel I must not give in to it too much. . . . It comes to me more & more every day how much of my liberty I have given up to you. . . ."

She would continue to write emotionally wrenching letters for the next year or two, a period when "Elliott partied frantically, with distressing consequences," one of which was that, occasionally, he didn't come home at night.

> Poor old Nell. I was so awfully sorry for you last night. . . .
>
> Please remember your promise not to touch any champagne tonight. It is poison truly & how I dread seeing you suffer.
>
> I am still hoping you may change your mind & come home this afternoon. Do take care of your dear, dear self.
>
> Ever most lovingly
>
> Anna.
>
> PS Ask any one you like for Thanksgiving night. . . .
> Do come back in less pain.

Although Anna's complaints were justified, the content of the initial letter above, about the exhaustion of playing tennis, was almost certainly exacerbated by her first pregnancy, which she found difficult and enervating, so much so that there were times when she wished she had not subjected herself to it in the first place. Anna knew that her brother-in-law Theodore's first wife had died as a result of giving birth; she began to fear that a similar outcome was waiting for her.

And when her due date arrived, and, right on schedule, labor began, the physician attending her found himself sharing the fear. Anna struggled more than either of them had ever anticipated. But she survived, although not in the best condition, and gave birth to a baby girl on October 11, 1884. The parents had been hoping for a boy, a "precious boy," and although Anna's next two children would be male—Elliott Jr. in 1889, and Hall, two years later—her first issue was Anna Eleanor, who would never be known by her first name.

As for Elliott, he surprised everyone in the family by being thrilled, forgetting his desire for a boy the moment he looked at his baby. She was "a miracle from heaven," he thought. He was enchanted from the moment he saw her, stroking her tenderly, and soon gave her the nickname that had been his own in childhood. To her father, Eleanor became, in all sweetness, "Little Nell."

Her mother's response could not have been more different.

Almost unconscious from her exertions, Anna took her first look at the infant and, to say the least, was not impressed. Was that the best she could do? A woman like *her*? With a man as handsome as Elliott? She did not understand.

For one thing, Anna thought Eleanor's nose was too long, and blamed it on her husband's seed, despite the fact that Elliott was not long-nosed himself. Neither, in truth, was Eleanor. Anna also thought her infant was "a more wrinkled and less attractive baby than the average," and that would in time suggest a nickname for her. As Eleanor later wrote, "I am told that I was to come down at tea time to the library and stood bashfully at the door till my mother saw me and called, 'Come in, Granny.'"

Granny. The first of her life's many insults. The child was barely two years old at the time, but to Anna she brought to mind an old woman, an image that had begun to form on the day of her birth.

"She is such a funny child," her mother told friends as Eleanor moved toward her third birthday, "so old-fashioned." Her friends seemed to agree.

And so "Granny" she remained for much of her early childhood, at least to a small circle of Anna's intimates. Remembering the sobriquet as an adult, Eleanor said that whenever she heard it, she "wanted to sink through the floor in shame, and I felt I was apart from [my brothers]." Sometimes she would look into the library with her finger in her mouth and watch her mother play with the two younger boys, so obviously her favorites. Too timid to enter without permission, Eleanor would wait until she heard the familiar "Come in, Granny," which Anna would invariably speak "with a look of kind indifference." Then she would sit with her mother.

In time, psychologists would believe that a child who puts a finger in her mouth is expressing a hunger for love, or at the very least attention. That discovery had not been made yet, but would be a fitting one for the young, precious, and lonely little girl.

"From the beginning," many people believed, "[Anna] made Eleanor feel homely and unloved, always outside the closed circle that embraced her two younger brothers."

Sometimes Anna would read to Eleanor; at other times, as she grew older, Eleanor would do the reading, perhaps some of the poetry she had begun to write. Her brothers listened, too, although not understanding. After a few minutes, Anna might interrupt to put the boys to sleep. Sometimes she would return. Sometimes Eleanor would wait futilely, as her mother stayed with the boys, or remembered something else she had to do.

In the opinion of biographer Blanche Wiesen Cook, it was Anna's growing doubts about Elliott that were the main reason for her lack of feeling toward her daughter. "Always correct and generally aloof," Cook wrote, "Anna Hall Roosevelt was not a woman of spontaneous emotion. The problems in her marriage caused her to become more walled off from her feelings, as she struggled to ignore as much as she could, hoping to notice less, to care less, to numb herself from hurt. Since to love a child is to open oneself to the most profound feelings, little Eleanor could only have seemed a threat to Anna's quest for composure. From the first she was the recipient of her mother's coldest attentions."

⟨◈⟩

WHETHER ELEANOR EVER FORGAVE HER mother for her behavior, of which "Granny" was the hurtful summary, we do not know. But in one of her volumes of memoirs, she would explain her mother's cruel appellation as if she were writing about someone else. She even seemed to excuse Anna, "for I was a solemn child, without beauty and painfully shy and I seemed like a little old woman entirely lacking in the spontaneous joy and mirth of youth."

But Eleanor was not completely lacking in joy. One of her favorite sources was sweets, although she had been warned about eating too many by the family doctor.

> I loved candy and sugar, so when we had dinner parties and there were sweets to go on the table, I stole into the pantry, and if I could find a paper bag with any of the sweets, I not only ate them but once or twice, fearing I would not have a chance to eat them on the spot, I took the whole bag and decided the best hiding place was down the front of my dress.
>
> I remember sitting on the lap of my brother's nurse, who was very strict with me, and when she felt something crackle she demanded to know what it was. I evaded the question, and, of course, was discovered at once. She scolded me, and then I was taken in to my mother, who scolded me again and sent me to bed in disgrace.

Disgrace. Forty years later, the word was still with her. "I was always disgracing my mother," Eleanor recalled. Eating sweets was the least of it.

⬦

ALSO FORTY YEARS LATER, ALTHOUGH she had no more skill at writing fiction than did her father, Eleanor was asked to write a short story for a magazine. The challenge appealed to her. She did not need much time to think of a plot.

The story's heroine, a woman named Sally, is thinking back over memories from childhood, memories that define her in the present.

> Her forty-fifth birthday. . . . As she looked [into the fire] pictures formed in the dancing flames, first, there was a blue-eyed, rather ugly little girl standing in the door of a cozy library looking in at a very beautiful woman holding, oh so lovingly, in her lap a little fair-haired boy. Through Sally's heart passed the old sensation, the curious dread of the cold glance which would precede the kindly and indifferent "Come in[,] Sally, and bring your book."

Another magazine asked Eleanor to select the "Seven People who Shaped My Life."

> The first were my mother and father. I suppose it is natural for any person to feel that the most vivid person-alities in early youth were those of his parents. That was certainly true in my case.
>
> My mother always remained somewhat awe-inspiring. She was the most dignified and beautiful person. But she

51

had such high standards of morals that it encouraged me to wrong-doing; I felt it was utterly impossible for me ever to live up to her!

My father, on the other hand, was always a very close and warm personality. I think I knew that his standards were nowhere near as difficult to achieve and that he would look upon my shortcomings with a much more forgiving eye. He provided me with some badly needed reassurance, for in my earliest days I knew that I could never hope to achieve my mother's beauty and I fell short in so many ways of what was expected of me.

I needed my father's warmth and devotion more perhaps than the average child, who would have taken love for granted and not worried about it.

❖

BUT DIFFERENT ATTITUDES TOWARD THEIR daughter were not the only points of contention in the Roosevelt marriage. In fact, by the time Eleanor was born, her parents' wedded state was already beginning to fray. As she would write in later years, "I doubt that the background of their respective lives could have been more different. His family was not so much concerned with Society (spelled with a big S) as with people, and these people included the newsboys from the streets of New York and the cripples whom Dr. Schaefer, one of the most noted early orthopedic surgeons, was trying to cure." For the most part, these were not people of whom Anna was even aware, much less those to whom she would have given her time or attention.

Surprisingly early in the marriage, Anna considered ending it, divorcing Elliott. But it would have been such a drastic step for a member of her class. She would, at best, be whispered about behind her back; at worst, she would be shunned by the very society that mattered so much to her. She felt herself trapped, and for the time being could think of no other course than to immerse herself all the more in the world of the Swells, for which

> she organized countless charity balls. She was the founder and creative director of an "Amateur Comedy Club" . . . She liked activity, and she enjoyed engaging company. But she was embattled. More and more, she hid her rage within the confines of headaches and ennui. She became impatient and distraught. Above all, Anna was irritated by her solemn daughter, Elliott's "Little Nell," who looked about her with sorrowful eyes reflecting fully the feelings her mother could not express.

The headaches that hid her rage were almost certainly migraines, and there were days when, like her mother before her, she could not get out of bed. Sometimes she remained under the covers for several days in a row.

Migraines had never plagued Anna before, and they produced a heartfelt tenderness in her daughter. "I know now that life must have been hard and bitter and a very great strain on her," Eleanor wrote many years later. "I would often sit at the head of the bed and stroke her head. . . . As with all children, the feeling I was useful was perhaps the greatest joy I experienced."

It is, perhaps, surprising that Anna would allow Eleanor's ministrations. Even more surprising is that, after her mother fell asleep, Eleanor would ease her way down to the foot of the bed and curl up, joining Anna in slumber, her repose shaped like that of a faithful puppy.

❖

GIVING BIRTH, HOWEVER UNENTHUSIASTICALLY SHE might have felt about it, was probably the most motherly act Anna ever performed. Other than that, she was a woman of "cold virtue, severity, and disapproval, while [Elliott] embodied everything that was warm and joyous in [Eleanor's] childhood."

Although Elliott did not read to her as often as Anna, he did introduce her to *The Old Curiosity Shop*, whence their nicknames had derived. In the first chapter of the Dickens classic, a deeply loving relationship is revealed between Nell and her grandfather, who, on one occasion, is advised by the first-person narrator to take more care of the girl. The grandfather was incensed.

> "More care!" said the old man in a shrill voice, "more care of Nelly! Why who ever loved a child as I love Nell?" . . .
> "I don't think you consider—" I began.
> "I don't consider!" cried the old man interrupting me, "I don't consider her! Ah how little you know of the truth! Little Nelly, little Nelly!"

In Eleanor's case, of course, it would have been her father, not her grandfather, who was indignant. But in both cases, the feeling was the same. No one ever loved a child as much as the two men, one fictional, the other real, loved their little girls.

PART TWO

NELL'S HOMELINESS

H AVING BEEN RAISED TO BELIEVE that beauty was a virtue rather than either an accident or a trifle, Anna could not rid herself of the shame of her daughter's appearance. It was not just the long nose Anna had imagined the moment she first saw her child, nor the wrinkles that were really there, as they are in most newborns. As Eleanor grew older, she grew disproportionately taller, always the tallest girl of her age or, later, in her class at school. Eventually she would reach a height of six feet, uncommon for a female even now, and virtually unheard of a century ago.

Perhaps, Anna thought, if Eleanor had been more coordinated, her height would not have made her appear freakish but rather would have given her a powerful yet elegant demeanor. Instead, it did just the opposite. She could not manage to appear graceful even when standing still. In motion, thought some who watched her, it appeared that various parts of her body were headed in different directions at the same time. As pointed out previously, the proud set of the head on the shoulders was a notable feature of the Halls, but Eleanor's head was not set proudly; it was simply attached to the neck, and sometimes jiggled as if the attachment were a loose one.

It did not jiggle too much, though, for it was a head that functioned superbly. She was not only the tallest of her peers, she was the smartest, and the most intellectual in temperament. Then as now, the smartest girl in the class is seldom the most popular girl, especially if she is burdened with other peculiarities. So it was with big Little Nell.

Topping her head, and adding to the impression it gave of jiggling, was a mass of hair, wild and unmanageable. She piled it atop herself as best she could; it nonetheless insisted on curling down the sides of her cheeks and over her shoulders and who knew *where* it would stop. Her parents could have taken her to what we would today call a styling salon, so that her mane appeared managed, if not precisely chic. For some reason, they did not. Elliott, perhaps, because he loved her without concern of her appearance; her mother, perhaps, for lack of interest.

❖

By consensus, Eleanor's least becoming feature was her overbite. Even her aunt Edith, Uncle Theodore's second wife, who was fond of the girl, could not withhold comment. "Her mouth and teeth," she said, "seem to have no future." Some people thought that the overbite made Eleanor sound peculiar, that there was a slight whistling quality to her voice at times. About this, Edith did not comment; it does not seem to have been true. But Edith did concede that all was not lost, not yet—that "the ugly duckling may turn out to be a swan." She gave no reason, however, for her optimism.

Anna's "gawky daughter who seldom smiled" would have had more reason for smiling, and less to dwell on her overbite, if—once again—her family had only cooperated. But, whatever their reason for not having their daughter's hair more fashionably shaped, they had an even stronger reason for not having her overbite repaired. As far as they were concerned, the latter would have been a violation of high society's tenets; "at the time, upper-class New York felt that orthodontia was only for showgirls."

The result, according to the son who Eleanor would name after her father, was that "Mother grew up convinced . . . she was physically ugly, with a mouthful of teeth so prominent that they gave a look of weakness to her chin." It was an opinion that Eleanor had no choice but to share, on more than one occasion referring to herself as "an ugly little thing." It is a chilling opinion for a child to have of herself, a powerful obstacle to overcome.

And then there was the back brace she had to wear for a time, producing small but unsightly lumps in her dresses and making a comfortable stride all the more difficult. She even struggled to find a relaxing posture while sitting.

There would be no mistaking Dickens's lovely Little Nell for Elliott's.

<hr />

As an adolescent, Eleanor dreaded the social events that were obligatory for offshoots of the Swells. But one could plead illness only so many times.

The entrances Eleanor made—to the ballroom, the banquet hall, the theater lobby, the salons of her parents' friends—usually followed a pattern. She would keep her head down, trying to deny others a good view of her. Sometimes she would walk slowly to seem more poised than she felt. Other times she would walk quickly to reach a corner where she could stash herself away like an artificial plant, unable to see the eyes she believed were upon her, or hear the insults that she had made up her mind were directed her way. If others bothered to talk about her, Eleanor had convinced herself, they did so derisively. That there was no proof of this occurring didn't matter; a child like Eleanor does not need evidence to justify her feelings.

Often, she was forced to attend events for which orchestras had been hired. "I was a poor dancer," she said of these debutante days, "and the climax of the party was a dance. I still remember the inappropriate dresses I wore—and, worst of all, they were above my knees. I knew, of course, I was different from all the other girls and if I had not known, they were frank in telling me so! I still remember my gratitude at one of these parties to Franklin Roosevelt [her fifth cousin, once removed] when he came and asked me to dance with him!" She accepted, and prayed, with successful results, that she would not trip over his feet or hers.

But, as she had done so often in the past and would continue to do even as the best-known woman in America, Eleanor underestimated herself. She was a good, or at least average dancer, not a poor one. In fact, years later, the "Eleanor Roosevelt Reel" would be named after her, although one suspects that the name commemorates achieve-ments that were political in nature as much as terpsichorean. But in any case, she did catch the eye of the young Franklin.

❖

SHE AND FRANKLIN HAD KNOWN each other for a long time, although, as befit their branches on the family tree, distantly. The first time they met, Franklin was four years old and Eleanor two. "A gentle and overprotected boy with a large imagination, he watched her for a moment" before deciding to act. "Then he asked if she wanted to play 'horsey' and then took her to the nursery and began a game that required her to ride on his back."

Once they both reached dancing age, Eleanor began to hear rumors that handsome young Franklin might want to marry her. She did not believe them at first, fearing, as had been the case once or twice in the past, that she was being made the butt of jokes. Still, just to be certain, she decided to send Franklin a note. "I am plain," she wrote him. "I have little to bring you."

Anna, of course, agreed with her daughter, "and from the time Eleanor Roosevelt was a little girl, she was constantly reminded by her mother that she was plain."

It was for this reason that Anna so assiduously instructed her daughter on the rules of etiquette, and Eleanor knew it, knew that it was not parental love behind her mother's concern, knew it "as a child senses those things." Anna had decided that, since beauty could not be taught, she would teach manners. What Eleanor lacked in appearance, then, she would atone for by knowing what fork to use for salad, which for dessert. She would embarrass no one, least of all herself, at the dinner table.

But her mother's diligence was torment for her pupil, who found that "[My mother's] efforts only made me more keenly conscious of my shortcomings." And, in fact, Anna admitted as much, looking at her daughter more than once in utter frustration. "Eleanor, I hardly know what's going to happen to you," she said. "You're so plain that you really have nothing to do but be *good*."

That word again. *Plain*. It was better, at least, than *ugly*. Better than bringing her mother more "disgrace." It could almost be construed as neutral. Almost.

❖

ELEANOR WAS MATURE FOR HER years even when her years were few. She came to accept her appearance and to reach a truce not only with the way she looked but also with the opinions of others. She realized there was a human being inside her exterior—someone special: sentient, bright, caring, and capable. Her emphasis, then, should be on developing that human being to her fullest, not on denying her because of something so irrelevant as the shell that encased her. She took a deep breath of determination. She would indeed develop that human being.

But she was just a child. She could not always keep up her resolve. There were occasions when she lapsed again into thinking the worst of herself, yielding to "those who mock the person, focus on her teeth and voice and other cartoon characteristics." In her book *This Is My Story*, she wrote, "I knew I was the first girl in my mother's family who was not a belle, and though I never acknowledged it to any [potential suitors] at that time, I was deeply ashamed."

As a result, Eleanor became withdrawn at times, her connections with family and friends often tenuous. A young relative recalled that she "took everything—most of all herself—so tremendously seriously." It is not a surprising observation. A little girl who has so many times been dismissed as ugly is unlikely to be light-spirited in her manner.

❖

FEW PEOPLE SPOKE UP FOR Eleanor at the time. There was the dowager, her name unrecorded, who, observing the girl at a ball, found that she was "most attractive" and "very much sought after." Whether Eleanor learned of the comment is not known. Whether she would have believed it can easily be inferred.

No one took Eleanor's side more adamantly than Uncle Theodore's daughter by his first wife. But Alice Roosevelt did not make her feelings known until both women had reached adulthood. Alice "usually had a tongue that could take paint off a barn wall"; in this case, however, she did not feel such treatment was warranted. As she wrote after both she and Eleanor were adults, too late to influence her formative years:

> She was always making herself out to be an ugly duckling but she was really rather attractive. Tall, rather coltish-looking, with masses of pale, gold hair rippling to below her waist, and really lovely blue eyes. It's true that her chin went in a bit, which wouldn't have been so noticeable if only her hateful grandmother had fixed her teeth. I think that Eleanor today would have been considered a beauty, not in the classical sense but as an attractive, rather unusual person in her own right.

Alice was right. In some ways, and from some angles, Eleanor *was* an attractive girl. After all, Franklin was a handsome young man, and he was drawn to her, and in his social circles the appearance of a potential mate could not have been more important.

Yet this is not to say that Alice was either friendly or consoling to Eleanor during their early years. To the contrary, Alice was as cruel in her way as others were in theirs. According to historians Peter Collier and David Horowitz,

> Alice was strong and supple while Eleanor, with her protruding teeth and recessive chin, gave off a downtrodden air. Her behavior was calculated to win sympathy, yet there was something in Eleanor—a combination of

smugness, vulnerability, obtuseness, not to speak of an ability to absorb emotional pain—that made an individual like Alice want to punish her. She was a gifted mimic and could "do" her buck-toothed cousin exactly. But for the most part, her assault was more subtle. Knowing that Eleanor was shy about sex, for instance, Alice once got her so upset by talking about the "begats" in the Bible while they were staying at Bamie's house that Eleanor tried to sit on her head with a pillow to stop the prurient talk.

Whether Eleanor was in reality smug and obtuse is open to debate. It is more likely that others attributed these qualities to her than that she actually possessed them. And more likely still that these qualities were attributed to her because she was usually so ill at ease with others.

⤜◆⤛

THE MOST SUPPORTIVE PRESENCE IN Eleanor's life, despite his being so consistently absent from home, was her father. To Elliott, his daughter was not just his Little Nell; she was his "little golden hair." He whispered the three words to her as she lay in bed at night, and more heartily spoke them when he saw her in the morning, rubbing her eyes for wakefulness. "Little golden hair." Anna might have been baffled "over her little girl's precocious sense of right and wrong and the sadness in her appraising eyes. But these same traits amused and charmed her father." Further, he admired them; they drew him ever closer to her, and she to him. He would never talk to her about those who denigrated her; instead, he treated such people as if they didn't exist, were unworthy of the effort it would take to return the denigration. And he would not allow her to speak of them in his company, believing that their time together was too precious to let others intrude on it.

Elliott's behavior toward his daughter, his belief in the irrelevance of her appearance and how others perceived it, is apparent even in an interview that Eleanor gave more than sixty years later. In the August 1958 issue of *Datebook* magazine, she answered questions from a man named Art Unger.

"What advice do you have for a girl who is physically unattractive?" Unger wanted to know.

"*Bear it!*" she said, in her best approximation of a drill sergeant's tone. She had nothing more to offer on the subject.

NELL'S SHYNESS

M R. AND MRS. ELLIOTT ROOSEVELT lived in New York at a time
when money was easy to come by if you had the right name
or right parents, and when respect, or a facsimile thereof, was
easy to come by if you had enough money. The Roosevelts' nighttime
activities, which have been sketched into previous chapters, usually
occupied them four or five times a week, perhaps more—causing men
as well as women to make lists of the attire they had worn here and
the attire they had worn there so that they did not repeat themselves
any more than necessary.

During the day, Manhattan was aswirl with the moneymaking
passions of the Gilded Age—some legal, some not; ruthlessness
more common than gentlemanliness, although the former was often
disguised as the latter. As for Elliott, he did not go along with such

practices. He had mastered the motions of employment in run-amuck capitalism, but neither the substance nor the timing; instead, he kept sneaking out of the office earlier and earlier to play polo and carouse with friends afterward. As for Anna, she enjoyed gossiping with her own set of friends while sipping a beverage and watching others cavort at tennis; further enjoyment came from such events as kennel and horse shows, and she met her civic duties by attending an occasional board meeting of one or two philanthropic groups. She "had her coupe in town and ordered her dresses from Palmers in London and Worth in Paris while Elliott stabled four hunters at Meadow Brook." Their existence was a breathless one. The object was to enjoy it.

For the Roosevelts and the other right people of the time, Manhattan was a "golden secure world in which the significant or even ominous events around the globe were hardly noticed." It was lush, arrogant, envied, expensive, exclusionary, and painfully tumultuous. It was life at the speed of light, with emptiness at the core of both public discourse and private party-going. Motion was all, contemplation a pastime for the poor and idle.

Which is to say, it was the worst possible place for a girl like Eleanor Roosevelt to be raised.

⟨◈⟩

No one would ever think of calling her a Swell. Not as a baby, not as an adolescent, certainly not as an adult. Among other things, Swells were prattling and garrulous, especially in the company of one another. Eleanor remembers herself as timid even at the age of two, insisting that her memory went back that far. She also recalls that the experience she describes here happened more than once over the course of a few years:

My earliest recollections are of being dressed up and allowed to come down into what must have been a dining room and dance for a group of gentlemen who applauded and laughed as I pirouetted before them. Finally, my father would pick me up and hold me high in the air. All this is rather vague to me, but my father was never vague. He dominated my life as long as he lived.

The so-called "dancing" was an ordeal for Eleanor, although of a different kind than the dancing of her later debutante days, and she believes she never smiled once during an entire performance. If it weren't for her father, she would not have been able to go through with it at all, frolicking about a roomful of strange men—for she knew, at some level, that they applauded and forced their laughter not because they were entertained but because the little girl was making a fool of herself for their amusement, which was all the more amusing because of her odd appearance.

But Elliott was oblivious. He did not realize the embarrassment he was causing his "little golden hair." Unable to read the situation, he seems instead to have been proud of the attention Eleanor was attracting. And Nell was too adoring of her father to reveal her true feelings, if she was even aware of them yet.

Much more to Eleanor's liking was a different kind of show, one that she performed privately, displays of the little girl's affection for her father that went unseen by a roomful of coarse and unfeeling strangers. He "was always devoted to me . . . and as soon as I could talk," Eleanor wrote, "I went into his dressing room every morning and chattered to him[,] often shaking my finger at him as you can see in the portrait of me at the age of five which we still have. I even danced for him, intoxicated by the pure joy of motion, twisting round and round until he would pick me up and throw me into the air and tell me I made him dizzy."

⬥

A FEW YEARS LATER, INSPIRED by her father's labors on behalf of the needy, Eleanor volunteered at a settlement house and a newsboys' club, the latter another place that Theodore Sr. had founded. As young as she was, she tried her best to educate other youngsters who, for one reason or another, did not attend school. Perhaps they had to work to help support their families; perhaps they simply could not be bothered.

But a shy child is often a self-critical child, and Eleanor constantly found her efforts lacking. "I feel sure I was a very poor teacher." Worse, and even more untrue, she pronounced herself lazy. "I rather imagine that by spring I was quite ready to drop all this good work and go up to the country and spend the summer in idleness and recreation." She simply did not have the self-confidence to credit herself, no matter what she was doing.

And after some more years had passed and a sophisticated social life intruded on her charitable efforts, her opinion of herself remained at the same nadir. "Eleanor dreaded her debut," according to biographer Jan Pottker. She was as uncomfortable being the center of attention as other girls of the upper classes were when they were *not* the centers of attention. "Her memory was colored by her own self-doubt and insecurities."

Once again it was distant cousin Franklin who tried to come to the rescue, assuring Eleanor that she was being too hard on herself. "I hasten to tell you," he wrote to her, "that you are far too modest about your appeal to the gilded youth of 1902."

His words cheered her, even if she could not make herself believe them.

"Try to forget about yourself and get interested in other people," Eleanor told Art Unger in *Datebook*, when, decades later, he asked her to give advice "for the girl who is shy." But it is much easier said for an adult than done for a child.

✦

EVENTUALLY, OF COURSE, ELEANOR AND Franklin would wed, but as a newly married woman in her early twenties, there were times when her feelings about herself reached levels that seemed to supersede mere shyness.

As Blanche Wiesen Cook writes, "Eleanor Roosevelt never used the word 'depression'; but during these years she never missed an opportunity to mock her own ignorance, her clumsiness, her many and various inadequacies as a young wife."

But she was a grown woman then, if a young one, and she still seemed no more confident in her abilities, or the perceptions of others in her abilities. "In 1922, she joined the Women's Division of the Democratic State Committee. Painfully shy, she forced herself to make speeches and official appearances and discovered, to her surprise, that she was not only good at politics, but that she liked it."

Only, though, after it was over. In the moments, sometimes even the days, preceding a speech or official appearance, she was nervous to the point of fright.

Even when she reached the status of First Lady of the United States at the age of forty-nine, a long-time companion said

> She never thought of herself as exceptional or extraor-
> dinary or important. Whenever we traveled, she was
> genuinely surprised that people made a fuss. Once, when
> she returned from a tour to promote the United Nations,

71

we landed in an airport that had laid down a red carpet and there were children with flowers and quite a display, and she said, "Oh, look! Somebody significant must be coming in."

❖

DANCING FOR HER FATHER'S FRIENDS might have been one of her first memories, but there were others almost as early. The locale for one of them was a cherry tree on the property that surrounded the Roosevelts' summer house in Hyde Park, New York. Out of the tree grew a thick, tenderly curving branch that Eleanor found remarkably comfortable, an embrace of sorts. She took up residence there while taking solace in her books. She nestled into the branch as comfortably as her brace would allow and found refuge from her social inadequacies by immersing herself in poetry and fiction. When she was finally rid of the dreaded back brace, the branch felt like a feather bed.

Eleanor's capacity to lose herself in her reading caused her to miss many meals. Nothing ordinary could be relied upon to "bring me out of the world between the pages." To the young ER all of Longfellow and such poems as "The Wreck of the Hesperus," "The Skeleton in Armor," "Evangeline," and "The Building of a Ship" were favorites—as were Tennyson and Scott: "What young person can read the 'Revenge' or 'Marmion' or parts of 'The Lady of the Lake' and 'The Idylls of the King' without being stimulated to dreams of a different age."

As an adult, Eleanor encouraged children to follow her example, to "read the Chanson de Roland, Le Cid, some of Dumas, some of Victor Hugo, some of German poetry, Heine, Goethe and some of the more modern German novelists and dramatists. . . . Every child should read the translations of Indian and Chinese poetry. We know too little of the thought of these far distant races and the beauty of the imagery in which they hide their precious kernels of thought and philosophy."

It is a profound thought, nicely expressed. What she nowhere acknowledges, however, is that a child might be led to books as often by timidity as by a love of learning, or that the two might exist in combination, one feeding the other. Reading, after all, can be a means of spending time in the company of others without actually having to endure their presence, feel inferior to them, or suffer the bite of their criticisms on her psyche. The characters in a book, after all, ignore the reader, just presenting themselves for observation. It is an ideal recourse for the faint of heart. In Eleanor's case, the written word would be an escape for her all her life.

"I have to this day," she wrote much later, "an insatiable interest in every kind of romance and story which grew I think from the first forbidden tales and novels, which I purloined as a child and read as far from the house as possible, perched in a cherry tree where I could eat cherries and watch the approach of any grown up who might disapprove of the type of literature I had chosen."

Apparently, this seldom, if ever, happened. "No one tried to censor my reading," she would admit in her autobiography, "though occasionally when I happened on a book that I could not understand and asked difficult question [*sic*] before people, the book would disappear. I remember that this happened to Dickens' *Bleak House*. I spent days looking for it."

⊰◈⊱

WITH HER TIMIDITY COMPELLING HER, it was but a short step for Eleanor to go from reading to writing, thereby providing herself with an even greater opportunity to elude all that made her young life so hard to bear. She was always more advanced with the pen than her years would suggest.

On one occasion, perhaps as much to inspire herself as to explore the topic, Eleanor wrote an essay she called "Ambition."

> Some people consider ambition a sin, but well-trained it seems to be a great good for it leads one to do, and to be things without it one could never have been.

Later in the piece, after pointing out the role of ambition in the lives of great military leaders and great artists, she said:

> Of course it is easier to have no ambition and just keep on the same way every day and never try to do grand and great things, for it is only those who have ambition and who try to do who meet with difficulties and they alone face the disappointments that come when one does not succeed in what one has meant to do. . . .
> But those with ambition try again, and try until they at last succeed.

And, perhaps even more, she enjoyed writing the poetry that she was sometimes able to share with her mother. As was the case with "Ambition," she was more often than not didactic, producing her rhymes to instruct and urge herself on.

> To be the thing we seem
> To do the thing we deemed enjoined by duty.
> To walk in faith nor dream
> Of questioning God's scheme of truth and beauty.

"It is very hard to do what this verse says," Eleanor would in time confess, "so hard I never succeed. . . . I am always questioning, questioning because I cannot understand & never succeed in doing what I mean to do, never, never. Suppose I don't really try. I can feel it in me sometimes that I can do much more. . . . I mean to try till I *do* succeed."

And, of course, she did succeed, so magnificently and for so many years that the adult does not seem to have grown out of the child, but to be a different person entirely.

❖

ELEANOR WAS ALWAYS A SUCCESS academically. Well, almost. But, as she began the formal process of learning, there was, on random occasions, a forbidding presence in the classroom, observing her, silently judging. As a result, she "remembered her first days in school as a time of agony and mortification. She was asked to spell simple words such as 'horse' that her Mother knew she knew, but frozen by shyness and the presence of her mother, who sat in on the class, she misspelled every one."

Eleanor was as bewildered by her performances as she was ashamed. Believing that her fellow students were ashamed of her too, that they secretly giggled at her ignorance, she would not speak to them for the rest of the day, and ran for the cherry tree to open a book the moment her class was dismissed.

Anna never explained why she paid her visits to school. Nor is it known what she said to her daughter when she returned home on days like this, or whether she said anything at all. Perhaps she, too, was ashamed, without realizing her role in everyone's discomfort.

❖

As a young girl, Eleanor had to cope with tension more often than adults ever do. It was part of the daily routine, like eating her meals and brushing her teeth. Her only means of coping, the only person with whom she would have shared the tree branch with her, had there been room, was her father. With him, she said, "I was perfectly happy." He had kind words for her when no one else did, and just the *right* kind words. He had a smile. He had a hug.

"He was the one great love of my life as a child," she wrote, when childhood was far behind her, "and in fact like many children I lived a dream life with him; so his memory is still a vivid, living thing to me."

It was a dream life of rich detail. When Eleanor was nine, "Father's own little Nell" received a letter from him about the dreams he would make come true for her, of "days through the Grand snow clad forests over the white hills, under the blue skies as blue as those in Italy under which you and I and Little Ellie [Eleanor's younger brother] . . . used to sail over Naples Bay to beautiful Capri."

Elliott would later be accused of building up a little girl's hopes unfairly, of taking advantage of her vulnerable state for his own emotional needs, not hers. It was not so. The child in him, whom his sons did not bring out nearly as much as his daughter, meant every word he ever wrote to the child that was Eleanor. Unfortunately for him, and sorrowfully for Nell and the rest of the family, there would come a time when, in lieu of actually whisking her off to faraway, exotic locales, he would not see her at all. Instead, he would have no choice but to describe his visions to her on paper rather than utter them excitedly to her face. Nor make them a reality.

But to the extent that his mind was still capable in those days, he still believed. Would believe until the end.

NELL'S FEARS

THE YEAR 1887. ELLIOTT ROOSEVELT continued to be a restless soul, hardly living the kind of dreams he shared with his daughter. He might have seemed a glamorous figure from the outside, might have continued to be portrayed as one in the society columns. But inside he was churning with a sharply edged angst. He did not say why. Most likely, he did not *know* why. He did, however, think he knew what to do about it.

Once again, he needed a change. Once again, his destination would be Europe. He had to get away from the tedium of New York real estate and the empty clatter of Swells' gaiety—all those homes entombed in opulence, all those dinner parties with the silverware shining so brightly that it reflected off the chandeliers and made a fellow squint. He even had to get away from the polo fields for a time. He had to leave everything that was familiar behind him.

This time he did not go alone. Accompanied by Anna, her sister Tissie, two-and-a-half-year-old Eleanor, and the child's nurse, he embarked on the cruise ship *Britannic*. The plan was for "an extended tour of the continent." He would put an ocean between himself and his troubles, whatever they were.

It was not to be.

❖

THE SHIP'S FIRST DAY AT sea was a foggy one and visibility wavered between poor and nonexistent. A steamer called the *Celtic*, chugging its way to port in New York and within a few miles of its goal, lost its sense of direction completely. It crashed into the side of the *Britannic*, heading the other way. Actually, the *Celtic* practically crashed *through* the ship carrying the Roosevelts, penetrating it by more than ten feet. The result was death, alarm, and screams that pierced the fog like the arrows of a bowman. The number of people who lost their lives is not certain, but one of them was a beheaded child. Several hundred passengers on both ships were injured, including another child who lost an arm.

Elliott responded heroically. He helped his wife, sister-in-law, and the baby nurse into a lifeboat, and then called for little Eleanor, clinging frantically to a crewman, to be dropped into his waiting arms. But Eleanor would not let go. She screamed and cried. The din all about her was terrifying. Her abiding memory was her profound fear of being dropped from the deck into her father's arms. The crewman finally freed her fingers, and Eleanor always remembered that fall, the feel of plummeting from the deck high above into the pitching lifeboat below, surrounded by "cries of terror." And shouts for help.

Eleanor landed without a scratch in her father's grasp, crying in relief. Or was there another reason for the tears?

Yes, she was happy to have been saved. But as young as she was, she never forgot the horror of the experience, not the result of the leap but its anticipation. When, a year or so later, her parents decided they would once more try a cruise to Europe, Eleanor begged to be left behind. Elliott and Anna pleaded with her to come, the latter with less enthusiasm than the former, but their little girl was adamant. She would run and hide from them when the topic was even mentioned. Even her father's soothing ways, his vows of assurance, could not get through to her. So, reluctantly, her parents left their daughter at the Gracewood estate of Elliott's uncle and employer, James King Gracie. They sailed abroad by themselves.

At first Eleanor was mollified. But that is not the same thing as being pleased. She did not want her mother and father on a different continent from her. Further, she did not know her great-uncle well, nor his family, and could not easily accustom herself to the care of strangers. However, she had no choice, for "the accident [had] left Eleanor with a fear of heights and water that was connected to a lifelong sense of abandonment. If she had not cried, if she had not struggled, if she had not been afraid, if she had only done more and been better, she would be with her parents."

Despite making countless journeys in her lifetime—by land, sea, and, later, air—Eleanor never entirely lost the fears with which her experience on the *Britannic* had left her. Her fear of abandonment would become a dread of special poignancy in the years just ahead, when, before her eleventh birthday, she would be abandoned twice, both times in the most horrifying of ways for a child.

❖

At the age of seven, Eleanor developed another fear, that of boys and girls who were new to her. Not just adults, like the Gracie clan, with whom she had ended up spending an entire summer; now it was children as well. There seems to be no explaining it, either the fear itself or the time when it first seized her. But seize her it did, and so powerfully that she was often forced into isolation, which, by this time, was already a comfortable place for her.

In the Roosevelts' social circle, it was common for parents to treat their children to parties on Saturday afternoons. Eleanor tried to go but could not. She could not spend time with boys and girls she didn't know in a house with which she was not familiar, no matter how pleasant the occasion otherwise.

Of course, she *did* know many of these children, who were in fact schoolmates Eleanor saw every day. But she did not know them well, did not allow herself to know them well, and in their presence at a social occasion she "would break into tears and have to be brought home. Anna arranged to have some boys and girls come in on Friday afternoons to play and stay for tea so that Eleanor could begin to make some friends, but the plan was never carried out."

Eleanor didn't want it to be. She wanted her mother to leave her alone. "In Eleanor's later portrayals of these years," Joseph Lash writes, "she emerges as a child who was full of fears—of the dark, dogs, horses, snakes, of other children. She was 'afraid of being scolded, afraid that other people would not like me.' She spoke of a sense of inferiority that was almost overpowering coupled with an unquenchable craving for praise and affection."

❖

As late as 1917, with her husband serving his fourth year as assistant secretary of the navy and spending much of his time in Washington,

DC, Eleanor's fear of being abandoned, which had never really released its grip on her, tightened once again. This time it was Franklin, she believed, who was abandoning her—and deliberately so. The feeling "was not relieved by FDR's breezy letters, and the summer of 1917 [with the United States having entered the Great War and Roosevelt busier than ever at his job] seemed the longest summer of her life." She wrote to him in gloom and anger. "I don't think you read my letters for you never answer a question and nothing I ask for appears!"

As was the case with most of his wife's pleas, Roosevelt did not reply. Her letters did not make sense to him and, even if they did, there was nothing he could do about their being separated. Truth to tell, he was becoming disappointed in her. Did she not understand the gravity of world events that kept them apart? Was she *that* wrapped up in her own life?

But at the beginning of August, with her husband having been hospitalized by a throat infection, Eleanor was finally able to answer her longing for his company. She took a train to Washington and spent almost two weeks with her husband, all of them in the hospital. But then it was time to go, and Eleanor made sure Franklin knew that her emotional struggles had returned as soon as she'd gotten home and withdrawn a sheet of stationery. The first letter she wrote upon departing from the nation's capital, after his release from the hospital, said, in part, "I hated to leave you yesterday. Please go to the doctor twice a week, eat well and sleep well and remember I *count* on seeing you the 26th. My threat was no idle one."

The words are harsh, her insecurity great.

A mere five days later, her husband was not only enjoying his return to work but was also feeling healthy enough for an outing to Harpers Ferry, West Virginia. Three friends accompanied him. One of them, Lucy Mercer, who would later be employed as the

First Lady's social secretary, was already becoming more than just a friend to Franklin, and Eleanor's eventual suspicion that he was romantically entwined with Mercer would turn out to be the most perceptive of all her fears.

Her son would later write about Eleanor's instability in a biography of her. "'I was always afraid of something,'" Mother remembered, "'of the dark, of displeasing people, of failure. Anything accomplished had to be done across a barrier of fear.'"

⸻◈⸻

IT IS NO SURPRISE THAT the only person capable of easily crossing the barrier was Eleanor's father, and there was no prospect to her more frightening than letting him down. It did not happen often, but when it did, Elliott could respond in what struck Eleanor as a totally un-Elliott-like manner. In fact, he could be "shockingly mercurial with the daughter who adored him." But he was always quick to realize his inappropriate behavior and apologize for it. Eleanor in turn was always forgiving, eager to resume their usual ways, *not* eager, or even willing, to question the reasons for an atypical burst of behavior.

Elliott was probably at his most mercurial after a long and wearing struggle to persuade his daughter to join him and Anna for yet another trip across the Atlantic. This time Eleanor agreed, and she would look back fondly on the beginning of the family's adventures overseas. "I remember my father acting as gondolier," Eleanor wrote in her autobiography, "taking me out on the Venice canals, singing with the other boatmen, to my intense joy. I loved his voice and, above all, I loved the way he treated me." For a time, Eleanor wanted to become a singer when she grew up, believing it would please her father.

But then a different Elliott appeared, also in Italy. One day, as he and Eleanor and some others set out by donkey to explore the countryside near Sorrento, the young girl found herself suddenly terrified by the terrain. The riders had been trotting along pleasantly and peaceably, the sun warming them and the land rolling gently, when they approached a steep downward slope, almost a crater in the ground. Eleanor, taken aback by both the height of the abyss and the possibility of falling off her animal and hurting herself, reined him in. Passing her, Elliott did not even slow his mount, and as he and his companions rode down the plunging hillside, he shouted back up to his daughter, "I never knew you were a coward."

The words were like a snakebite to her. More than four decades later, when she wrote of them, she could still remember "the tone of disapproval in my father's voice."

His disappearance also stung. One moment Elliott rode next to her, the next he had vanished as if the earth had swallowed both him and everyone else in the party. Eleanor gently prodded her donkey to the edge of the slope. She sat there alone, watching as the men reached the bottom. Her father said nothing else to her and did not look back.

After a few minutes, she began to explore her surroundings and found a path around the descent. Proceeding with as much caution as forward motion would allow, she made her way—a long way—back to her party, which had climbed back up the other side of the chasm and, in the process, grown impatient waiting for her. Her father, however, greeted her with a big smile on his face. It took no more than an instant for her smile to be a match for his.

Elliott and his daughter continued their ride as if nothing out of the ordinary had just happened, as if he had not frightened Eleanor just a short time before. His girl was happy again, in the place she most liked to be, at her father's side.

Another incident from the trip to Italy, also involving elevated ground, stayed with Eleanor for years to come, as well.

> I remember my trip to Vesuvius with my father and the throwing of pennies, which were returned to us encased in lava, and then the endless trip down. I suppose there was some block in the traffic, but I can remember only my utter weariness and my effort to bear it without tears so that my father would not be displeased.

Eleanor did not blame her father for causing her trepidation, in this case or any other. She knew he loved her. Always thinking the best of him, she might have assumed he was trying to toughen her up, prepare her for the difficulties that all children will face in the years ahead. Or she might have assumed he had some other reason, benevolent in purpose if harsh in the execution. At all times, she gave him the benefit of the doubt.

In time, however, she would learn that he did not always deserve it. She would learn that her father was cursed with a special darkness, one that was fated, in the near future, to drop over him like a shroud, shaping itself to his very contours. But she also learned—knew already, in fact—that his love for her was a constant, and as her savior in childhood and spectral mentor for all the years to follow, she would love him through all the turmoil that the future would bring.

NELL'S LONELINESS

T HAT ELEANOR WOULD BE A solitary child was perhaps, at least
when considered with a literary sensibility, destined to be. As
has been suggested, "Between her parents' disappointment
that she was not a boy and the death threat that her advent into
the world represented to her mother, Eleanor, in a sense, came
into the world guilty and had to reinstate herself." It would be a
long process, inevitably difficult, inevitably isolating. One thinks
of the Roman Catholic notion of original sin, and how a lifetime
must be devoted to eradicating its stain.

Or, to look at the matter in a secular fashion, one might think of
what the novelist and playwright Thornton Wilder would one day
say. "Many do not want a life after death, but do want a loneliness
mitigated in this." Eleanor would never completely achieve such a life.

Loneliness, if not always a curse, always threatened. And sometimes even comforted, for to be lonely is sometimes to be inured to pain.

⬦

THERE WOULD COME A TIME when Eleanor, still a little girl, would be sent away—not to live with her father, which they both so desperately desired—but instead, to live with her maternal grandmother. Other members of the opéra bouffe household in which Nell would find herself included two uncles, two aunts, and one of her two younger brothers, Hall. "Eleanor's uncles were already alcoholics," reports biographer Hazel Rowley. "Her aunts were beautiful, talented, unmarried, and frustrated. Eleanor was acutely aware of the tensions in the house."

According to most accounts, Mary Livingston Ludlow Hall was not the best of guardians. She had, after all, joined with her late husband to raise a girl who would venerate the superficial, and, perhaps for that reason, had no choice but to become an inadequate mother to Eleanor. "Strict and adamant," writes Blanche Wiesen Cook of Mary, or Grandmother Hall, as she came to be known, "she spent many hours alone in her darkened room with the windows closed and the shades drawn, emerging only to issue orders, and to conduct the prayer services that began and ended each day. Everyone in the household attended these services, including the entire staff." It was Grandmother Hall who insisted that Eleanor dress in the way that humiliated her, wearing "short skirts, hideous black stockings, and outrageously unfashionable high-ankled shoes."

But there also seem to have been qualities of the late Anna's mother not easily perceived. It has been said, with some authority, that Grandmother Hall gave Eleanor "a new sense of belonging," enabling her, for the first time in her life, to feel "secure and wanted."

Perhaps because the presence of a child under the roof was such a novelty, Eleanor's grandmother and others in the Hall family made her "the center of attention." They saw to it that she learned French and German, and took classes in dancing, ballet, and piano. She learned to play lawn tennis, to ride horses, and to shoot rifles. In other words, for no reason that history records, Grandmother Hall raised Eleanor in stark contrast to the way she raised her own daughter.

The only problem, other than her attire, was that, with the exception of Alice Roosevelt, who was being raised nearby after her own mother died during childbirth, Eleanor had no children her own age with whom to play. And Alice was seldom available to share her time. Was Eleanor sad about those circumstances? Art Unger asked for *Datebook*.

"No, not sad," she told him. "Lonely, but not sorry. I was the oldest of the children and there was nobody else. So, I was alone most of the time and I was lonely. But I never wept. If I wept . . . yes, when I wept . . . it was over books. I can remember weeping over books."

And so, as Eleanor became accomplished at languages, dance, and music, she also became even more withdrawn; as she became active in the life around her, she turned ever inward for sustenance. Her loneliness further contributed to her feelings of homeliness, shyness, and fearfulness, creating an unholy stew of emotions that plagued her even during her most courageous moments.

⬥

AFTER A WHILE, AND WITHOUT really knowing it, Grandmother Hall did Eleanor the greatest favor ever bestowed on her. She had begun to think that her charge might "benefit from a year or two away from her increasingly erratic uncles." One of Eleanor's aunts suggested that she be sent to a boarding school outside of London called

Allenswood, the domain of Mlle. Marie Souvestre. Although reluctant at first, Eleanor eventually agreed to the plan. She could not have decided better.

> The three years Eleanor spent there were the happiest of her life, she remembered. It was at Allenswood, a cousin recalled, "that [she] for the first time was deeply loved . . ." Eleanor was especially proud when she was elected captain of the field hockey team and eventually became the most admired girl in the school.

At Allenswood, she outgrew at least some of her ungainliness, and her appearance was not an issue with the other girls. Nor was her bookishness, her intelligence, except in a positive sense; the other girls at the school were also bookish and bright, meaning that Eleanor was no longer a square peg amid round-holed peers. She was, rather, a friend of others with whom she engaged both intellectually and emotionally. Never before, as far as she could remember, had she encountered circumstances into which she slipped so naturally.

But for that reason, she was beset with loneliness again when it came time to depart. "The summer [of my third year] was now approaching," she wrote, "and I knew that I must go home for good. Mlle. Souvestre had become one of the people whom I cared for most in the world, and the thought of the long separation seemed hard to bear. I would have given a good deal to have spent another year on my education, but to my grandmother the age of eighteen was the time when you 'came out,' and not to 'come out' was unthinkable."

And so Eleanor departed from what had been a home for her, stimulating and accepting, and returned to New York, to a house that had never been a home, to circumstances oppressively Swell.

BUT SHE RETURNED A YOUNG lady with an even greater depth of, and quest for, learning. She was quite a different person from the one who had departed. Elliott would have been proud. A few years earlier, he had written a charming letter to her, one that she never forgot. In it, he advised her to think of masons building a house, placing

> one stone after another . . . and then think that there are a lot of funny little workmen running about in your small head called "Ideas" which are carrying a lot of stones like small bodies called "Facts," and these little "Ideas" are being directed by your teachers in various ways, by "Persuasion," "Instruction," "Love" and "Truth" to place all these "Fact" Stones on top of and alongside each other in your dear Golden Head until they build a beautiful house called "Education"—then! Oh, my dear companionable little Daughter, you will come to Father and what jolly games we will have together.

I could not locate a response to this letter, but it is certain that Eleanor was captivated by the sentiments. Many years afterward, she wrote as follows:

> Learning and living. But they are really the same thing aren't they? There is no experience from which you can't learn something. . . .And the purpose of life, after all, is to live it, to taste experience to the utmost, to reach out eagerly and without fear for newer and richer experience.
>
> You can do that only if you have curiosity, an unquenchable spirit of adventure. The experience

can have meaning only if you understand it. You can understand it only if you have arrived at some knowledge of yourself . . . which teaches you to cast out fear and frees you for the fullest experience of the adventure of life.

ELEANOR'S LONGEST, MOST HEARTRENDING PERIOD of loneliness was not in 1902, when she returned home to formally enter society. Rather, it was as an adult, beginning in the late fall of 1909. That spring, her second son, Franklin Delano Roosevelt Jr., was born. He was, thought FDR Sr.'s mother, Sara, "A sweet sight, but my heart sank a little because Baby looks so delicate and exquisite."

Too delicate, as it turned out. In October, young Franklin and some of his older siblings came down with influenza, but it was the former who was most severely stricken, and with more than just the flu. Different doctors offered different diagnoses. He might have had a murmur in his heart, might have had anemia, might have been breathing more rapidly than he should have been. The final diagnosis, however, was endocarditis, an infection of the inner lining of the heart. The disease was fatal. Franklin Delano Roosevelt Jr. passed away on November 1, 1909, having known life for a mere seven months and fourteen days.

That Eleanor was saddened is beyond doubt. But she was also beset with guilt. By her own admission she was not a good mother, neither warm nor playful, neither vigilant nor free with her time. Did she blame her mother for the example she had set? Nowhere does she explore the notion. "She had viewed motherhood as a duty rather than a joy," according to biographer Jan Pottker, "and now blamed herself for her baby's death." She could see no other explanation. "I felt . . . in some way I must be to blame," Eleanor said. "I even felt that I had not cared enough about him."

Criticizing herself as she did after baby Franklin's passing, she recoiled from the company of friends and relatives who sought to console her. She did not want consolation, did not want to surround herself with those who offered it. Instead, she sank into a loneliness that was familiar to her but at times seemed the blackest and most frigid of nights. "Although Eleanor saw no 'alienist'* to diagnose her terrible sadness and hopelessness—in 1910, psychiatry was scorned by social New York—it would not take a medical specialist to determine that she was severely depressed."

When Eleanor finally, and gradually, allowed people back into her life, they urged her to join them for parties, concerts, the theater, meals at the city's finest restaurants or most elegant residences—the kind of life her parents had lived. At first she resisted. But perhaps, she thought, such frivolity would be helpful to her now, a series of mindless activities in which she could lose her doubts and sorrows. By the time she consented, however, she found herself pregnant with a son she would name Elliott, and unable to return to the social whirl. Pottker opines that "a pregnancy at this time was probably the worst thing for her emotional well-being."

❖

YEARS LATER, WITH HER SURVIVING children grown and most of them succeeding in one way or another, she was still blaming herself for not raising them properly. "It did not come naturally to me to understand little children or to enjoy them." And so she was more likely to turn

---

* The word *psychiatry* was not in common usage at the time. One who practiced it was known as an alienist.

the children over to nurses and nannies and devote herself, often in solitary fashion, to her work.

In fact, Eleanor did not even take pleasure from the act responsible for bringing children into being. To her daughter, Sara, she admitted that she did not enjoy sex, had never enjoyed it. It was, rather, an "ordeal to be borne." It is a troubling statement to read, this admission that she could not step out of her solitary state even long enough to share what is, at its best, one of the greatest joys of humanity.

⟡

ELEANOR EVEN FOUND HERSELF LONELY in March 1933, on the eve of her becoming the nation's First Lady. She "worried that her talents would not be used; that she would become a shut-in, a congenial hostess in the political shadows politically sidelined." Rather than demand a role in the nation's governance, which she would later do insistently, she yielded to what she seemed certain the future would hold, and once again shut herself off from others. "Her great friend Lorena Hickok was so impressed by ER's initial distress that she titled her subsequent biography *Eleanor Roosevelt: Reluctant First Lady.*"

It was, in fact, in a letter to Hickok that Eleanor made the following confession:

> My zest in life is rather gone for the time being. If anyone looks at me, I want to weep. . . . I get like this sometimes. It makes me feel like a dead weight & my mind goes round & round like a squirrel in a cage. I want to run, & I can't, & and I despise myself. I can't get away from thinking about myself. Even though I know I'm a fool, I can't help it.

By summer, Eleanor's zest for life had returned, but she was not deceived. It would depart again, and then return, and then depart, return; it was the pattern of her life, cycles of inevitability. She might have been at her loneliest when Hickok, a journalist for whom Eleanor did step out of solitude, was away from her, on assignment.

The two women exchanged letters that took friendship to such an extreme that many people suspected they were lovers. Although there was such a thing at the time as a "Boston marriage," in which two women lived together in a passionate but nonsexual relationship, it is probably true that Eleanor and Lorena *were* physically intimate. Friendship is seldom carried to such an extreme that it invokes desperately expressed longing on the one hand, or jealousy on the other. In Eleanor's case, it invoked both. The latter was especially troublesome to her. And to Hickok. Eleanor was not only unhappy when Lorena was out of sight; she was vigilant. "Frequently flirtatious, Hick met women in her travels who found her attractive, who squired her about, took her home for dinner, and for weekends. . . . ER's letters indicate that she was in no mood to entertain dalliances. When Hick confided that a new situation with yet another had emerged, ER wrote firmly: 'How hard for you to have a lady who is in love in her mind with you. Well if she is in love you can tell her how to snap out of it!'"

And Hick did just that. Eleanor was as important to her as she was to Eleanor.

Ultimately, though, details of their physical relationship are as unknown as they are irrelevant to the present story. Lorena Hickok is best thought of as a woman to whom Eleanor allowed enough proximity to ease the pangs of her lifelong loneliness. Leave it at that.

NELL'S COLDNESS

THERE WERE TIMES, COMING SELDOM but spectacularly, when Eleanor's demeanor was unrecognizable as described in the preceding pages. It was, in fact, the opposite, displays of an insensitivity hard to fathom. Perhaps it was her mother's genes, not that anyone knew anything about genes then; perhaps it was an occasional need for revenge against the hurtful circumstances of her life and those responsible for them. Or even those *not* responsible; anyone would do, for Eleanor might have been lashing out generally rather than specifically in a manner that had more to do with letting off steam than striking specific targets.

Her inability to be a warm and loving mother might have been, at least in part, a means of "getting even" with her own mother, although a statement like this gets too close to psychobabble for comfort. Still, her refusal to answer calls to come home when ensconced in her cherry tree with book in hand surely was a snub to her family, especially to her mother, as much as it was a sign of engagement in a particular tale.

"She was not a saint," it has been accurately stated, especially in the days leading up to her residence in the White House. Writes Blanche Wiesen Cook, in a passage almost chilling in its mean-spiritedness:

> [T]hough long-suffering, ER could be mean and cold and disagreeable. Initially she went everywhere with rambunctious dogs. They growled and snarled, barked and nipped, bolted and chased. . . . ER's dogs represented an unacknowledged part of her character, and served various purposes. ER often admitted to feeling "low in my mind," discontented and depressed. She rarely expressed anger directly. But when she grew cold, she could freeze the stoutest heart . . . and she parted with her dogs only after they had lunged at several children, and bit at least one diplomat, one senator, and one friendly woman reporter.

The senator was Hattie Caraway from Arkansas, the first woman ever elected to serve a full term in that office, and one of Eleanor's beasts sank his teeth into her arm deeply enough to draw blood. Caraway was as surprised as she was horrified. It would have been an inexcusable occurrence under any circumstances, but the senator was ambushed at Eleanor's first Gridiron Widows party, one of the most significant social events of the year for Washington's women. One is usually safe from animal attack at so festive an occasion.

The dog in question was a German shepherd named Major, and Blanche Wiesen Cook understates the case when she calls him "a large, distracting presence." Nonetheless, Eleanor, having learned nothing, and perhaps even taking a sort of mean-spirited pleasure from her experience at the Gridiron Widows party, also brought Major to her first press conference. The journalists waiting to question her were aghast, having never seen anything like this before. Major stood by his mistress's side, sharing the podium, cold black eyes flitting about the room as if wondering whom to attack first.

Fortunately, he attacked no one. Still, bringing a dog capable of violence to a press conference was not the best idea the First Lady ever had. He might not have lunged at any of the reporters, but he barked at everyone who spoke, except Eleanor, which is to say that the First Lady had a hard time hearing the questions, and as a result did not always provide the kind of answers the reporters wanted to hear—Major acting protectively, the German shepherd as press secretary.

At another event, a different member of Eleanor's canine corps sought revenge for the First Lady by chewing on the face—yes, the face!—of Bess Furman. She was the "friendly woman reporter" referred to in the previous passage from Cook, but had recently written an article about the inappropriateness of Major's presence at governmental events. Several stitches were required to close the wound and traces of a scar remained with her for the rest of her life.

Also required was a profound apology. The stitches were quickly provided, but the latter—inexplicably—never came. Neither Eleanor nor anyone acting on her behalf ever wrote contritely, or at all, to Furman after the attack. It took "other incidents" before the First Lady finally agreed to stop behaving like the grande dame of a police state.

This was the Eleanor Roosevelt America had come to know and love? *This* was the woman it would come to know and love all the more as her husband continued in office in the years afterward? *This* was the national mother figure, benign and welcoming, champion of the underdog?—no pun intended. One struggles to explain it but cannot. Nothing foreshadowed this and other instances of casual cruelty and remorselessness.

She couldn't have contented herself with a Chihuahua?

"One might argue that ER had an imperious temper, even a cruel streak. But saints and melancholy Griseldas are generally unconscious of such impulses, and tend to regret them when confronted by their impact."

Apparently, Eleanor was one of those who did *not* regret them—at least not so that anyone would know. What she *did* regret was the pressure, coming from all quarters, to exile the dogs from the White House. About their eventual departure, the First Lady said, with incomprehensible callousness, "That was a sad day for me and no one thought it wise to say too much to me about dogs for a long time."

❖

BUT EVEN WITHOUT CANINE COMPANIONSHIP, there was still the occasional outburst, puzzling and atypical. Eleanor "once became very annoyed at a child who seemed to be crying all over the White House halls, and insisted he find a bathtub to sit in until he was through." The parents quickly took the child out of Eleanor's hearing.

A few years later, after she and Franklin had had several disputes over domestic policy, "the White House became during the winter of 1935 an exceedingly frosty place. ER might have thought she was subtle, might have believed her husband failed to notice her prolonged silences, might even have imagined her blue tones of cold invisible. But he knew them as well as anyone. He had witnessed those icicles that might at any moment dart from behind her eyes, and linger unspoken as she pressed her lips."

But—and it cannot be repeated too much—occurrences like these were uncommon, and perhaps understandable given the torments of Eleanor's childhood that still, at some level, festered within and took strange forms when they erupted. Only one person would have understood this side of her, could have soothed her, could have explained her to herself after her rare bursts of irrationality.

But by this time, he was no longer mortal. He had now assumed the role of guardian angel. Only Eleanor knew that, despite his rapid deterioration, which is about to be described, he met all the qualifications for the job.

PART THREE

SECOND NOTE TO READERS

THE CENTER OF THE MURAL

W E ARE WELL INTO THE story. But I believe there is something that should be said at this point before it continues.

I have taken some liberties so far, not with the truth but with my method of telling it. I have skipped back and forth in time between Eleanor Roosevelt as a child and Eleanor as an adult. I have taken smaller skips, but skipped nonetheless, with her father. In short, I have been more concerned with theme than chronology; that is, more concerned with Elliott's background and, later, his remarkable influence on Eleanor, than with writing a diary of their relationship, heeding the dictates imposed by a calendar.

It is for the same reason that I am about to do even more skipping, this time taking not steps but leaps. This will allow me to fill in the blanks hinted at but not detailed in the preceding chapters. Henceforth, Elliott will appear only during a period of thirty-four years, ending in 1894. As for Eleanor, she will not appear until 1917, when the Great War, later known as World War I, forces her out of her cocoon and into the realm of politics already occupied by her husband. There will, thus, be no intercourse between them except for flashbacks and memories, although many of these will appear. They will provide evidence of a bond that itself makes a leap—in this case a leap over time, not only ignoring the calendar but transcending death.

Again, I am allowing theme to trump chronology, and asking for the reader's patience. I am trying to tell the story in what I believe to be not only an engaging manner but also a "factual" one, factual as Ralph Waldo Emerson once employed the term. "If a man wishes to acquaint himself with the real history of the world," Emerson wrote, ". . . he must not go first to the state-house or the court-room. . . . It is what is done and suffered in the house, in the personal history, that has the profoundest interest for us. . . . The great facts are the near ones."

Elliott and his daughter could not have taken more divergent paths in life. In most cases, a circumstance like this creates a gulf between parent and child that cannot easily, or ever, be bridged. Especially given the path that Elliott took, however much against his will, however due to perversities of his nature that were as unwanted as they were uncontrollable.

But this did not happen with the two Roosevelts. Despite their divergent paths, Elliott would be the most important person in Eleanor's life for all of her days, even to the last one, even when he was no longer corporeally present. Theirs was a relationship for the ages,

fascinating to contemplate if not always easy to understand. The role
of the parent in the growth of a child is one of the deepest and most
important of human mysteries, one that cannot be predicted or, as
it seems with the Roosevelts, solved even after the fact.

As I worked on *Someone to Watch Over Me*, I thought of a painting.
Most biographers who write about America's longest-serving First
Lady try to tell the complete story of her existence, from unprom-
ising start to esteemed world figure. This means telling of war and
peace, of conversations and disputes with the most influential men
in the world, of leadership in a wide variety of spheres, of opinions
that mattered, expressed in a wide variety of forums. It means, as
well, telling of one of the most extraordinary transformations that a
human being has ever made from child to adult.

Biographers, then, think of her story as a mural, and they are correct to do so; Eleanor's was among the richest, most widely ranging
lives of a public figure in the twentieth century.

What I have chosen to do, and I believe with equal validity, is
something altogether different. I have focused on only a part of the
painting, one small section, perhaps easy to overlook but to me, a
section of particular interest, where the action is more intense than
elsewhere on the canvas and the meaning more significant. To me,
that small section is in the center of the mural, and I believe that
from that position all the rest of the painting, all the rest of the
qualities that made Eleanor Roosevelt the unique person she was,
may be said to radiate outward.

The mural cannot be taken in with one glance. To understand
it, to appreciate the wide-ranging aspects it reveals, one must know
where to cast his or her gaze initially. I trust that I have found the
proper place and, further, that the description of it that follows, is
more complete than any presented before.

FATHER

1873–89

I T IS HARD TO SAY when it all started to go wrong for Elliott. Probably when he was thirteen, although there might have been signs earlier, and there were definitely indications a year later. Easier to state are the symptoms, and how they showed themselves— gradually at the outset, and then at an ever-increasing rate. What can be stated with certainty, fatal certainty, is when and how the symptoms finally ceased.

Elliott seemed an unlikely candidate to be struck with "mysterious problems," an imprecise term that was as precise as anyone could at first attach to the boy's difficulties. As author Allen Churchill writes, "Handsome Ellie, youngest of the brood, always seemed the best adjusted of the children. But something had happened."

Something had happened. It is a simple phrase that Churchill uses, yet in Elliott's case an ominous one.

Blanche Wiesen Cook's speculations cover a lot of ground. "Whatever was wrong with Elliott," she writes, "whether he had a brain tumor or epilepsy, whether he was having a sexual coming-out crisis as he entered adolescence, or whether he was the one who acted out the emotional turbulence of his family, we will never know."

The earliest days of Elliott's troubles roughly coincided with Theodore's gains in strength and vitality, Elliott's no longer needing his older brother's protection as he surpassed him in most physical endeavors, from lifting weights to running long distances, from boxing to wrestling to sheer muscularity of appearance. Whether this timing was coincidental or cause and effect, no one can say. It is, however, suggestive, surely a point worth considering.

When he was thirteen or fourteen, probably the former, Elliott began to suffer what are commonly known as seizures. More specifically, he was "experiencing fainting spells, blood rushes to the head, blackouts, severe headaches, and an inability to concentrate on his studies . . . he had fits during which he babbled incoherently." It was more than a young man could cope with. "The doctors called it 'hysteria.' His family called it 'Elliott's weakness.'" It is possible, however, that even before this, Elliott, like his wife some years later, had begun to struggle with migraines, an unusual occurrence in one so young. But the year in which his migraines began cannot be pinpointed.

Theodore's biographer H. W. Brands described the earliest days of Elliott's lengthy demise like this:

> He . . . began to show symptoms of a worrying emotional or neurological disturbance. He grew nervous easily,

fretting over whether he would amount to anything in life, and suffered debilitating headaches and occasional seizures. "I jump involuntarily at the smallest sound and have a perpetual headache," he confided to his brother, adding that he was "nearly always low in spirits."

Brands's reference to Elliott's concern about whether he would amount to anything in life supports the notion that, at some level, envy of Theodore played a role in his unhinging. The latter, as all Roosevelts seemed to sense when Theodore was but a boy, would one day be a stunning success at something or other. He was brilliant; he was determined; he would not be pushed aside. Elliott, on the other hand, was simply charming, and charm is no guarantee of accomplishment. Besides, in time his charm would begin to wane. Except to one person, that is, one who always responded to the best in her father, even when he was not able to display it openly.

❦

Tired of working with tutors at home, a lonely occupation but one that was common among children of the Swells in their earliest years, Elliott persuaded his father to let him attend Saint Paul's School, a prestigious prep school in Concord, New Hampshire. There, he told Theodore Sr., he "could make more friends" than he could studying with only a single adult present. And there he could join his cousin and best friend, Archibald Gracie, upon whom he would be able to rely for emotional stability. His father, although dubious, agreed.

But the summer before he was to enter Saint Paul's, Elliott again found himself felled by seizures. He was not ready for boarding school, Theodore Sr. decided, and delayed his entrance for a few months to take the boy with him on a business trip to Europe. So often in those days were changes of scenery thought to be cures for one malady or another. So seldom did they actually turn out to be, and so it was with Elliott. It was in Europe, in fact, that he suffered his worst attack yet. His older brother speculated on the reason.

> It came from overexcitement but of so natural a kind that I foresee it will be very difficult to guard him from it. A pillow fight was perhaps the principal cause. . . . It produced congestion of the brain with all its attendant horrors of delirium, etc. The doctor says that there is no cause for anxiety as it is only necessary to avoid all excitements for 2 or 3 years and he will entirely outgrow it. He is perfectly well again now, but of course weak and confined to his bed.

When Elliott returned from abroad, his brother noted the change in him, making his own youthful diagnosis. "He is nervous," Theodore said, "although he stoutly denies it. He sleeps in my bed." The need for Elliott to have a nighttime companion in his adolescent years should have set off more alarms in the family than it did. Theodore, though, did not seem to have minded, or at least did not think he could afford to mind. "I should be afraid to leave [Elliott] alone," he said, and, unfortunately, he knew firsthand whereof he spoke.

Theodore had demons of his own as a youth, and they took a toll, of which most people are unaware. He was "haunted by nightmares and monsters, headaches and stomach upsets, and on occasion, an acute case of asthma, which completely incapacitated him." So much so that there were times when his breath was weakened to the point at which he could not blow out the candle on his nightstand.

But by the end of Theodore's sixteenth year, which was Elliott's fourteenth, he had both worked and willed his maladies away. He was exercising tirelessly, reading voraciously; his father had demanded that he "*make* your body," and Theodore had done just that. In fact, he went even further, making his mind as well.

Elliott had watched Theodore transform himself with awe, and, as previously noted, encouragement. But the more he saw, the more certain he became that he could never perform such feats himself. He was far from being a weakling, but he was neither as tough nor as dedicated as his brother. Nor as committed to learning. In fact, he had begun to think he did not measure up to Theodore in any way. And thus the gulf between the two brothers' futures widened.

❦

PERHAPS BECAUSE, AS YOUNG AS he was, he was already susceptible to so many maladies from within, Elliott seemed unusually receptive to others from the outside, too. For instance, he caught colds more often than most boys his age. And he was said to have been the victim of "an undiagnosed disorder and fainting spells, which some of his relatives subsequently called epilepsy." About this latter point, Elliott's relatives were almost certainly wrong.

As is the judgment put forward so confidently by Eleanor's son, who never knew his grandpa. "In his schooldays," Elliott the second would write, "a tumor developed in her father's brain."

❦

AFTER THE BUSINESS TRIP TO Europe with Theodore Sr., Elliott was allowed to enrolled at Saint Paul's after all, and got off to a promising start. As Theodore's biographer Nathan Miller tells us, "Out of the family orbit for the first time, he did well. 'I think all my teachers are satisfied,' he wrote his father in September 1875." His cousin, also at Saint Paul's, agreed. Elliott seemed at home on the campus and, said Archie, he "studied hard and worked late."

But it didn't last. In October, only the second month of the school year, Elliott wrote another letter to his father, a frightful one.

Private

During my Latin lesson, without the slightest warning I had a bad rush of blood to my head it hurt me so that I can't remember what happened. I believe I screamed out, anyway the Doctor brought me over to his house and I lay down for a couple of hours; it had by that time recovered and after recovering and after laying down all the afternoon I was able to go on with my afternoon studies. I lost nothing but one Greek lesson by it. . . .

You told me to write you everything or I would not bother you with this, but you want to know all about me don't you?

P.S. II [*sic*] Don't forget *me* please and write *often*.

Love from Ellie

Also in the letter, Elliott told his father that he was running out of "anti-nervous medicine" and wanted more. Theodore Sr. sent it, but with misgivings. Medicine, he realized, could be no more than an anodyne for his son, not a cure. And a cure was difficult to arrive at with the causes of Elliott's disease, or diseases, being so uncertain.

His father wanted him to come home. But Elliott persuaded him otherwise, to give him one more chance to be normal. Again with misgivings, Theodore Sr. relented, and son remained at Saint Paul's without incident for two more months, leading the same life as the other students, and with better-than-average results.

Then came the incident that all in the family would long remember, perhaps the beginning of serious dread.

One day, after finishing his lunch, he stood at his table, about to begin walking out of the cafeteria. He could not even manage a step. He suddenly became dizzy. Trying to steady himself by grabbing on to the edge of the table, he failed, fainting and tumbling to the floor. After regaining consciousness, he was able to sit up, but seemed unsure where he was or what had happened. In fact, he would never quite remember.

His father dispatched Theodore to Concord to bring his younger brother home. Elliott went gratefully on the one hand, but in anguish on the other, puzzling over the nature of his health. Was this the life he was fated to live?

His father, in no less anguish, could think of only one more course of action to prescribe for Elliott. He would send him out west, put him to work on the range, settle him down and build him up in an environment unlike any he had known before. It had worked for Theodore, had been part of his "making"; there seemed no reason it wouldn't work for Elliott. Or so his father hoped.

ELLIOTT WAS SENT TO FORT McKAVETT, an army outpost in the hill country of Texas, a desolate patch of the American frontier where his father had a friend who could keep a careful eye on him, as well as make him into a hardier soul. The initial results were encouraging. As Elliott approached his sixteenth year, he seemed to be on the way to at least a partial recovery.

Dear Father:

I have gone through some regular roughing since I last wrote you . . . After we left there we came on slowly camping at night and shooting all that we wanted to eat for we have never been on short rations yet thank goodness. The weather up to last night was very warm and pleasant but suddenly one of those frightfully cold north winds sprang up and from being too warm with our coats off, the addition of blankets, ulsters and mufflers of all kinds did not keep us even tolerably warm. . . . In this manner I shivered through the night up to five when "breakfast gentlemen" brought us all to our feet and without more ado we ran for the fire . . . and were served by the old lady still pipe in mouth with bacon and bread a frugal meal but if you laugh at it think I had not a mouthful since six A.M. the day before, roughing it! eh?

Elliott signed the letter "Your affectionate Son."

If his nights were often a trial, his days were spent pleasurably, riding the range, shooting wild turkeys, and listening with eagerness to his older companions tell him stories of lives so different from his own. Sometimes they related their exploits in the Mexican War, at other times their battles with Indians, those savages who still lurked on the plains, refusing to peaceably surrender their land to the white man. But they told Elliott not to worry; there were no Indians within hundreds of miles of them now. They had become an endangered species.

It all seemed just what the boy needed, especially since he was building up his body—not to Theodore's proportions, to be sure, but into someone more closely approaching manliness than he had been back in the land of the Swells. And he even gave Theodore reason to be proud of him, for Ellie "had a good deal of experience in buffalo-hunting, and once or twice was charged by old bulls but never had any difficulty in either evading the charge or else killing the brute as it came on."

But before long, Elliott began to feel guilty; he was spending his days as a cowboy when he should have been back in the classroom, like Theodore, like his sisters. Instead, here he was spending his father's money "as if I was ill." Spending his father's money was something that would not bother him a few years later.

⊰◈⊱

BUT, THE ISSUE OF EXPENSE aside, Elliott enjoyed his sojourn in the Wild West so much that he made a few return trips. In fact, Theodore visited him once, the brothers meeting in Chicago "to rest and restock. There," we know, "Theodore wrote a letter to Corinne that was to haunt the family's future."

> We have come back here after a weeks hunting in Iowa. Elliott revels in the change to civilization—and epicurean pleasures.
>
> As soon as we got here he took some ale to get the dust out of his throat; then a milk punch because he was thirsty; a mint julep because it was hot; a brand smash "to keep the cold out of his stomach"; and then sherry and bitters to give him an appetite. . . .
>
> Elliott says these remarks are incorrect and malevolent; but I say they pay him off for his last letter about my eating manners.

Theodore did not say anything to Elliott about his drinking, perhaps believing it an isolated incident, brought on by circumstance

115

more than need. But his older brother began to wonder, and would pay more attention to Elliott's thirst in the future.

Actually, Theodore or someone in the family should have started to pay attention earlier. Elliott had begun to drink well before his binge in Chicago. Perhaps his drinking followed in the wake of his first seizures; it is also possible that he had begun to drink before that, at much too young an age, and the alcohol had contributed to the seizures, even exacerbating them. Regardless of the order of events, Elliott was on a path to destruction in his earliest teens.

But the Swells didn't know this. Anna Hall didn't know. Only the closest family saw the signs.

◈

BY THE TIME HE HAD married, Elliott "was drinking heavily," according to Theodore's most definitive biographer, Edmund Morris, "although his good looks and athletic bearing tended to disguise the fact." But Elliott was a full-fledged alcoholic even before he became a suitor, and a truth of that magnitude could not be disguised for long. Morris continues:

> There had been a complete physical collapse in 1889, followed by such desperate drinking during the early part of 1890 as to shock even himself into awareness of his impending doom. Swearing never to touch alcohol again, he left the United States for Europe that summer, taking his wife, six-year-old daughter, and baby son with him. From Vienna, in September 1890, came news of the inevitable relapse, followed shortly before Christmas by a *cri de Coeur* from Anna. She was pregnant again,

and was afraid of spending the winter alone with her unstable husband.

Later on their trip, the family went to Italy. It was then that Elliott and Eleanor went for the donkey ride when he called her a coward. The explanation for his sudden change in behavior is now apparent. He was under the influence, under many influences. What was mercurial about him was almost certainly the result of his intake of foreign substances, and a physical and emotional makeup not nearly so vigorous as it appeared to others.

Still later on the trip, although Eleanor would downplay the event in her memoirs, Elliott was institutionalized for the first time, entering the Bavarian spa in Bad Reichenhall. "Anna wrote that [he] was taking the baths and drinking the mineral waters and getting better little by little except for 'awful attacks of depression.'" She was probably too optimistic. Her husband was *not* getting better, little by little or any other way.

We do not know what Eleanor was told to explain her father's absence for several weeks on the vacation. Probably that he had taken ill and had to be hospitalized. But he would be fine, it was nothing serious, she should not worry. Various historians and biographers have written different sequences involving the episodes in these months abroad, and there is no archival material definitive enough to get at the truth. These details simply are not agreed upon. We are well enough served to return with the family, Elliott in tow after his failed Bavarian rehabilitation, to New York.

❧

ELEANOR WAS ABOUT SEVEN WHEN she first learned that something was not right with her father, something more serious than whatever it was that led to his admittance to Bad Reichenhall. She believed it was a physical problem, which is at least partially true, and she believed that even her father did not understand its cause. Also true. But it was a little girl's conclusion, too general to be meaningful, and also a model of stubborn avoidance. Or, to be more precise, it was Eleanor's way of protecting her perception of the man who would live in her heart, forever.

The truth, unfortunately, was more grim than Eleanor realized. Even when Elliott seemed his old self, when he *was* his old self as a father, at least on the surface, something was happening inside, something was roiling. He had begun madness, and it was beyond his control or that of anyone else. He sometimes felt as if he were going to explode from the exertion of holding back a dreadful new self. But one step at a time. For now he just wanted to make sure his daughter didn't know what was happening to him. He did not want her to *see* what was happening, whatever it might be, when devilish forces overcame him. So far, so good.

∐◈∑

THE CHILD WITH WHOM ANNA was pregnant abroad was her third and last, her second boy, who would be known by his middle name of Hall, and sometimes by the nickname of Brudie. The baby boy who accompanied them to Europe, child number two, was Elliott. But although his attitude would later change, Eleanor's father was not especially pleased by the appearance of his namesake child. Unlike Eleanor, he was *not* a miracle from heaven. As Blanche Wiesen Cook writes:

> The birth of his first son seems to have plunged Elliott deeper into depression. He worried about money, and

feared that he was doomed to failure. He became suspicious of his wife, and wrote jealous notes suggesting that while he was struggling at work in the city [continuing at the Gracie firm] she was gay and carefree on Long Island. Throughout the autumn and winter of 1889, Anna patiently tried to comfort him in her letters: "poor darling old Elliott . . . Please don't worry darling. Start off firmly making up your mind that you will be happy. Say to yourself that *you* know I am true, & that you will trust people. It would make you feel so much happier if you truly could, & I tell you there is *nothing* to fear. Please believe me—And as to success, remember that you are God's child. . . . I seldom worry when I tell Him everything, all my troubles."

The addition of Hall to the family only sank Elliott into a deeper misery. "Anna still loved her husband and longed to help him," biographer Hazel Rowley relates, "but she was suffering from chronic headaches, and occasionally became hysterical herself under the strain." As there was little she could do for her own condition, there was even less she could do for the no-longer-dashing young man she had married.

One cannot help but sympathize with Anna. At the same time, it is surprising that she did not recognize Elliott's symptoms earlier. Unfortunately, she had had the necessary experience. "Anna's own father had been a wild drunk who had reformed and . . . reached sobriety—to deaf ears, as both her brothers were alcoholics. She knew enough to see the warning signs, but she married Elliott nevertheless."

NEVER LOSING HIS PHILANTHROPIC IMPULSES, Elliott agreed to take part in an amateur circus, with all proceeds going to charity. But he would do more than just take part: he would be the star of the circus, the daring young man on the flying trapeze. He was the only person to volunteer for so demanding a feat. But he was also a natural athlete, proficient at a variety of sports as a boy; he had no doubt that he could master an aerial act, at least at an elementary level, in his young adulthood.

One day he was practicing and, as had been true on other days, he seemed to be doing rather well in the air. But then something distracted him; there was a moment's loss of attention and the loss of his grip as a result. Elliott tumbled from his bar to the ground, landing painfully from an unspecified height. According to one account, he was attempting a double somersault at the time, which would have been a preposterously difficult trick no matter how skilled an athlete he had once been.

"His leg was broken," Eleanor later wrote, "and later it had to be rebroken and reset. I remember the day well, for we were alone in his room when he told me about it. Little as I was I sensed that this was a terrible ordeal, and when he went hobbling out on crutches to the waiting doctors, I was dissolved in tears and sobbed my heart out for hours. From this illness my father never quite recovered."

And further, said his daughter from the perspective of advanced years, the accident "completely broke his nerves." She did not know, of course, what Elliott had suffered in the years prior to breaking his leg, nor did she know how her father tried to medicate himself after falling through space. He turned to alcohol to lessen the pain, and when it didn't work, he kept increasing the dosage. His wife knew, however, and her longing to help him was now stretched to the breaking point. She no longer believed there was anything she could do, nor was she able—or was it willing?—to make the effort. She believed now that she, and her marriage, were doomed.

Most perceptively, Cook writes about the effect of Anna's alienation on the daughter from whom a degree of alienation had already taken root. "Unable to find any real comfort anywhere, and under ever-increasing pressures from her desperate family situation, Anna forged a hard, untouchable armor that warned those around her to keep their distance. Once forged, that armor seemed to her firstborn daughter created especially for her."

Even had Eleanor heard such a nuanced explanation at the time, she was too young to understand it. She was also too young to understand precisely what was happening to her father, but there were occasional frightening moments at night. "Sometimes I woke up when my mother and her sisters were talking at bed time," she wrote about her experiences at the uncomprehending age of eight, "and many a conversation which was not meant for my ears was listened to with great avidity. I acquired a strange and garbled idea of the troubles which were going on around me. Something was wrong with my father, and from my point of view nothing could be wrong with him." Although but a child, she "was well acquainted with insecurity, self-hatred and guilt." Her father, whatever his failings, was the balm for them all.

Even after the episode at the Knickerbocker Club.

⬥

IT WAS LATE ONE AFTERNOON when Elliott asked Eleanor to take a walk with him. Also in their company were three excitable terriers, straining at their leashes. It is not certain that the club, a favorite haunt of Elliott, was his destination this day, but as they approached it, he told Eleanor he wanted to go inside for a few minutes. Just a few minutes, he assured her, and she believed him. He flashed her a smile, then climbed up the steps to the front door, leaving Eleanor outside with the dogs. She did not mind. She would tend to the dogs, despite their wild efforts to break free. She would wait for her father.

Elliott went straight to the bar and began drinking. And drinking. And, finally, forgetting. His daughter waited for him for an hour, then another hour, and finally *six hours*, by which point both Eleanor and the dogs were exhausted, and by which point Elliott was so drunk that he had to be carried out of the club by several of the members and stuffed into a cab, which took him home. Somehow, Eleanor did not see her father's pathetic exit, or else did not know it was he.

"Finally," Eleanor's eldest grandson, Curtis Roosevelt, related, "the doorman said, 'Young lady, who are you waiting for?'"

"And she said, 'I'm waiting for my father, Mr. Roosevelt.'"

"And he raised his eyebrow, probably, and said, 'Well, young lady, I think we'd best get you a taxi, because your father left quite a while ago.'"

It might have been this incident that first made Eleanor aware of her father's alcoholism. She realized that he "began to drink, and for my mother and his brother Theodore and his sister began [a] period of harrowing anxiety . . ."

It was not, however, a harrowing time for her. "Like most children of alcoholics," it has been written, "Eleanor felt that she could never do enough to protect her parent, to care for him, to ward off danger, or change or try to control the situation." Perhaps she thought she was having some success. "When he was not drinking," Doris Kearns Goodwin has written, "he was loving and warm, everything Eleanor wanted in a father." The same as always. She had begun to feel that, just as her father was good for her, she was now good for him. And the opportunity to help him, to repay him for her unfailing love, made her bond with him all the more secure.

◈

Although Theodore Sr. had left him a considerable inheritance, Elliott was doing his best to drink his way through it, having swilled down the interest within a few years of returning from India and now beginning to take gulps of the principal. True, much was left but, then again, much drinking was still to be done. And there would be other expenses, the most shameful yet for the family.

But Theodore was already worrying about Elliott tarnishing the family name. "It is," he said, "a perfect nightmare."

In truth, it was more of a nightmare than Theodore knew. As he sought relief from the ordeal of his broken leg, Elliott had turned not only to liquor in greater quantities than ever before, but to drugs. He continued to ingest the drugs, and copiously, long after his leg had healed as much as it was ever going to. He was now addicted to more substances than ever, and in combination they exerted an unbreakable hold. According to FDR biographer Jean Edward Smith, Elliott enjoyed "frequent recourse to laudanum and morphine—painkillers to thwart whatever demons stalked him."

They didn't work.

"It is all horrible beyond belief," Theodore declared, stepping up the pace of his disgust. "He is a maniac morally as well as mentally . . . a flagrant male-swine."

Eleanor did not hear judgments like these. Even if she had, it would not have mattered. She still "preferred her warm and affectionate father to her cold and self-absorbed mother. At least with her father, she said, she never doubted that she 'stood first in his heart,' whereas for as long as she could remember she felt that her beautiful mother was bitterly disappointed, almost repelled by the plainness and the ungainliness of her only daughter."

She would not be budged from her position, no matter what others thought of Elliott, no matter what kind of behavior they witnessed from him. She only knew what she saw herself, and how happy and accepted she was when the two of them were together. He "dominated my life as long as he lived," Eleanor reflected in her book *This Is My Story,* "and was the love of my life for many years after he died."

DAUGHTER

1917–28

E UROPE WAS AT WAR AND the United States would join the Allies in 1917. With her husband working for the navy, and no end to his tasks in sight, Eleanor eventually joined him in Washington, where it did not take long for her to feel an unusual restlessness. She started to dwell less on herself and the problems that had long plagued her and began to think she might find a larger and more distracting role in the larger world, where such turmoil and violence now reigned. It is another way of saying that, perhaps for the first time in her life, she sought a purpose for herself, a purpose outside of herself, "the opportunity to move beyond her limited social circle" and into the virtually unlimited realms of politics and world affairs. It was a move that did not come easily.

Years earlier, when her "Uncle Ted" took the presidential oath of office, "politics still meant little to me," Eleanor admitted, and further confessed, referring to his inaugural address, that "I have no recollection of what he said!" Some time after that, while traveling abroad with her husband, she found herself in the company of Sir Ronald Ferguson, the governor-general of Australia, and his wife, Helen.

> One afternoon at tea I was alone with Lady Helen, when she suddenly asked me a devastating question: "Do tell me, my dear, how do you explain the difference between your national and state governments? It seems to us so confusing."
>
> I had never realized that there were any differences to explain. In fact, I had never given a thought to the question. I knew that we had state governments, because Uncle Ted had been Governor of New York State. My heart sank, and I wished that the ground would open up and swallow me. Luckily, Sir Ronald and my husband appeared at that moment for tea, and I could ask Franklin to answer her question. He was adequate, and I registered a vow that once safely back in the United States I would find out something about my own government.

Just as her knowledge of politics did not come easily, neither did it come quickly. When Eleanor and her children finally moved to Washington, several months after the United States had declared war on the Central Powers, she discovered that, as the wife of a member of President Wilson's subcabinet, she was automatically assigned to tedium. Initially, says Franklin's biographer Jean Smith, her days "had been almost as circumscribed as her life had been in New York, restricted to paying formal calls and leaving visiting cards, entertaining and being entertained, while supervising a household that grew larger each year," eventually numbering six children and various quantities of household help.

Supposedly, she was working on behalf of the Allied cause, but for the life of her she could not see how. By talking up American involvement at minor social events, by pleading for assistance for the troops and reciting platitudes that were supposed to boost morale—preaching, in other words, to the choir—she was not doing enough to suit herself.

Eleanor matured later in life than most people, and in a sense the process was just now beginning. Before long, she stopped handing out calling cards, declined invitations to social events, and took her first tentative steps toward becoming the Eleanor Roosevelt that always lay within, finding a way to do more for the American fighting man. But, at the start, it was not much.

Joining thousands of other women across the country, she picked up a pair of extra-long needles and started turning out blankets for the soldiers, to keep them warm in the trenches. "I did very little war work that summer beyond the inevitable knitting which every woman undertook and which became a constant habit. No one moved without her knitting. I had always done a certain amount but never had achieved the ease which the war brought as a natural result."

But Eleanor's goal was not greater proficiency with knitting needles. She knew from her first stitch that she needed a different kind of role, one that would not be merely helpful to the war effort but indispensable. It could not help but become a priority of hers, having relocated to Washington and dwelling in the midst of so much dedication to keep the world safe for democracy. Her father had taught her, when she was a child, to do what she could to assist those less fortunate than she. Once, the less fortunate had been children with various disabilities, including poverty. Now they were grown men whose lives were threatened daily.

Besides, her husband was busier than he had ever been before and, even though they were living in the same city now, she saw him remarkably little. But she did not feel abandoned as she had previously; rather, she felt free to devote herself to the national interest, to invigorate herself through meaningful activity. So, two or three days a week, she volunteered at the Red Cross canteen, for which duty she wore a sharply pressed khaki uniform and a cap resembling the woolen hats worn by doughboys overseas. She worked the day shift, getting home in time for dinner, and was proud to have her children see her in such official attire.

> Everyone in the canteen . . . was expected to do any work that was necessary, even mopping the floor, and no one remained long a member of this Red Cross unit who could not do anything that was asked of her. I remember one lady who came down escorted by her husband to put in one afternoon. I doubt if she had ever done any manual labor before in her life, and she was no longer young. The mere suggestion that she might have to scrub the floor filled her with horror and we never again saw her on a shift.

In that long ago letter of his, Eleanor's father had wanted her to lay one stone on top of another to build a wall of education for herself. She was now doing so, although hers was a wall of self-confidence as well. Stone upon stone. It occurred to her that soldiers who had not yet gone to battle, or had returned for home leave or recuperation from injuries, should have a meeting place, that it was important for warriors to gather with their mates, to swap experiences and reflections, to console each other, perhaps to shoot a game of pool. To her own surprise, she was not shy about advocating such a haven. "I went to the Red Cross and begged them to build one of their recreation rooms, which they did." At one point, her uncle Theodore cabled money to Eleanor for her military activities; it is likely that she donated some of it to rec room construction.

Still under the aegis of the Red Cross, Eleanor was sent to Saint Elizabeth's, a naval hospital and the primary mental institution in Washington. She didn't want the assignment, didn't believe she could handle it. "I cannot do this," she thought, but then: *You must do the thing you think you cannot do.*" So once a week she went to the hospital, where she "took flowers, cigarettes and any little thing that might cheer the men who had come back from overseas." Many of them had returned with injuries that would never heal, some physical and some emotional. To be in the company of such wounded men was an experience Eleanor never expected to have, and she was not only aghast at seeing the ravages of war directly in front of her; she was toughened. And educated, in a way even the best school could not have taught.

One boy—for he was just that, little more than a child—seems to have caught her eye more than the others. He was young and his hair was the color of wheat.

The sun in the window placed high up, well above the patients' heads, touched his hair and seemed almost like a halo above his head. He was talking to himself incessantly and I inquired what he was saying. "He is giving the orders," said the doctor, "which were given every night in Dunkirk, where he was stationed." I remember my husband telling me that he had been in Dunkirk and that every evening the enemy planes came over the town and bombed it and the entire population was ordered down into the cellars. This boy had stood the strain of the nightly bombing until he could stand it no longer, then he went insane and repeated the orders without stopping. . . .

I asked what chances he had for recovery and was told that it was fifty-fifty, but that in all probability he would never again be able to stand as much strain as before he had had this illness.

Eleanor's work at Saint Elizabeth's did not go unappreciated, either by those on the hospital staff or, at least in one case, by the parent of one of her patients. "I want to thank you," a mother wrote, "as one of the boys who was in the Naval Hospital at Washington from the first of April until July 8th for the kind words—the little favors—the interest you took in my son . . . He always loved to see you come in. You always brought a ray of sunshine with you, always had something to say to him."

That she was gratified by the note goes without saying. That she was appalled by conditions at the hospital was no less true. Stepping out of character—the character we have known so far, at least—she wrote to her husband's friend, Secretary of the Interior Franklin K. Lane. It was the first time she had taken advantage of her union with the assistant secretary of the navy, and she had not asked his permission.

She urged Lane to visit the hospital, to see the abysmal conditions for himself. He declined. But she refused to take no for an answer. She wrote again, telling him there were not nearly enough attendants to provide proper care for the patients, or even to keep them company in their suffering. This time Lane was motivated to investigate Eleanor's complaints and he found them valid. He thanked her for alerting him, and increased the funding for the hospital; more attendants were immediately hired.

It was all Eleanor's doing. Yet to no one did she admit her pride, perhaps not even allowing herself to feel entitlement for what she had accomplished. "Out of these contacts with human beings during the war," she wrote later, "I became a more tolerant person, far less sure of my own beliefs and methods of action, but I think more determined to try for certain ultimate objectives. I had gained a certain assurance as to my ability to run things, and the knowledge that there is joy in accomplishing a good job. I knew more about the human heart, which had been somewhat veiled in mystery up to now."

Her childhood memories of loneliness and the cruelty of indifference would always be with her. But they were slowly beginning to recede, drifting further back in her consciousness. All of those except the ones involving her father. To him she would have admitted her pride in having come so far. To her he would have expressed his confidence that she would do so.

And, in its own way, the conversation probably did take place.

⬥

WHEN THE WAR ENDED, FRANKLIN left the navy and the family moved back to New York. He joined a law firm, became vice president of a surety bonding house, headed the local Navy Club and the Greater New York Boy Scout Council, and served as an overseer for his college—Harvard, of course.

He was, in other words, as busy and distant from his wife and children as he had been in Washington. Eleanor took it as a sign. No longer dismayed by his absence, she resolved to continue on her own path, to make a life of her own. And so she began to gather even more stones for her wall.

The first few toppled quickly. With the world at peace, she could see no obvious direction for herself. "If I had to go out and earn my own living," she said, "I doubt if I'd even make a very good cleaning woman. I have no talents, no experience, no training, for anything." Not long after assessing herself so pessimistically, she tried, as she had done once before, teaching. The pessimism remained. "I can't say I am set up by the exams my children did," she wrote to her husband, whose mind was on his future in politics, not his wife's seeming lack of a future. "I only flunked one, but the others were none too good." Of course she blamed herself for her students' poor showing, not the students themselves.

Still, she did not give up, and in 1920 finally found a place for herself in the world of politics—a small one, to be sure, but a toehold nonetheless. In *This Is My Story*, she writes:

> In New York I had begun to do a fairly regular job for the women's division of the Democratic State Committee, and was finding work very satisfactory and acquiring pride in doing a semiprofessional job. We started a small mimeographed paper with which Mr. Howe [Louis Howe, one of Franklin's top advisers and unyielding supporters] gave me considerable help. . . . I learned a great deal about advertising, circulation and make-up. . . . I learned how to make a dummy for the printer, and . . . I became quite proficient in planning, pasting and so on.

It sounds as if Eleanor learned more about the trade of printing rather than that of politics, which was more and more becoming her goal. But, as she surely realized, a long wall begins with the place-ment of but a few stones.

And then came 1921, and the world suddenly spun off its axis.

❖

THE YEAR BEFORE, FRANKLIN DELANO Roosevelt had been the Demo-cratic Party's brightest young star. He had lost his bid for the vice presidency of the United States, but the defeat was rightly blamed on the man at the head of the ticket, Senator James M. Cox from Ohio, who had been thumped in the election by Warren G. Harding. Roosevelt, meanwhile, was viewed as having acquitted himself well in the campaign. Presidentially, some even said. Privately, he allowed himself to agree.

The following summer, a few months after Harding and Calvin Coolidge began to occupy the nation's top two offices, Roosevelt was vacationing with his family on Campobello Island, off the coast of New Brunswick, Canada. With the future seeming to hold such promise for him, he was exuberant. One day, despite a strange and lingering ache in his legs, "Franklin and the chil-dren splashed and whooped into the water, and swam to the other side, then they hurried up and over a low ridge, ran across several yards of sandy beach, and hurled themselves into the frigid Bay of Fundy." He thought the exercise would help, that the cold water would stimulate him, soothe him—but his legs still ached. He did not feel "the glow I'd expected."

Nor would he ever feel it again. He became increasingly fatigued, and that night started to shiver. Despite the summer tempera-tures, Eleanor piled all the blankets in the house on him. The next morning, getting out of bed after a largely sleepless night, "his left leg buckled beneath him." His back was now hurting as much as his legs and his temperature had soared to 102. He climbed back into bed, afraid to venture even a few steps. And even more afraid of the future. Franklin Delano Roosevelt had contracted polio.

Perhaps because it was such a blow to her, perhaps because she was by nature a private woman, and perhaps because the whole world would learn of it in time, Eleanor would write little of this momentous event in the future. But the disease upended her life as much as it did that of her husband. Louis Howe, one of Franklin's most trusted advisers, not to mention greatest admirers, was nonetheless quick to accept the new reality and the most Machiavellian in his assessment of its political ramifications. There were a number of Democrats who had looked askance at Roosevelt because of his upper-class background, perhaps secretly envying him. Howe believed that those same people might now be persuaded to view the man differently, to sympathize with him. Howe reasoned, then, that the sympathy would cancel out the envy and make FDR an even more powerful presence in Democratic circles. If, that is, he could somehow remain a viable political figure. It would not be easy. There had never been a handicapped man in the White House, which was already Howe's vision as well as Franklin's.

How could Americans be made to believe Roosevelt was up to the job when mere locomotion could seem a job in itself? What kind of image would such a man project of the country he led? The questions seemed so large as to defy answers. That was where not only Howe came in, but Eleanor.

And so, for months—for years, actually, but especially in those first months, when she was always at his side—she worked tirelessly in his behalf. ER brought friends and political associates to his bedroom to keep him informed and entertained. She clipped newspaper items for him, marked editorial he would either enjoy or abhor. She insisted, during the days of dread and despair, when he struggled without success to move his limbs or even his toes, that he continue to take a vital interest in the political world. In concert with Louis Howe, she kept up a running commentary on the current political scene—on who among FDR's associates was feuding with whom on any given day, what deals were being made with and without his approval, for or against his interests.

Eleanor amazed herself that *she*, she of all people, could instruct her husband in politics, both the gossip and substance of it, instruct him so well that no one would know, from talking to him, that he had been felled by a vicious disease. But that is exactly what she did. And, as a result of her unceasing effort, her constant questioning of Howe and other government insiders, and the application of her own growing intellectual acuity, she kept her husband so informed that his voice could not be ignored. She had moved well beyond the nuances of the printing press now.

"'Mrs. Roosevelt's activity with the Democratic women,' the *New York Herald Tribune* wrote in 1927, 'has caused a revival in Tammany circles of the talk the Governor [Al] Smith favors Franklin D. Roosevelt . . . as Democratic candidate for Senator.'" Instead, Smith would be the party's presidential candidate, losing to Republican Herbert Hoover in 1928, and Roosevelt, with his nominating speech for Smith at the convention, would spring back into presidential consideration by taking Smith's old position as governor of New York. It was, for its time, a remarkable accomplishment.

WHAT IT MEANT WAS EVEN more work for Eleanor. But she welcomed it. Determined to prepare herself, she enrolled in business school to learn shorthand and typing, while at the same time signing up with the League of Women Voters. The latter would prove to be the most formative of all early influences for a life devoted to public service.

Once again, Eleanor amazed herself. Her interest in politics might have been ignited by her husband's, but only she could fuel an ongoing commitment. And fuel it she did. She soon became a member of the league's board of directors, and took an active role in fund-raising for the group's initiatives. A constitutional amendment had given women the right to vote in 1920, but the league had so many more items on its agenda:

> [N]ational health insurance, unemployment insurance, state and federally funded old-age pensions . . . an end to child labor, maximum-hour and minimum-wage legislation, the Sheppard-Towner Maternity and Infant Protection Act, pure-milk-and-food legislation, federal aid to education, civil-service reform, full citizenship for women "whether or not married to U.S. nationals," the participation of women at every level of national life, the promotion of international peace and membership in the League of Nations.

It is impossible to imagine a more ambitious list of goals. To one degree or another, Eleanor involved herself in all of them, and reported back to members of the league on how their programs were progressing through the legislative process. It was a series of time-consuming, often complicated tasks, and often disappointing in their outcomes. No matter. Eleanor Roosevelt, once shy, was exhilarated.

And although there is no evidence to suggest that she spent much time now thinking about her mother, it is intriguing to contemplate Anna's decision to teach her daughter etiquette. She had done so because she believed Eleanor could aspire to nothing more than good table manners. As it turned out, there was an entire world of more important matters to which Eleanor could aspire, and in which she would play increasingly important roles. It was a world that involved her attendance at a number of dinners to raise both money and awareness, as well as to plot strategies. Eleanor attended many of them, demonstrating that she knew not just what utensils to use, but what arguments to make for her evolving positions.

⸺◆⸺

ALTHOUGH RAISED A REPUBLICAN, to the extent that she was raised in a political culture at all, she was now a Democrat—and not just because of Franklin. "I believe that the best interests of the country are in the hands of the Democratic Party," she said, without going into further detail, "because I believe they are the most progressive." As for Republicans, "well, they are more conservative, you know, and we can't be too conservative and accomplish things."

And her desire to accomplish things was beginning to match that of her husband, whose increasing political ascendancy might have surprised even Louis Howe's ambitions for him. Having crossed the country on Smith's behalf in 1928, despite having to drag his legs beneath him, proved to be evidence of strength and courage, not a handicap. And as governor of New York, his patrician bearing now made him appear more dignified than elitist.

Eleanor's involvement in her husband's campaign for Albany was little short of superhuman. She stepped up her duties with the New York Democratic State Committee and the League of Women Voters, and began to turn out even more pieces for a monthly New York publication called the *Women's Democratic News*, to which she had already been contributing her time. "She wrote the editorials, solicited contributions from prominent Democrats . . . and kept in touch with a network of correspondents in *every county.*" [Italics added.]

One of the editorials composed by this woman, who only a few years earlier could not explain the difference between state and federal governments, was called "Our Foreign Policy—What Is It?" She bemoaned the fact that "we do nothing constructive to build up good feeling, and we drift into a very difficult situation. . . . Can it be that we, 'the big brother of all nations on this side of the Atlantic' are playing the part of the bully?" About the other side of the Atlantic, Eleanor believed US policy was dismissive, writing that, since "we do not wish to be entangled in European difficulties, our government's only concern is to collect what money is due us."

Other than the editorials, Eleanor did not write for the *Women's Democratic News* herself, but everything that appeared on its pages reflected her emerging views, and at this time affairs overseas remained her most abiding concern.

> The Republican Administration has no foreign policy; it has drifted without plan. This great nation cannot afford to play a minor role in world politics. It must have a sound and positive foreign policy, not a negative one. We declare for a constructive foreign policy based on these principles:
>
> (a) Outlawry of war and an abhorrence of militarism, conquest and imperialism.
>
> (b) Freedom from entangling political alliances with foreign nations. . . .

(d) Non-interference with the elections or other internal
      political affairs of other foreign nations. . . .

(k) We condemn the Republican Administration for lack
      of statesmanship and efficiency in negotiating the
      1921 treaty for the limitation of armaments . . .

With statements like these, Eleanor seemed to be rehearsing for the part she would play in just a few years, when the prize her husband sought was not the governor's mansion, but the White House. It was a place she would occupy as forcefully as her husband.

⊶◆⊷

OF COURSE, ELEANOR'S CONTACTS AND labors—the speeches she gave, the articles she wrote, the contacts she made, the funds she raised, the campaign literature she helped to disseminate—were hardly the sole reason that her husband won election as president of the United States in 1932. But that it was helpful, and that the groundwork she had laid in preceding years was an important part of Franklin's victory cannot be denied. She had opened doors through which he was able to make his way with ease when the time came, helping him to amass 22,821,513 popular votes, compared to 15,761,532 votes for Hoover, the Depression-riddled incumbent. The future, once so promising for Franklin Roosevelt, and then apparently denied him, had been realized after all.

It was a miracle in American politics.

And Eleanor, still at some level the lonely, fearful little girl who agreed with her mother and other adults close to her that she was so unattractive as to be ugly, this little girl was about to become the First Lady of the United States. Although, as she had stated to

Lorena Hickok, she would do so against her will. "If I wanted to be selfish," she insisted, "I could wish Franklin had not been elected." She went on to say that "I never wanted it, even though some people have said that my ambition for myself drove him on. They've even said that I had some such idea in the back of my mind when I married him. I never wanted to be a President's wife, and I don't want it now." Hickok listened to her attentively, but there was something in her expression that Eleanor could read instantly. "You don't quite believe me, do you?"

One recalls Eleanor's childhood essay, "Ambition." At the same time one is certain that the desire she expressed to succeed did not extend nearly this far.

FATHER

1890–92

O N THE SAME TRIP TO Europe during which Elliott and Eleanor
went donkey riding, and during which Anna began to show signs
of being pregnant with Hall, the family took a house in Neuilly-
sur-Seine, just outside of Paris, for her confinement. Well, most of the
family. It was a small abode, and thought to be too small for Eleanor,
what with nurses hovering and friends and family coming to call. And
the place was certain to feel even smaller when the baby was finally
born. That, at least, was the excuse for sending Little Nell, then just five,
to a convent school for a few months, where she would be out of the way.

Eleanor did not want to go. She "saw this as banishment. She was
made to feel like an outsider by the other little girls, whose religion

she did not share and whose language she spoke awkwardly." It was not a happy experience, not nearly like her later years at Allenswood with Mlle. Souvestre. "I was not yet six years old," she later wrote, "and I must have been very sensitive with an inordinate desire for affection . . ."

One day, a classmate of Eleanor's swallowed a penny, and all the girls were titillated by the feat, admiring her, even jealous of her courage. "[S]he was the center of everybody's interest," Eleanor said. "I longed to be in her place." So she tried. She let it be known not only to the other students at the convent, but to the nuns who presided over the school in typically draconian manner, that she, too, had swallowed a penny. But her story was unconvincing, obviously untrue, and lying, no matter how inconsequential the topic of the lie, was a sin.

The nuns sent for Eleanor's mother to pick her up and take her home. She had been banished from her place of banishment. Eleanor recalled Anna's appearance at the convent, so pregnant that it appeared as if she had attached a balloon to her midsection.

> She took me away in disgrace.
>
> I remember the drive home as one of utter misery, for I could bear swift punishment far better than long scoldings. I could cheerfully lie any time to escape a scolding, whereas if I had known that I would simply be put to bed or be spanked I probably would have told the truth.
>
> This habit of lying stayed with me for years. My mother did not understand that a child may lie from fear; I myself never understood it until I reached the age when I realized there was nothing to fear.

What is most interesting about the incident is not Anna's believing that she had cause, yet again, to be disgraced by her daughter's behavior, nor is it Eleanor's admission that she had become a liar as a result, which, if true, was a habit that did not last long. No, what is most interesting is her father's reaction. Elliott, rapidly becoming an intolerable burden to the entire family, was drinking more than ever, and his addictions to morphine and laudanum were worsening, destroying his health and beginning to erode his sanity. "I am sorry to say," Eleanor wrote about her father's ongoing presence in Paris, "he was causing a great deal of anxiety, *but he was the only person who did not treat me as a criminal!*" [Italics added.]

And so the pattern continued: Even at his worst, Elliott was the best man for, and to, his daughter. Against all odds, through his fog of liquor and drugs, he managed to convey his certainty that Eleanor was a worthy child. He let her know, as soberly on this occasion as on so many others, that she deserved not only love but respect, even though his own life affirmed to his family that he himself deserved neither.

❖

AND HE HAD NOT YET reached the bottom of his abyss. But the nadir was soon to come, and would arrive in stages, each more embarrassing and self-destructive than the previous one.

After Eleanor was dismissed from the convent school, Elliott checked himself into another sanitarium. It was his fourth, the previous place of incarceration being Mariengrund in Graz, Austria, prior to the family's moving on to France. Fortunately for the Roosevelts, this was all happening abroad and the press did not learn that Elliott had been institutionalized. But just as the treatments at Mariengrund proved anonymous, so did they prove ineffective.

Elliott's next attempt to rid himself of addiction came just outside the French capital, but it was not like the others. To the others he went willingly. This time he did not want to be put away, especially in what was commonly referred to as an asylum. In fact, he claimed that his wife and his sister Bamie had kidnapped him, handing him over to physicians at the Château de Suresnes against his will. No one believed him, however; no one *should* have, and thus he began yet another round of futile treatment.

As he did, Anna, Bamie, Eleanor, and her brand-new baby brother sailed back to America, with Eleanor's pleas to stay behind being ignored. She wanted to remain with her father—near to him, at least. She was still too young to understand either the details or the causes of Elliott's breakdown, continuing to know only that there was something "seriously wrong" with him, something about which she was told more often than it was something she observed. But this was all the more reason, she believed, for her to stand by his side, as he was always standing by hers.

No one listened. No one cared. In fact, her mother and Bamie were growing angry with her continuing displays of affection for a reprobate, the family's black sheep. Eleanor had no choice but to board the ship that would put an ocean between her and her father.

When the Roosevelts arrived home, Anna stepped ashore with something new and troubling on her mind. It was not that, in his drunken rages her husband had accused her of becoming impregnated with Hall by someone other than himself; she was by this time used to such mindless raving. But in Paris, prior to his hospitalization, he had added a new quirk to his behavior. Actually, something more than a quirk. He was not just drugged and befuddled by liquor, as usual; he was suddenly less communicative, even silent for long periods of time. His stillness was almost worse than his ravings.

In addition, when not institutionalized, he was often missing. It had happened a few times during their courtship, but Anna had not been seriously troubled then. It was nerves, she thought, albeit a severe case, brought about by his upcoming nuptials. And she knew where to find him, or at least thought she did. He was either on his polo mount or alone in his room, sometimes for as long as a day or two. He needed to be by himself, he told her; from the floor below she could hear him pace, and then stop to write down his feelings in an attempt to make more sense of them.

But this was different. In Paris there were nights when he came home later than he ever had before. There were periods of several days when he did not come home at all, and when he did he had nothing to say about his absence. Where did he go? Anna asked. With whom was he spending his time? Doing what? Why? Elliott would not answer any of her questions. For the first time in their marriage, Elliott was becoming not just a burden but a stranger.

❖

IT WAS BECAUSE OF ELLIOTT's confinement at the Château de Suresnes that the Roosevelts finally ran out of luck. Journalists learned of Elliott's plight, and in the process began to ferret out the facts about his past, the years of drugs, drunkenness, irresponsible behavior—and they made headlines, big and bold and black. Eleanor might have brought disgrace to Anna; now her father brought disgrace, true disgrace, to the entire clan.

The *New York Herald*'s coverage was the most sensational.

ELLIOTT ROOSEVELT DEMENTED BY EXCESSES
Wrecked by Liquor and Folly, He Is Now Confined in an Asylum for the Insane Near Paris.

Proceedings to Save the Estate.

Commissioners in Lunacy Appointed on Petition of His Brother Theodore and His Sister Anna with His Wife's Approval.

Even back then, the *New York Times* was a more restrained publication.

ELLIOTT ROOSEVELT "INSANE"

HIS BROTHER ASKS FOR A COMMISSION

TO PASS UPON HIS CONDITION

Elliott Roosevelt, a brother of Theodore Roosevelt, is insane, and, upon the petition of Theodore, Judge O'Brien of the Supreme Court yesterday appointed a commission to legally pass upon his condition in other that a committee may be appointed to take charge of his person and estate. He is now in the Chateau Suresnes [*sic*] near Paris.

Before Elliott left this country for Europe in July, 1890, Theodore says, he saw him very often and he gave many indications of a failing mind. He is unable to state how far this was due to excessive drinking and to other extremes. Before 1890 he noticed that Eliot [*sic*] was unable to bring his mind to bear upon any one subject for any length of time. . . .

In the Winter of 1890 he says that nearly every time he saw his brother he appeared to be irrational. He did not seem to know what he was doing and on occasions was violent. Three times he threatened to commit suicide.

The Roosevelts, all of them, were horrified. Oddly, it was Anna who seemed most under control. Even when Elliott had disappeared for more than a day, even though she suspected the reason for his absences, she wrote to him plaintively from New York upon his dismissal from the Château de Suresnes. "Try to remember that I do love you and will always be true loyal. Goodbye again[,] darling Boy. Goodbye from your loved Baby Wife."

Did she really love him? It is hard to believe. More likely, her note was an attempt to placate him. And herself. More likely, what she felt for Elliott was sorrow. She cared about his well-being because it affected her own; she wanted to save his reputation because hers would be saved in the process.

Elliott, however, paid her no mind. Not now, not in the midst of such publicity. It was the newspaper stories that consumed his attention, and he had enough coherence remaining to be enraged at them, despite their veracity. He wasted no time in responding to the story of his downfall in a letter to the editor of the *Herald*.

> You publish in your edition today a most astounding bit of misinformation under the title "Is Mr. Elliott Roosevelt To Be Adjudged A Lunatic?" I wish emphatically to state that my brother Theodore is taking no steps to have a commission pass on my sanity with or without my wife's approval. I am in Paris taking the cure at an establisse-ment hydrothérapeutique, which my nerves shaken by several severe accidents in the hunting field, made necessary.
>
> My wife went home at my request to spend the summer with her mother, Paris not being a good place for children during the hot months. I hope you will give this letter as great prominence as you today gave the invention—or worse—of your misinformant.
>
> Elliott Roosevelt,
>
> Paris, 18 August, 1891

The *Herald* published the letter, but without comment and without undoing any of the damage already done.

Eleanor knew nothing about it. She did not yet read newspapers and was being carefully protected from the reactions of those who did.

⊰◇⊱

THE HEARINGS OF THE COMMISSION that the *Times* had mentioned were a jumble of ineptitude and confusion. There were times when Elliott, still in Paris, seemed to cooperate with them, other times when he didn't, instead accusing Anna of being "abominable," which made him seem to her a "madman." Further, the family was not united behind Theodore's decision to take the matter to court, objecting to the continued public notice. This infighting delayed a decision on Elliott's fate, and on the disposition of the $175,000 that remained from his inheritance, until finally Theodore had had enough stalling and decided to act on his own.

He sailed to Paris in January of 1982, "[s]poiling for a fight," and "after a week of browbeating, moral rectitude, specific threats, and familial blandishments," got the concessions he wanted from Elliott. He told his brother that he would be released from his latest asylum and permitted to come home; the legal machinery that had been slowly grinding against him would cease.

But in return, he had to place two-thirds of his remaining money into a trust to benefit his wife and children. He also had to agree to continue all attempts at ridding himself of his dementia—both in France, where he would *not* be freed from the Château de Suresnes until he finished his current regimen, and at the famed Keeley Clinic in Illinois, where, if necessary, he would begin his efforts anew. During these periods, he would try his best to find steady employ-ment, and if he found it, he was to dedicate himself to it, nose to the grindstone, while spending his off-duty hours continuing his therapy, keeping his nose to the grindstone at that as well.

As for Anna, she had a demand of her own. After writing tenderly to her husband in the note cited on page 146, the "Baby Wife" toughened. She and Elliott would remain separated for a year while he tried to reassemble his life; there would be no resumption of conjugal life, perhaps a brief visit or two, nothing more. Theodore had an even longer period of time in mind. As far as rejoining the family was concerned, he told Elliott that he would be permitted to do so only after two years of good behavior, which would prove he was a changed man. Two years. That would be sometime in the fateful year of 1894.

One can only imagine Elliott's reaction. He would not see his Little Nell for more than 730 days! He must have been bereft, spoiling for a fight of his own with Theodore. But what choice did he have? Of course, he knew even when he *acceded* that he would spend time with his daughter, sneaking in visits at some time or another. He consented only verbally; in his heart he could never agree to Eleanor's removal from his life.

❖

UNAWARE OF WHAT LAY AHEAD for the Roosevelts, Theodore was proud of himself. "In certain respects," writes biographer H. W. Brands, "the confrontation represented the climax of the sibling rivalry that had long created tension between the two. Theodore interpreted it so, at any rate, for when he persuaded Elliott to give up a large part of his money and to separate from Anna . . . he commenced his report to Bamie with the single word, 'Won.'" He continued, in self-congratulatory manner, in his January 21 missive from Paris, with "Thank Heaven I came over."

When Theodore returned to the United States, he described the brother he had left behind. Elliott "surrendered completely," he related, "and was utterly broken, submissive and repentant. He signed the deed for two-thirds of *all* his property . . . and agreed to the probation. I then instantly changed my whole manner, and treated him with the utmost love and tenderness. I told him we would do all we legitimately could to help him to get through his two years (or thereabouts) of probation; that our one object now would be to see him entirely restored to himself; and so to his wife and children. He today attempted no justification; he acknowledged how grievously he had sinned; and said he would do all in his power to prove himself really reformed."

⧊◊⧋

First, though, Elliott had more to do in France than finish his treatment at Château de Suresnes. He had to do something about which no one in the family knew, something that might completely sever the few ties that remained between himself and others with the same surname. He had to write to a woman named Florence Bagley Sherman, an American divorcée from Detroit whose home was now New York, but who was living in Paris for a few months with her two children.

Before Hall's birth, Elliott had begun an affair with Sherman, even though he was drug-addicted, besotted, and subject to violent and irrational tantrums. Apparently, though, he was on his best behavior with her—whatever "best" meant for him these days—and she satisfied the lusty impulses that his wife no longer tolerated. And he, obviously, satisfied something in her.

Now, however, Elliott had to visit Mrs. Sherman to tell her that their relationship was over. He didn't want it to be, but his family had left him no choice. Mrs. Sherman told him she understood. She was also broken-hearted.

This morning, with his silk hat, his overcoat, gloves and cigar, E. came to my room to say goodbye. It was all over, only my little black dog, who cries at the door of the empty room and howls in the park, he is all that is left to me. So ends the final and great emotion of my life. "The memory of what has been, and what shall never be" is all my future holds. Even my loss was swallowed up in pity—for he looks so bruised, beaten down by the past week with his brother. How could they treat so generous and noble a man as they have. He is more noble a figure in my eyes with all his confessed faults, than either his wife or brother. She is more to be despised, in all her virtuous pride, her absolutely selfish position, than the most miserable woman I know, but she is the result of our unintelligent, petty, conventional social life.

So Elliott had been, in addition to his other malfeasances, an adulterer.

⊰◈⊱

THE FOLLOWING MONTH, ELLIOTT FOUND himself in Dwight, Illinois, where he began taking the "Keeley Cure" for addiction. There were numerous remedies for alcoholism in the United States at the time, but according to William H. White in his book *Slaying the Dragon*, none "was more famous, more geographically dispersed, more widely utilized, and more controversial than Lesley Keeley's Double Chloride of Gold Cure." It was administered both orally and by injection. Ironically, 27.55 percent of the cure's oral version was alcohol. The rest consisted of such horrible-sounding chemicals as tincture of cinchona and ammonium chloride. As for the shots, one of the ingredients was sulfate of strychnine. Neither mixture of ingredients contained gold.

Unfortunately, what Keeley provided was all too typical of "cures" at the time. Recidivism was high. Side effects were often painful. Elliott wanted nothing to do with them. Keeley's notion of medicine was "wicked and foolish," he insisted, and he wanted to return home so that he could recover from his addictions, once and for all, "*in my family* with the aid and strengthening influence of Home."

In fact, even before he went to Dwight, he wanted to see Anna so that she could "see me as I *am*. Not as she last saw me, flushed with wine, reckless and unworthy but an earnest, repentant self-respecting gentle-man."

But, whether conscious of the fact or not, Elliott was unable to realize the truth of his condition. Anna knew it, however, and reminded him they were to remain separated for a year. It was harder for her to do than it should have been, but she insisted, nonetheless.

As his treatment at Keeley dragged on, Elliott seemed to mellow, at one point writing to thank Bamie for the books she had sent him on his birthday. "As I regain my moral and mental balance," he said, "I am able to appreciate more fully the hideousness of my past actions and I grow stronger daily in my determination to live rightly and do *anything* required of me by my loved ones. . . . Try and think lovingly and forgivingly of me."

Long after Elliott had died, and long after the adult Eleanor had learned in detail of her father's addictions, she wrote of them sympathetically. She produced an autobiography and at least four volumes of memoirs, and she refers to her father's substance abuse in them only briefly, and in a manner suggesting that her father suffered from little more than a lingering cold. About his affairs, she never said a word. Not even about the most notorious of them, with Katy Mann.

This was the bottom of the abyss.

DAUGHTER

1932–36

I N HER MONTHS OF PREPARATION to be a First Lady like no other
before or since, Eleanor made a "most momentous decision . . .
to pay tribute to her father." And in more ways than one.

Few people knew anything about Elliott Roosevelt as late as 1932;
most people who heard his name thought of Eleanor's son, not her
father. But those who did still recall the latter found him a controversial figure—disdained by some, eliciting no more than a bewildered
shake of the head from others. These were people who believed that his
daughter had succeeded despite his influence, not because of it. It was
not an unreasonable assumption. It was also the most fundamental
of misunderstandings.

Eleanor was advised *not* to pay tribute to her father. Or at least not now, and certainly not in the manner she proposed. But she wouldn't listen. She wanted to do something to express her gratitude for all that Elliott had meant to her, and continued to mean to her. And so what better time than the present, on the eve of her residence in the nation's manse, to acknowledge the man who had been her only ally and champion in her troubled youth. Regardless of what others might think, she believed her father was more responsible for her coming eminence than anyone else.

So she began honoring Elliott by collecting his correspondence, a portion of it, at least. She omitted much, including his most personal and revealing messages, especially those to her. Most of the letters, in fact, had been written before she was born. She edited them and published a book called *Hunting Big Game in the Eighties: The Letters of Elliott Roosevelt, Sportsman.*

Eleanor explained her decision to publish the book at such a crucial time, a time when millions of Americans would begin forming their opinions of her, in the foreword. Conceding that he had "many short-comings," she went on to repeat a familiar and heartfelt theme. Her father, she said, "was the one great love of my life as a child, and in fact like many children I lived a dream life with him; so his memory is still a vivid, living thing to me." Since she would soon learn that her secretary, Lucy Mercer, was doing double duty as her husband's paramour, and later learn that there had been others, she might also have added that her father was her one great love as an adult, too, certainly her most constant, even though he had long since passed away.

Blanche Wiesen Cook goes on to provide more insight into Eleanor's decision to release her father's letters to bookstores at this time:

> Although it was not her intention, the book . . . estab-
> lished Elliott and his daughter in a social tradition of

fabulous wealth and international privilege. Her father's life was one of global travel and big-game hunting that depended on an Anglo-American club of sportsmen and colonial rulership that seemed during the 1930s in rapid decline.

But ER ignored that aspect of her father's legacy and emphasized rather his "great love and tenderness" for his family and her impression of his sense of personal democracy: "He loved people for the fineness that was in them and his friends might be newsboys or millionaires. Their occupations, their *possessions*, meant nothing to him, only they themselves counted." However exaggerated her impression, that trait represented the core of her father's bequest to her.

Perhaps more than publishing the book, the First Lady–to-be's "most extraordinary tribute to her father" was her unannounced decision to take the stage at the New York's Metropolitan Opera between the first two acts of *Simon Boccanegra* shortly before Christmas 1932. With America sinking ever deeper into the Depression, and more descent on the way, she was inspired by Elliott to make a plea for the kind of philanthropy in which he believed and practiced.

"When you come face to face with people in need, you simply have to try to do something about it," she told an audience even more startled by her message than her presence. She further told the grandees in the audience a story about a man who had been out of work for several months. "There was no heat at home, no food, and even the gas had been turned off. And there were five children." She asked those before her to think of that man and so many others like him, and to donate all they could to the Emergency Unemployment

Relief Committee. "After all," she concluded, "this is the richest country in the world. We cannot allow any one [*sic*] to want for the bare necessities of life."

Like an overcoat, Eleanor might have been thinking, the kind of garment her father gave away one frigid night when she was a child.

❦

ELEANOR BEGAN HER TERM AS First Lady in a most unconventional way: by disputing the policies of her husband, the president. Some of his policies, at least. For instance, Franklin believed it was necessary to eliminate or curtail spending on a number of government programs. Eleanor opposed him on a few of them, such as programs aimed to create jobs and provide food without cost to those who needed it most. These programs were necessary, she declared, even though "we will have to pay for [them] through taxes and our people might just as well face this fact. . . ." In other words, the most common pejorative applied to Roosevelt's New Deal by upper-class Americans, that it showed the president to be a "traitor to his class," belongs as much to Eleanor, as it does to her husband.

In addition to domestic affairs, Eleanor also disagreed with Franklin's positions on a number of international affairs. For one, his isolationism, the backbone of which was a number of laws that had been in effect since the end of the Great War, and were in fact the result of it. She also believed that one of the most necessary steps toward solving the Great Depression was to forgive, in their entirety, debts owed to the United States by foreign nations; this, she insisted would "end the worldwide depression and the rising tide of bitterness that threatened world peace." Franklin did not think so, and was certain Congress would rage at him for even suggesting such a measure, believing it would worsen, not solve, the Depression at home.

That Eleanor took different stands from her husband on so many issues, in a few cases before he was even inaugurated, revealed more than anything else yet the distance she had come from the little girl who would shrink at the opprobrium of others. She was no longer shy. She did not fear controversy or hide from it in a tree. The transformation was remarkable, and required a great deal of support.

⊰◈⊱

JUST AS FRANKLIN HAD ASSEMBLED his famed "Brains Trust" (although seldom used, the plural is the correct term) to serve as architects of the New Deal, Eleanor had her own circle of advisers helping to form her own views. They included such little-known but influential figures as Esther Lape, Molly Dewson, Elizabeth Read, Earl Miller, Louis Howe, and Malvina "Tommy" Thompson, her secretary and personal assistant. As Blanche Wiesen Cook tells us,

> With her activist team ER contemplated the traditional fate of a First Lady. She was expected to give up her own life and stand by her man, affirming and silent.
>
> She could not do it. Unlike her predecessors, ER claimed her right to a public role. Between Thanksgiving and Christmas 1932, she boldly broadcast her conviction that the tragic economic conditions which prevailed were due to the "blindness of a few people who perhaps do not really understand that, after all, the prosperity of the few is on a firmer foundation when it spreads to the many." She believed that everybody would soon realize there were only man-made reasons for so much deprivation in a land of overproduction. And now, because of her husband's election, she sensed a new spirit of giving all around her,

and she hailed the renewed impulse toward generosity. "We are going through a time when I believe we may have, if we will, a new social and economic order. . . .

On 3 March 1933, the eve of FDR's inauguration, she gave her last commercially sponsored broadcast in a series that had become increasingly controversial. On one occasion, she ignored prohibition and counseled women on moderate alcohol consumption. The Women's [*sic*; it is singular, "Woman's] Christian Temperance Union (WCTU), and church groups attacked her as America's primary "Jezebel."

Perhaps Eleanor smiled when she heard this. So long ago, she had heard so much worse.

However, Eleanor did not ignore Prohibition so much as try to make it more workable, less unrealistic. She did favor a ban of some sort on alcoholic beverages, and this was one of the major points of contention between her husband and her. But her feelings about the Eighteenth Amendment were "complex," by her own admission. "ER had hoped that Prohibition might result in 'less drinking now among young people than there was among our fathers.'"

The phrase could not be more telling. If only, Eleanor thought, there had been a workable prohibition when her father was young. If only . . .

In large part because of Elliott, his daughter abstained from alcoholic beverages, and supported most of the aims of the Woman's Christian Temperance Union. But "she now believed that the United States faced more critical issues," and Prohibition was no longer the priority it had once been.

As for Franklin, his stance was simple. Although once a supporter of the Eighteenth Amendment, he had changed his mind and campaigned against it, although waffling his opposition rather than speaking out directly. Having it both ways, the candidate's dream; it seldom works. But it did in this case. Since Hoover stood foursquare behind a dry America, Roosevelt, however timid his dissent, seemed by comparison his Republican opponent's avowed foe, and in the process might have accumulated enough votes to win the election on that issue alone.

He knew, of course, what alcohol had done to the man who would have become his father-in-law had he still lived, but decisions like this were matters of realpolitik, not personal experience.

Franklin had also shifted his position on the League of Nations and World Court; again, he once supported them, but had become an opponent well before Election Day 1932. "Eleanor, on the other hand, continued to work with Esther Lape for ratification of the World Court," Blanche Wiesen Cook tells us. "Pleas for action over her signature were sent to all Democratic senators, and she asked the Democratic national committeewomen from their states to get after any senators who did not respond."

Further, Eleanor and Franklin were at odds over the president's attitude toward Tammany Hall, the corrupt New York City political machine. Although never a supporter of either its power or its practices, Roosevelt was in its debt; it had thrown its considerable resources, not all of them ethical, behind his gubernatorial and presidential campaigns, playing a major role in delivering America's largest city— and thus the state—to the Democrats in both elections. So, once in the White House, FDR was measured in his criticism of the group, especially since, after running New York for almost eight decades, Tammany had begun to age and was a more feeble organization than it had been when William Marcy "Boss" Tweed was its head.

But Eleanor didn't care; aging or not, lacking its previous power or not, Tammany and Tweed were blights on democracy, and she wanted her husband to think of them as public enemy number one, or something close to it. Franklin found her a nag on the issue, as she was once again urging him to take a completely unrealistic position. And there were more: despite agreeing with his wife, the president had to dismiss her pleas to pass tougher laws on child labor and increase the amounts of money for unemployment compensation. Did this woman realize there was a Depression going on? Did she realize that introducing such legislation now would lead, not to higher wages but to bitter resentment in Congress?

Eleanor was, as well, one of the first advocates of more jobs for women in federal government, and a greater role for women in all workplaces. But at the same time, she believed that many women already working were being forced to spend too much time at it. In 1925, before Franklin was even governor, Eleanor spoke before the New York State Assembly, expressing her support for a bill that would reduce—by six, one per day—the number of hours women had to spend on the job each week. She told the legislators that the "great majority of the working women of this State are really in favor of this bill and would like to see it become law. I can't understand how any woman would want to work 54 hours a week if she only has to work 48 and could receive the same rate of wages." And, as Joseph Lash tells us, "The battle for the 48-hour law went into the 1926 and 1927 legislatures where she again clashed with the lobbyists for industry."

Members of the New York State Assembly shook their heads. This Eleanor Roosevelt wanted more jobs, yet fewer hours! Franklin, for his part, believed that women should stay home with the children.

❖

AS HER HUSBAND STARTED UPON his presidency, Eleanor began a practice that would not be tolerated today. She accepted payment from outside the government to serve as editor of a magazine called *Babies—Just Babies*. "Although it did not last," said the authors of *The Eleanor Roosevelt Encyclopedia*, "its overriding theme, education for motherhood, fitted well with new ideas on parenting in the 1930s as middle-class couples reduced the size of their families and attached more importance to raising the children they did have."

In fact, *Babies—Just Babies* went out of business after six months, but that was long enough for controversy to form. During that time, not only was the First Lady taking money for outside employment, which seemed improper to some and had never been done before; she was doing so by supporting, at least implicitly, birth control, which seemed improper to even more people.

Eleanor gave second thoughts to none of her actions. The money she made editing the magazine went to charities of her choosing. She had decided that if the government was not funding needy causes, it was up to the individual to do so, even if that individual was the president's wife.

Nor was she troubled by a far less significant matter, her occasional decision to travel by public transportation instead of a government vehicle when she felt like it. She enjoyed contact with the people she believed she represented. And, if she wanted privacy, there was her occasional decision to walk, refusing the escort of a military aide.

One morning, instead of having breakfast at the White House, she decided on the nearby Mayflower Hotel. Warren Delano Robbins, the president's cousin in addition to being the State Department's chief of protocol, met her there with his wife and a limousine to accompany her back to the executive mansion. It was a nice day, she said; she preferred a stroll.

"But Eleanor, darling, you can't do that," Robbins told her. "People will recognize you! You'll be mobbed!" The argument between the First Lady and the protocol chief went on for several minutes, attracting the attention of people at nearby tables. In the end, however, Eleanor won. With only Lorena Hickok by her side, she made her way back to the White House. Un-mobbed, as it turned out. She would do things, all things, large and small, her own way.

Franklin respected his wife's tough-mindedness, so absent when he first became acquainted with her. But he was not always pleased with it. In truth, though, he and Eleanor were in accord more often than in dispute on the issues of those troubled days, and even after Eleanor found out about Lucy Mercer, she continued to respect her husband as the nation's leader and a master politician who sincerely wanted to help the little man rise out of the Depression's mire. Both Franklin and Eleanor strongly believed in the country's future economic growth, and that the fruits of that growth should be shared as equitably as possible among all Americans.

❖

HOWEVER, MANY OF THOSE WHO had the president's ear were upset by Eleanor's independence, believing, according to precedent, that First Ladies should be seen, not heard. Or, as Joseph Lash put it, "Franklin was the politician, she the agitator." No one shared that opinion more than Secretary of the Interior Harold Ickes. "She is not doing the President any good," Ickes believed. "She is becoming altogether too active in public affairs and I think she is harmful rather than helpful."

But Ickes was only one of those who sang in the chorus against Eleanor.

> Some of Roosevelt's closest advisers—Sam Rosenman, his counsel and speech writer, and Doe O'Connor, his law partner and a political counselor, thought Eleanor

was dangerously idealistic. Not long after Rexford G. Tugwell was drafted as a member of the Brains Trust in the spring of 1932, he was stunned to hear O'Connor say to him and Ray Moley, Columbia University professor and the first to be recruited into the Brains Trust, that he hoped they knew one of their first jobs was "to get the pants off Eleanor and onto Frank." Sam agreed. Eleanor's "well-meant probings" annoyed them, so much so that they tended to avoid the dinner at the mansion that preceded a work-out with the Brains Trust.

Others, apparently, avoided White House social functions as well. It was said, one hopes with exaggeration, that the "Roosevelt receptions and parties were 'so carefully avoided by the "nice people,"' and 'a Washington cave dweller was heard to say, that Eleanor "had to invite the people who worked for the government in order to have any attendance at all.""'

It is true that outside of her circles of friends and advisers, Eleanor's supporters during the early months of her husband's first term were few. Perhaps the most influential was the syndicated newspaper columnist Heywood Broun, who founded the American Newspaper Guild, now known simply as the Newspaper Guild. Like Eleanor, he was a champion of the little man who would not be muzzled by so-called political necessities, and he pronounced himself "delighted to know that we are going to have a woman in the White House who feels that like Ibsen's Nora, she is before all else a human being and that she has a right to her own individual career regardless of the prominence of her husband."

Even though few other columnists wrote on her behalf, Eleanor was by consensus "the most influential woman in Washington." Further, she "became the most outspoken first lady this country has known—the most active, the most independent, the most courageous, the most admired, the most savagely mocked. She dealt, as a woman in the political arena, with constant condescension. 'Any woman in public life needs to develop skin as tough as rhinoceros hide,' she said." Continuing with the animal metaphor, she stated that a woman could be successful in politics only if she combined "the wisdom of the serpent and the guileless appearance of the dove." But the dove, under whose wings she had hidden as a child, was only a disguise; and in some cases it wasn't the serpent's wisdom that proved necessary; it was the fangs.

Her fangs came in much later than her teeth, but Eleanor accustomed herself to them quickly and was not afraid to bare them, although she seldom seemed unladylike when she did so. As a result, Joseph Lash is correct when he points out that, after FDR had been in office for a hundred days, it was Eleanor

as much as her husband [who] had come to personify the Roosevelt era. She as much as he had captured the imagination of the country. Far from being a prisoner of the White House and having to content herself with riding, catching up on her reading, and answering mail, as she had predicted to friends, she found herself so busy that she had no time to have her hair washed . . . Her [own] mail, which at the end of the hundred days was heavier than ever, showed that hope was returning to the country, and that morale and self-confidence were bounding upward. That represented the nation's response to Roosevelt's fulfillment of his pledge of "action, and action now," and it also expressed the nation's recognition that in Eleanor as well as in Franklin it had again found leadership.

Theirs was not, as was said back then and is still believed by some today, a "co-presidency." But the term was occasionally heard—as a compliment by those who admired Eleanor's tenacity, as an insult by those who believed that, of all American women, it was the First Lady who most belonged at home with the kiddies, even if home was the White House.

⬥

MORE OFTEN THAN NOT, FRANKLIN tolerated his wife, sometimes seeming amused by her earnestness. Occasionally, it even inspired him to act. But there was no doubt that the commander in chief was commanding. "He was a showman," says Joseph Lash, accurately, "and his charm and magnetism were so overpowering that the household naturally gravitated around him; everyone's interests were subordinated to his. A woman in love with a man could accept this, but that kind of love had died with the Lucy Mercer affair, Eleanor told herself. She was not in love with him. Yet she was prepared to render him a labor of love by serving his work . . . if he would be thoughtful, considerate, and treat her as a partner and confidante."

And he often did.

⬥

THERE WERE TIMES WHEN ELEANOR had to get away from it all. She had not been raised in the world of politics, and was still puzzled, and occasionally beaten down, by the degree to which an honest statement of ideas (hers) could rouse such hostile responses (theirs). So she would retreat to a cottage that had been built in 1924 on the Roosevelt property in Hyde Park. When not in the White House, she and Franklin would spend an occasional weekend—longer, if possible—in their prepresidential home, the so-called "Big House"; the cottage, named Val-Kill, a Dutch word that means "valley stream," was about two miles away. It was there that "she could entertain whoever she wanted, stay up reading as late as she liked, and be alone if she chose." It was there, Eleanor said, "where I used to find myself and grow. At Val-Kill, I emerged as an individual."

Actually, there were two buildings on the site, the Val-Kill Cottage itself, and a smaller structure known as the Stone Cottage. Initially, the former was a small factory whose operations were overseen by the future First Lady and three of her friends. "They hoped to train local people in craft skills that they could use to supplement their income from agriculture without having to move to the city. The high quality reproduction Early American furniture Val-Kill Industries made did well in the 1920s."

As for the Stone Cottage, Eleanor spent as much time as she could there with Nancy Cook and Marion Dickerman, friends and fellow "executives" in Val-Kill Industries. When the company went out of business, Eleanor had the factory converted to a house and moved in, part-time, leaving the Big House to her husband and the Stone Cottage to Cook and Dickerman, who lived there together for the next twenty-one years.

The solitude of Val-Kill was a restorative for Eleanor, a tonic for her psyche. The Big House remained her primary, or at least nominal residence, but the cottage always beckoned and always received her in warm, silent, and familiar welcome. When her husband died, Eleanor, uncomfortable despite her upbringing in what she believed to be the falsity of grandeur, made the much more modest cottage her full-time residence. The Big House became a library and museum, attracting people like me, who saw an untold story in the past.

◆

As IT TURNED OUT, THE homage Eleanor paid to her father by publishing his letters was one of the least controversial actions she took in her early years as First Lady. But the letters she did not publish, which are kept in the Big House, several of them following in this book, tell a more gripping story. It is those messages, almost all of them brief, that reveal how Eleanor tried to help her father from afar during his last, agonizing days, and what Elliott Roosevelt meant to her, before, during, and long after those days had passed.

FATHER

1891

Not long after Elliott said good-bye to Mrs. Florence Bagley Sherman in Paris, Theodore learned of her existence and exploded, calling his brother "a maniac morally as well as mentally." Then, feeling that even more invective might be in order, he also pronounced his sibling a "flagrant man-swine."

But when Elliott said hello again to Mrs. Sherman in New York, as she and her children returned shortly after he did, he proceeded so cautiously that Theodore knew nothing about it. Initially, at least. Appalled by the publicity that had descended on her lover like a cloud of mustard gas, and the secretive measures he had to take to see her, Mrs. Sherman defended him against the mass of men who were "not large-souled enough to appreciate him."

But the lovers did not have much time to spend with each other. The timing is not certain, but it seems that soon after Mrs. Sherman appeared in New York, Elliott went off to Dwight, Illinois, for his failed attempt at the Keeley Cure. Mrs. Sherman said she'd wait. Unlike his wife, she told him self-righteously, she would be patient; she trusted him. She could not have spoken more foolishly.

When Elliott returned to New York, he again took up with his lover, and all was well between them for a while. But his state was now perpetually agitated, and it prompted him to increase the scope of his philandering. He added another mistress, a Mrs. Evans, about whom history records as little as it does about Mrs. Sherman.

After a brief, inexplicable stay with his wife, it was Mrs. Evans with whom Elliott moved in, and to keep their relationship secret from Mrs. Sherman, as well as from the Roosevelt family, he and his new paramour kept moving. Like criminals fearing the hot breath of the law, they changed apartments every few weeks, with Elliott altering not only his address but his name—although the latter with comic subtlety. Instead of Mr. Roosevelt, he was Mr. Elliott to those from whom he rented. First name unknown. Mrs. Evans apparently allowed herself to be dragged into this fugitive life without complaint. Mrs. Sherman, meanwhile, wondered why she didn't see Elliott as often as she had expected.

But it wasn't either of these affairs that led to his final shame. Nor was it either that led to his exile from the family. It was, rather, an earlier affair, or perhaps just a one-night stand, an act of sexual congress that occurred before the European trip that ended for Elliott at Château de Suresnes. The woman's name was Katy Mann. She was employed by the Roosevelts as a housemaid. And she was pregnant. In fact, she had her baby in New York within a few months of

Anna's giving birth to Hall in Paris. Unfortunately, Elliott was the father of both children.

❖

IT WAS ON A SHEET of stationery from Katy's lawyer that Theodore received the news. His first reaction was to call Katy Mann a liar. Yes, Elliott had lost his moorings, perhaps even his ability to differentiate moral rectitude from its opposite. But something like *this*! No, it wasn't possible, not little Ellie. Not, of all people, a Roosevelt!

Still, Theodore had to confront his brother with the accusation. When he did, Elliott seemed surprised. He swore the story was a fabrication, that the housemaid was a vicious opportunist who knew about his distressed circumstances and was trying to take advantage of them. It made sense to Theodore, and he allowed himself to be persuaded. But with an uncomfortable reluctance.

As the days passed, however, and the threat of legal action grew more imminent, Theodore continued in his role of interrogator, and in the process Elliott became less and less adamant. Eventually, he settled on a drunkard's defense. He "no longer denied sleeping with Katy Mann; he merely said 'he could not remember' doing so." And with that, Theodore sensed the truth. Further, as biographer H. W. Brands put it, he "realized that if [Katy Mann's] claim was true, it could destroy the family name forever—and certainly would do nothing good for the political career of one who made such a fetish of character and integrity." Meaning Theodore himself.

He was dumbfounded. How could even a reprobate like Elliott go this far? He found that the "hideous revelation hangs over me like a nightmare." It would not, as Theodore feared, destroy the family name forever, and in fact was known by relatively few people in the twentieth century and virtually no one in the twenty-first. But the young patriarch may be forgiven for hyperbole at so upsetting a time.

A later communication from Katy's lawyer revealed that he had proof of a relationship between his client and Elliott, a locket that he had given her. It was now in the lawyer's possession. As were several letters that Elliott had written to his client, letters that have never been discovered since. Believing now that they had no choice but to accept the truth of the allegation, the Roosevelts gathered en masse and decided to offer Katy between $3,000 and $4,000 to help raise her child.

It was not enough. And, the family was told, if Katy filed a paternity suit, as she was now on the verge of doing, the jury was almost certain to take the woman's side "if she can make out at all a plausible case. The character of the man is taken much into account. If it can be shown that he was apt to get drunk, or to be under the influence of opiates, or to go out of his head and become irresponsible, it would tell heavily against him." All of the preceding was, of course, easily provable.

To make matters even worse for Elliott, Katy had witnesses of a sort. Other servants in the Roosevelt household would testify that he had treated young Ms. Mann differently from the rest of them, more affectionately, never finding fault with her work. At least once, a few of the servants swore, they had heard his voice in her room late at night. Furtive whispers, followed by sounds that could not be misconstrued.

Elliott continued to insist that he did not recall ever having been intimate with Katy Mann. Or having treated her better than others in the household service brigade. Or having been admitted to her room in the midnight hours. Yes, it could have happened—yes, yes! Elliott *just didn't remember.* It remained for Theodore to stifle his rage long enough to explain to his brother precisely how matters stood.

If you and I were alone in the world I should advise
fighting her as a pure blackmailer, yet as things [are]
I did not dare . . . The woman must admit that on her
own plea she must have been a willing, probably inviting
party. But she has chosen her time with great skill.
During that week [of the alleged seduction] you were
very sick, and for hours at a time were out of your head,
and did not have any clear recollection of what you were
doing. You wandered much about the house those nights,
alone. She could get testimony that you were often wild
and irresponsible, either from being out of your head or
from the use of liquor or opiates. At present you are not in
any condition to go on the stand and be cross-examined
as to your past and your personal habits by a sharp and
unscrupulous lawyer.

So that however the suit went, it would create a great
scandal; and much would be dragged out that we are
very desirous of keeping from the public.

What Theodore refrained from saying was that the scandal could
not be kept from the public if Katy Mann's charges were heard in a
courtroom, and that the resulting frenzy in the public prints would
make Elliott's failed rehabilitations seem insignificant by comparison. A settlement of some sort was mandatory. Her silence, and the
child's welfare, had to be purchased.

⊸◈⊸

SOON THERE WAS NO LONGER a need to jog Elliott's memory, or to persuade him what to do, for the charge against him reached a conclusion that would have been deemed legally unassailable at the time.

When Katy's child was born, the Roosevelts hired a man named Cosgrove, an "expert in likenesses," to examine the infant. He did so meticulously, poring over every centimeter of the baby, then doing so again. Changing this angle, changing that, feeling his head, his limbs. Taking measurements, as if he were a phrenologist. There was no doubt, Cosgrove determined, and he was prepared to testify in a court of law. The child had distinctly "Rooseveltian features." His father was Elliott. Not needing the verification, Katy had already named her son Elliott Roosevelt Mann.

Theodore was livid and beyond. In biographer Edmund Morris's paraphrase, "he believed [alcoholism] to be a disease that could be treated and cured. But infidelity was a crime, pure and simple; it could be neither forgiven nor understood, save as an act of madness. It was an offense against order, decency, against civilization; it was a desecration of the holy marriage-bed. . . . Elliott had forfeited all claim to his wife and children. For Anna to continue to live with him now [which she had ceased to do] would be 'little short of criminal.'"

Elliott Roosevelt Mann's existence still had not been reported in the papers and to prevent such an occurrence, Theodore ruled that the baby's father must dig even further into his inheritance, and with contributions from others in the family, which Elliott had expected all along, increase the offer to Katy Mann. The new total, both for her child's needs and the mother's refusal to discuss the matter with anyone, was $10,000. The family would have probably increased the bribe even more if Katy would have agreed to change the infant's name, but, as much as she needed money, she insisted it was not for sale.

Despite the fact that historians constantly do it, there is no single means of determining how much $10,000 is worth today. Using the Consumer Price Index as a guide, the sum can be said

to equal more than $268,000 now. If the basis of comparison is
relative share of the gross domestic product, the amount soars in
excess of $11,200,000. There are other measures as well. Regardless,
$10,000 was a lot of money in 1891, and Elliott and his relatives had
no choice but to part with it.

It is not certain, however, that the payment ever made its way to
Katy, as intended. In fact,

> [w]hatever settlement was reached, there is now evidence
> that Katy Mann received no money, and that what-
> ever money was put in trust for her son was presumed
> "stolen" by the attorneys. On 26 November 1932, Elliott
> Roosevelt Mann and his mother wrote ER a letter of con-
> gratulations on the election results. ER responded: "I was
> very interested to receive your letter and to learn that you
> were named after my father."

The tone of Eleanor's note, and the fact that she replied at all, suggest that she knew nothing about Elliott Mann's provenance. Surely
the family would have done all it could to keep the news from her in
1891, and sending her to the French convent school might have been
done in part for this reason; the family had heard whispers of the
pregnant Ms. Mann even then. Regardless, as Eleanor was a child
of not quite seven years old when Theodore and various attorneys
sat behind closed doors, negotiating the terms of the hush money, it
would have been easy to keep the little girl in the dark even had she
remained with her kin.

Perhaps nothing about this entire matter upset Theodore more
than the fact that, although Anna knew about Katy's accusation,
and accepted its veracity, she and Elliott lived together for that
brief period of time before he moved in with Mrs. Evans. It is not

certain whether they shared a bed. Regardless, Anna's allowing him under the same roof with her and the children was an appalling act of indecency on her part, Theodore believed, and Anna was now as guilty as her husband, or at least an accomplice. He would have nothing to do with her for a time; she was, after all, not a Roosevelt by birth.

Theodore had lost patience with her well before this, however. For, showing either more courage than anyone had ever expected of her, or the abject foolishness of which many Roosevelts had always thought her capable, Anna insisted that Elliott be nearby when Hall was born. Attempts were made, and at high decibel level, to talk her out of such a demand. Anna would not be budged. And so there he was, Elliott Roosevelt, standing proudly in a Paris hospital, on June 28, 1891, cuddling the baby to which his wife had just given birth, despite the fact that, on March 11 of the same year, Hall's father was responsible for the birth of another son by another woman. Elliott was not, however, at Katy Mann's side.

As for Theodore's wife's reaction to Elliott, Edith was more restrained, if equally appalled. "He drank like a fish and ran after the ladies. I mean ladies not in his own rank, which was much worse." There were no Swells, in other words, on his roster of conquests, and, in fact, Elliott was now unrecognizable as the man swooned over just a few years ago by ladies of that ilk.

⬥

WHEN ELLIOTT WAS CONFINED IN his various sanitariums, he wrote a number of letters to his mother-in-law, Grandmother Hall, inadvertently revealing how much his grasp on reality had loosened. They were "rhapsodies of an idyllic time," one that never had existed, and never would.

He and Anna walked each morning in the beautiful park of the chateau. The weather was lovely, and they "read for two hours at a time while the children play." Eleanor was sent to the local school in the mornings, but joined them each afternoon and was pleased to feed the fishes and the ducks. "Sometimes in the afternoon Anna and I drive a jolly little pair of ponies we found at a Livery Stable down along the banks of the Seine or through the grand old forest."

It was precisely the kind of letter Elliott would write so often to Eleanor. That he believed deeply in all of his visions, both those expressed to his mother-in-law and daughter, cannot be doubted.

❖

KATY MANN SOMEHOW DISAPPEARED FROM notice shortly after giving birth, joining Mrs. Sherman and Mrs. Evans in historical anonymity. Today, of course, she would be starring in a reality show on a cable television network, but in the more restrained time of which I write, no one seems to know what became of her. And to those employed at various Roosevelt archival sites, she was not worth the research that would make her part of the official annals. To bring up her name in those precincts is to be eyed with a cold suspicion. The same may be said about her son, Elliott Roosevelt Mann. He was never taken in by any of the Roosevelts, never acknowledged as a member of the family. What is known is that he lived for eighty-five years, married at least once, and helped to raise two daughters. There is no evidence to indicate his life was anything other than respectable. He was, of course, the half brother of Elliott's cherished Nell, but, again, if she knew of their connection, she never acknowledged it to anyone. It is hard to believe that she never learned of it, but easy to believe that, if she did, she put it out of her mind and certainly out of her memoirs.

⊶◈⊷

THE BLEEDING FROM THE ROOSEVELT family's crisis had been stanched before it reached the newspapers. But that did not mean the crisis was over. Now the question became what to do with Elliott. Even before the paternity of Katy Mann's child was discovered, Theodore had told him that he was unfit to dwell among his kin, that he would be excommunicated for two years. Now he was more certain of that than ever. *At least* two years. But where would he be deposited? How could it be done without attracting journalistic attention? It would be Douglas Robinson Jr., the husband of Roosevelt's sister Corinne, who provided the answer.

But before he did, seven-year-old Eleanor realized that the grown-ups around her were deciding her father's fate, and that whatever it turned out to be, he would no longer live with his family, would no longer be as accessible to her as he had been in the past. Her reaction is nowhere recorded . . . unless, to stretch a point, it was done many years earlier by Charles Dickens. Just as the author had provided Eleanor's childhood nickname, and for a shorter period of time a nickname for her father, in *The Old Curiosity Shop*, so, perhaps, did he foreshadow Eleanor's reaction to her father's coming expatriation in *Hard Times*.

One day, Dickens tells us, Sissy Jupe, a circus girl of approximately Eleanor's age, discovers that her father, a clown in the circus, has suddenly disappeared. Sissy loves her father more than anyone else in the world, and he loves her; she does not understand his flight. The only thing she can conclude is that he must have left in shame, disappointed in himself for being nothing more than a jester, unable to rise through the ranks of the circus and provide a better life for the two of them. He has gone to make his fortune, Sissy decides, and as soon as he does he will send for her and the two of them will live their "dream life"—Eleanor's term, not Dickens's—together and forever.

Nonetheless, when Sissy first learns that her father has put the circus behind him, she is grief-stricken. "Oh, my dear father," she cries out, "my good kind father, where are you gone? You are gone to try to do me some good, I know! You are gone away for my sake, I am sure. And how miserable and helpless you will be without me, poor, poor father, until you come back!"

It is, of course, Dickens's fiction. But it so closely resembles what must have been Eleanor's reality.

DAUGHTER

1920s–1950s

Aftter decades of studying and writing about Eleanor Roosevelt, Blanche Wiesen Cook concluded that she "was forever attracted to people who evoked her father." She "felt understood and loved by [him]. He encouraged his little daughter to excel, to be courageous and bold. He promoted her interests and her education. He wanted her to be self-reliant and self-fulfilled." Which is to say, he wanted Eleanor to surround herself with people who were even-tempered and encouraging, who did not think ill of her because she lacked beauty as conventionally perceived, who took her side in disputes, who thought the best of her even when others were thinking the worst. As the constituency of her Brains Trust indicates, she found these traits most often in women; it was they who once constituted her Val-Kill Industries partners, and who now constituted the majority of her advisers. The most notable of the exceptions was her husband's indispensable aide, Louis Howe.

It was only natural, then, that women's issues would occupy a great deal of Eleanor's time—and not just when she was sparring with Franklin about more jobs, and more reasonable working hours, for the American female. Actually, the First Lady's passion for women's rights goes back at least as far as 1920, when Franklin was Ohio governor James Cox's vice presidential candidate. At the time, Eleanor was lobbying for women to be able to bargain collectively, to be the beneficiaries of a new federal agency that would ensure full employment, to receive the same pay as men for the same job, and to have full access to public education, including lessons on such sexual matters as birth control and venereal disease. She was an ally of Margaret Sanger, a member of the American Birth Control League, for most of her life, long before the cause was considered respectable.

As she wrote in one of her memoirs, when Eleanor began devoting her life to political issues, "I became a much more ardent citizen and feminist than anyone about me in the intermediate years would have dreamed possible." In some cases, her feminism was visionary, with a number of the goals she formulated being decades ahead of their time—and in the case of such matters as equal pay for women, still not having been universally achieved.

In 1899, a woman named Florence Kelley made news when she began demanding legislation to end fraudulent practices in advertising. "What housewife," Kelley said, "can detect, alone and unaided, injurious chemicals in her supplies of milk, bread, meat, home remedies?" Fairness in advertising was one of the first aims of the National Consumers League (NCL), which awarded a white label to products that met their standards. The NCL "became the most influential consumer movement of the early twentieth century. By 1906 there were sixty-three leagues in twenty states; by 1913 there were thirty thousand members. When National Recovery Administration codes were introduced in 1933, the NCL's white label campaign became government policy."

It seems to have been the NCL that first opened Eleanor's eyes to the plight of the working poor, who had to shop so carefully when they could afford to shop at all. "Luckily, I went with an experienced older woman to do some investigation in garment factories and department stores," she wrote.

> It had never occurred to me before that the girls might get tired standing behind the counters all day long, or that no seats were provided for them if they had time to sit down and rest. I did not know what the sanitary requirements should be in the dress factories, either for air or lavatory facilities. This was my first introduction to anything of this kind and I rather imagine that by spring I was quite ready to drop all this good work and go up to the country and spend the summer in idleness and recreation!

But she didn't. She couldn't. Having felt so many grievances of her own as a youngster, it was not in her nature to let the grievances of others go unheeded as an adult.

And so she worked, among other things, for the Child Labor Amendment, which would have given Congress the right to regulate working conditions for boys and girls eighteen years of age and younger, and about which her husband was lukewarm. So was much of the rest of America, and it has continued to be; there remains no such protection for young workers written into either the Bill of

Rights or statewide statute books. Eleanor Roosevelt might have grown into the most powerful woman in the United States, but even for her there were limits.

❖

PRIOR TO HER HUSBAND'S PRESIDENCY, as a board member of the League of Women Voters, her assignment had been to prepare reports.

Her initial response was typical. "I explained that I had had little or no contact in Washington with national legislation, that I had listened a great deal to the talk that went on around me, and that I would be interested but doubted my ability to do this work." But she did it—thoughtfully, comprehensibly and knowledgeably.

She became familiar with the International Congress for Women Workers (ICWW), the first session of which opened with a denunciation of the Treaty of Versailles because no women had been involved in formulating it. Eleanor got to know many of the ICWW's members, who came from nineteen different nations and informed her how women were treated in all of them; she was appalled to learn that conditions were usually worse elsewhere than they were in the United States.

She also acquainted herself with the Women's Trade Union League and the New York League of Girls' Clubs, among other organizations, lending support, encouragement, and, when she could, participation in the groups' events. Once in the White House, she would occasionally hold press conferences for female journalists only, something never done before or since and a practice denounced by many at the time. She was, in fact, the first First Lady ever to hold a press conference for anyone.

And, of course, the only First Lady ever to confront reporters with a beast at the end of a leash.

"Throughout the 1930s, ER and [her fellow occupant of the feminist trenches Molly] Dewson worked every channel of influence to promote women to positions of respect, prestige, power. Only women in power, ER believed, would consider the needs of women without power; men in power rarely, if ever, did."

❖

FOR ELEANOR, IT WAS BUT a short step from interest in women's issues to similar concern for other groups whom she believed were underrepresented in government or mistreated in society. Women's issues were merely the doorway; once she entered, she found an entire roomful of people with needs that, in her opinion, the government ruled by her husband was ignoring.

From biographer Blanche Wiesen Cook: "Long before her husband and most of his advisers, she publicly connected white supremacy in the United States with white supremacy in Hitler's Germany. To fathom America's failure to respond to the Holocaust, it is helpful to consider Eleanor Roosevelt's early and lonely public opposition to racism, as well as her own crusade against fascism in Spain and in support of Jewish refugees from Europe."

That support did not come immediately, and there had been a time when it seemed that Eleanor would never provide it. As a younger woman, she was an anti-Semite, although she was careful to keep her views as private as possible. "When, as wife of the assistant secretary of the navy, she was obliged to attend a party given by the Admiralty to honor [the Jewish financier and philanthropist] Bernard Baruch, then chair of the War Industries Board, ER wrote her mother-in-law that it was a party 'I'd rather be hung than seen at.'" She did, however, attend; Franklin insisted. But she found "[t]he Jew party appalling." Strong language. But were her feelings equally strong?

It is probable that Eleanor's anti-Semitism came from ignorance more than malice, from a blind acceptance of the views not only of her own family, in which Jews were not disdained so much as "tinged with a vague sense of otherness," but of the entire community in which she was raised. Tolerance was hardly the same virtue among the Swells as beauty.

But as she got to know Baruch and such other estimable figures as Felix Frankfurter, Henry Morgenthau Jr., and Sam Rosenman—men upon whom President Roosevelt depended, indifferent to their ethnicity—her views changed, and rapidly.

In fact, it was not long after the party for Baruch that the two of them found themselves sailing for Europe aboard the same ship. On more than one night they sought out each other as waltz partners. "He thought her gracious, interesting, and charming. She thought him gallant, interesting and unusual." It was one of the first concrete steps in her cure for her anti-Semitism, although it may have been her relationship with Morgenthau, back on dry land, more than Baruch who made her an activist.

Some years later, she went so far as to speak strongly in favor of the women's organizations in Germany that refused to expel their Jewish members, and at the same time advocating with no less vehemence the need to open the gates of Ellis Island to refugees from Hitler's pogroms.

By this time, she had begun to wonder at her previous self, at the source of her anti-Semitism. She thought back to the Swells who had surrounded her as a child, their often dismissive attitude toward Jews, the derisive comments she overheard some of them make. How had she ever managed to allow the prejudice of others to create one of her own, especially when the "others" were not people she respected, not even people around whom she was comfortable? How had she been so complacent?

Just as she came to despise the treatment of Jews abroad, so did she come to despise the mindless violence of Mussolini's fascism. "ER was disturbed by America's inaction concerning Italy's aggression and now joined Lorena Hickok's fantasy of new work as a war correspondent."

It remained a fantasy, of course; Eleanor never took to the front with pen and pad. But her views had set in by now, and she made use of whatever forums were available to her—and eventually there were more than she could accept—to plead with her fellow Americans to be receptive to the victims of Hitler, Mussolini, and tyrants everywhere.

◆

In *Go Set a Watchman*, Harper Lee's much belated prequel to *To Kill a Mockingbird*, the author recounts some snippets of the vitriol directed at Atticus Finch when he defended the black man, Tom Robinson, against fabricated rape charges. Someone accused Atticus of being just like "old lady Roosevelt . . . nigger-lover . . . entertains forty-five niggers but not one fresh white Southern virgin." It was an authentic touch by Lee. Epithets were constantly raining down on Eleanor for her efforts on behalf of better lives for African-Americans. It is likely that she was more constantly and ignorantly vilified for this position than any other she ever took.

When she was younger, she believed in the inferiority of blacks, a view that permeated her caste. But, as was the case with her anti-Semitism, "[h]er views changed slowly over time. She became an antiracist activist, although she began her public career steeped in the sensibilities of the Old South, filled with distorted and ugly images of blacks and Jews. The distance she traveled on issues of race, gender, and class, her ability to stand up for what she believed, involved conscious struggle."

Eventually, Eleanor's voice was one of the loudest and most persistent in supporting bills that made lynching a federal crime and eliminated poll taxes. Blanche Wiesen Cook believes that she "was among the first to see race relations as the primary issue America would have to confront if it were to move into its future as a united, liberal and progressive nation."

When the Washington Committee on Housing met in the spring of 1936, one of its principal concerns was better housing for African-Americans. After Eleanor concluded one day's session with a speech that was for the most part improvised, and in its totality sincere, the committee's secretary, Florence Stewart, spoke the next day about the effect of her words. Stewart said, "I was told this morning that a Negro who had been working for some time in racial relations had to retire in tears because she was so touched by the understanding and sympathy for her race that was expressed by Mrs. Roosevelt's manner as well as her speech."

Not long afterward, Eleanor used the word *darky* in a magazine excerpt from the second volume of her memoirs. Soon thereafter, she received a letter from a black woman, Esther S. Carey, a graduate of Tuskegee Institute in Alabama. She was not pleased. "Alas," Carey wrote, "as I was reading I came across two mentions of 'darky.' I couldn't believe my eyes. Surely no one of the Roosevelt blood could be guilty of using this hated term, and we do hate it, as much as the Jew hates 'sheeny' and the Italian 'dago' or 'wop.'"

It is not an exaggeration to say that Eleanor was stunned by the letter. She replied that she had grown up with the term *darky*, that it had been used by her beloved great-aunt, among others, but always with affection. No one in her family had ever told her that it brought offense.

The mail did not stop. Esther S. Carey was not alone in her disappointment in the First Lady. The following week, an attorney from

New York, probably a white man, told her that the word *darky* was simply unacceptable, being "offensive to many of your readers, and by many it is thought to do harm to the Negro as a race."

Again Eleanor replied promptly, this time promising action. "I am terribly sorry if the use of the word 'offends' and I will change it when my autobiography is published in book form."

And not only did she do that, but she excised the term from her vocabulary, never speaking it again. In addition, she cautioned those who worked for her never to use such a word, or any words that might bring pain to any group of Americans, even in private conversations. She gave the example of *pickaninny*, which Eleanor had used earlier in life as well as *darky*, not aware of its sting, but for which she had been excoriated by those who believed she was a friend of black Americans.

A year later, in 1937, when her memoir *This Is My Story* was published as a book, she made certain to show herself the friend of black Americans that she truly was. Although she did so, it must be admitted, in a way that would be offensive today.

> The colored race has the gift of kindliness and a fund of humor. Many difficulties of life are met with easy laughter and a kindly tolerance toward other people's failings. Though their eyes may mirror the tragedies of their race, they certainly have much to teach us in the enjoyment of the simple things of life and the dignity with which they meet their problems.

After another couple of decades had passed, and the Supreme Court had ruled that American schools be desegregated with "all deliberate haste," Eleanor criticized President Eisenhower's definition of *deliberate*. He is "about as aggressive as a meek little rabbit," the former First Lady charged. And when a crisis erupted at Little Rock Central High School because of Governor Orval Faubus's intransigence to the court's order, Eleanor said "that President Eisenhower should have gone down and personally led the nine Negro children into the school."

In his *Datebook* interview with Eleanor in 1958, Art Unger asked what advice she had for a white girl whose high school had just been integrated.

"First realize that you can be friends with people of any color or creed," Eleanor replied. "Then, when you accept this fact, you will find you naturally behave with equal dignity no matter who your friend is. But, remember, if you accept a girl as a friend, you should treat her exactly as you would any other friend."

And what about a Negro girl in a school that was previously all-white?

"Exactly the same advice!"

◈

IT TOOK GREAT INNER STRENGTH for Little Nell to become the Eleanor Roosevelt known to history, for her to transcend the biases of her childhood, to overcome the entire zeitgeist of her formative years. But she could not have transformed herself as thoroughly as she did without a unique form of assistance, one upon which only she could call.

FATHER

1892–93

Douglas Robinson's idea for Elliott's immediate future actually belonged to his wife, Corinne. She has been described as "the most sympathetic" of Elliott's siblings, and despite his dissatisfaction with his sister's plan, it was probably the most practical decision the family could have made. And the most sympathetic as well.

Corinne persuaded her husband to offer Elliott a job managing the Robinsons' newly acquired coal and timber businesses in Virginia. In addition he would oversee the thousands of acres surrounding them—except that it was not an offer; it was an ultimatum. Elliott accepted, and, as he thought of it, "went voluntarily into exile." Among others, he left behind Mrs. Sherman and Mrs. Evans, who would see him only on his occasional visits to New York for the next year and a half, and who, each without knowing of the other, missed him terribly.

Elliott's Elba, his Saint Helena, was the small town of Abingdon, 361 miles from Washington, DC, 581 miles from the Roosevelt home in New York, but, sadly, less than a short walk from the nearest neighborhood tavern. In fact, we learn from Mason White, "One evening, drunk and naked, he knocked over a lamp and burned himself badly."

It might have been this incident, or possibly a later bout with his spirituous demons, that led to the following, one of countless letters he wrote—or, in this case, dictated—to the daughter he could no longer see, the daughter who, as an adult, did not publish such correspondence:

> Dear little Nell:
> Father has your sweet note of May nineteenth and as he may not be allowed to write for a day or two has asked his nurse to drop you these lines to assure you as ever of his love. . . .
> I am much better, have had an attack of "la grippe".
> Yours affectionately and Devotedly
> Elliot [*sic*] Roosevelt

On another occasion, Elliott had to enlist someone other than a nurse to write a brief note to his daughter. Like the previous one, it was undated.

> Dear little Nel [*sic*]
> Your father is not well, and unable to write. He sends you lots of love, and hopes you are very well and happy.
> Sincerely,
> H. G. Moore

There is no way of knowing whether this letter, too, was the result of a drunken binge that, perhaps causing an injury, made it impossible for Elliott to hold a pen steadily. His earliest days in Abingdon were a torment for him. But that would soon change.

◈

To DISTRACT HIMSELF FROM HAVING to settle in what was, to him, so remote a part of the country, and the further travail of a puzzling new set of vocational duties, Elliott threw himself into a hobby that came naturally to him: horse breeding. His previous passion for polo served as a foundation for his interest, which was also a passion for many others who lived around him. Soon, in fact, he found that raising horses was not the only thing he enjoyed about Abingdon. His experiences there proved to be much more pleasant than he ever could have imagined.

In the spring of 1892, Abingdon was "a sprawling old Virginia village," with about fifteen hundred residents, fewer than the number who lived within a couple blocks of his childhood residence in New York. But even those men and women he met apart from the horse farms were, by and large, amenable sorts. He was not only at ease with them but also impressed. "Old families of the Virginia aristocracy type lived in mellowed houses within the corporate limits and on outlying plantations, or farms as they are called in this part of Virginia. Army officers, congressmen, State Governors and Supreme Court Judge, and men of their ilk had always been among the leaders of the community."

As for the life that Elliott Roosevelt lived in these far-from-urban environs, it was not only different from anything he had known before, but more demanding of his time.

My little Darling Daughter:

Father would write you a long letter if he could but he is very busy and even to send off these few lines is more than he so should do.

I hope my little girl is well and I thank her for the two precious little notes she wrote me.

And:

My darling little Nell:

What can you think of your Father, neglecting to write you for so long. Though you are the naughty pretty little recreant as you owe me one or two I think. . . . I have been very, very busy down here, working at things which someday you will be interested to hear about when you get older. . . . [G]ive everybody my love. Keep a great deal for yourself my little Nell.

Ever devotedly,

Your Father

Because of their separation, both Elliott and his daughter were extraordinarily sensitive to each other's epistolary needs. If one of them feared that he or she had let too much time elapse without a reply, the next letter always contained an apology. "We moved to the country," Eleanor told her father in the summer of 1894, "and that is why I have not written before we were in such a hurry to get of [*sic*] for it was so hot in New York."

In the hope of eliminating a delay in response, one was likely to urge the other on, as Eleanor did a month later, "Please write to me soon." And later it was "Write to me soon another letter. I love you very much. . . ."

More than once, Elliott had to apologize not for allowing too much time to pass before writing but for the likelihood that he would not see her in New York as planned. His absence would be especially poignant in the winter of 1892. After asking her for "a little list of Christmas wants so that I can prepare to tell Old Santa Claus about them," he was forced to say, "Goodbye. I may not see you at Christmas though I shall try to be up from Virginia at about that time. Everlovingly Your Father."

He did not see her that Christmas. He was too busy working; that, at least, was the excuse. In reality, he was forbidden by his family to visit Eleanor.

⊰◇⊱

THERE IS NO REAL NEWS in most of these letters, but that is of no significance. Rather, it is important to understand the cumulative effect of the messages that father and daughter exchanged, the reassurance that they were thinking of each other, the willingness they revealed to always find the time to write and then mail the messages. It is no small thing to keep up a frequent correspondence. For Eleanor and her father, it was a constant reaffirming of love and need—a presence in the midst of absence. That is the real content of the letters; that is what makes them indispensable in understanding the relationship between the pair. When they wrote to each other, Elliott and his daughter were solidifying the foundation, already in place, that would not only keep the bond between father and daughter firm despite the distance, but would also continue to support Eleanor when she needed propping up in the future, a future that her father would not live to see but that Eleanor ever attributed to his influence.

To his Little Nell, Elliott was always light and affectionate when he wrote, allowing no trace of his pining for her to appear and cause her to fret.

In addition, he knew that the more cheerful he seemed in his writing, the more puzzled Eleanor would be by his seclusion, which would make her more likely to plead for an end to it—to her mother, to Uncle Ted, to Corinne and Douglas, to Grandmother Hall. On paper, Elliott was able to seem the soul of cheerfulness in Abingdon. But, although he enjoyed it more than he expected, he did need to dart off for occasional escapes.

And Eleanor was able to believe in his good cheer, in the return of his normality, as she grew older and felt more and more the miles between them, each of the hundreds a pinprick of pain that the two of them felt equally. Historian Nathan Miller writes that Eleanor "lived for Elliott's letters to his 'Little Nell,' and carried them about as a talisman."

The last point is a crucial one in understanding Eleanor's years of ascent, still almost two decades away. In fact, it is crucial to understanding her entire life's underpinnings.

❖

IN HER COMPOSITION BOOK, ELEANOR wrote a story, dressed up as fiction, that was reminiscent of something Sissy Jupe might have written when she found that her father had disappeared in *Hard Times*.

"A child stood at a window. . . . Her father [was] the only person in the world she loved, others called him hard & cold but to him she was everything lavishing on him all the quiet love which the others could not understand. And now he had gone she did not know for how long but he had said 'what ever happens[,] little girl[,] some day I will come back' & she had smiled. He never knew what the smile cost."

❖

THE AIR IN ABINGDON WAS fresh, clean, crisp, scented bracingly.

And birds chirped. Elliott swore he could hear birds chirping, at the same time that he heard the faint rustle of leaves when they fluttered onto them and then through. Did birds chirp in New York? He had no idea. He could not remember. Perhaps they did but were drowned out by carriages clattering on cobblestone streets; machines that were tearing down old buildings and putting up new ones as Manhattan moved ever northward; newsboys standing on street corners braying out the latest tabloid headlines, with the loudest boy selling the most papers. Were birds smart? Probably not, or the word *birdbrain* wouldn't be one of the language's pejoratives. But a bird could be pretty dumb and still have the sense to flap itself away from the crowded din of New York for the peace and beauty of Washington County, Virginia, the huge, gently rolling green swards and endless white fences of horse country. So many places for them to alight contentedly. Maybe they were like him, exiles from Manhattan. But unlike him, they could return with ease.

Elliott Roosevelt's life in Abingdon involved not only a lot of responsibility but also a lot of territory.

> The Robinson properties covered a vast, almost primeval wilderness of virgin forest, laurel thicket, and high peaks, which the Douglas Land Company had decided to begin to tap. This meant bringing in railroads, improving mountain trails, settling boundary disputes, selling land to homesteaders.

In none of which occupations had Elliott so much as the slightest whiff of experience. But he did seem to possess the right instincts. Joseph Lash continues:

The work was difficult and hazardous but "by meeting the mountaineers upon their own grounds" Elliott was soon considered a "friend," the Washington County [Virginia] paper wrote. "Children loved him; Negroes sang for him usually when he was sick in bed: the poor, the needy and the unfortunate had reason to bless him; the young girls and the old ladies "fell for him;" and men became his intimate friends.

Elliott's social success in Abingdon seems, in large part, to have been the result of a single party, which his new acquaintances held in his honor, fearing that he might be bored with them and their existence, so rural and unsophisticated. Assuming—incorrectly, as had always been true—that Elliott was as lordly as his last name suggested, the upper crust of Abingdon decided that it would be wise neighborliness to make a friend of him.

The gathering started out, prior to the guest of honor's arrival, as "a very stiff and formal and altogether proper affair. He came. The stiffness thawed out, the formality disappeared, and the reception became one of the jolliest of their usual easy and natural parties. From then on he was simply one of the crowd, except that he was the life of every party and his presence in any gathering was a guaranty of a jolly good time for everybody."

❖

IN THE MONTHS AFTER THE election of 1932, the future First Lady of the United States would pay a visit to Abingdon, another homage to her father that, like publishing the book of letters, she was advised not to do. But, again, she refused to listen. She knew what she had to do, and that was to thank all the people who had been so gracious to Elliott when he lived among them. She had to know what they were like, to feel what her father felt in their midst. She had to make sure they knew what *she* felt about their kindness toward the man who was always kind to her.

❖

HIS SOBRIETY, IT SEEMS, WAS never an issue in Abingdon. Apparently no one, or perhaps just a few people, saw his unclothed self when he knocked over the light, and his burns might have been covered once he attired himself again. There is no other report of a public display of inebriation on his part. Which is not to say he was now sober, only under control. And which is not to say that he did not drink copiously when alone.

About this we obviously do not know.

What his fellow Abingdonians did see was something close to the Elliott Roosevelt that Manhattan high society saw only a few years ago—although how difficult it was for him to maintain this veneer is also something we don't know.

> "He dropped into homes and fitted into every family circle, eating apples by the open fire, reading poetry, talking of local things or about his own wife and children." He always functioned best away from his strong-minded wife and very successful brother but does not seem to have recognized this. And although he carved out a place for himself in Abingdon, his letters home were full of remorse and pleas that the "homeless and heartsick and lonely" sinner be forgiven and allowed to return to his family. "You know no sin which compares with mine," he wrote his wife, "can hardly know the *agony* shame and

repentance I endure and the *self* condemnation I have to face. I need indeed be brave to make my fight."

Such a different tone from the letters he wrote to his daughter.

But Anna was no less troubled than her husband. That she wanted him to recover and rejoin her family cannot be questioned; she wanted his help with the children, wanted the friendship and adoration of the man she had known as a suitor, who was then the envy of all in her circle. But that she believed it was unlikely to happen, no matter how hard he tried, was equally obvious. After receiving one of Elliott's emotional messages, perhaps the one just cited, she wrote to Bamie, "This letter from Elliott worries me so that I send it to you," she told her. "I am so awfully sorry for him. My heart simply aches and I would do anything I could that could really help him. . . . It seems to be dawning on him for the first time that he is not coming home this Autumn."

⟨◇⟩

INITIALLY, ELLIOTT LIVED OVER A store on Main Street. Hardly regal in the Rooseveltian sense. Soon, however, he moved up a notch, renting rooms in the home of Mrs. Mary Branch Campbell, the widow of a local judge and "a lovely old lady of motherly heart and infinite understanding of the ways of young men." For Elliott, these ways included the invitations he extended to the young ladies of Abingdon "to drive with him on the high seat of his swanky trap or in his two-seated yellow jersey wagon and he was a much sought addition to the masculine conclaves of men both young and old."

But there is no evidence, not even a suggestion, that Elliott ever did anything with an Abingdon woman other than ride with her and tell her tales, heavily edited, of his previous life. No attempted liaisons, no drunken revels. At least when others were present, especially those of the opposite sex, he seems to have been on his best behavior. Did he long for flesh, for the lusty responses of his two New York mistresses? Yet again, something we do not know. No letters between Elliott and either of the ladies exists. Or, if they do, they are certainly not housed in an official Roosevelt archive.

Elliott was also behaving on the job, despite Joseph Lash's previous description of it as "difficult and hazardous." For the first time in his life he seemed to enjoy going to work, helping to transform Abingdon into a more modern and economically thriving area. He even went so far as to tell some of his recently made friends that he was thinking of settling permanently among them.

He did not mean to fool them. Certainly, though, he was fooling himself. He could not stay in such rural environs. He needed the pace of Manhattan society again, even if he was excluded from it. More important, he needed the proximity of the large Roosevelt clan, which would make it easier for him to beg for forgiveness, to take him back and include him again in familial life.

And, of course, more than anything else, he needed his daughter, needed to call her "Little Nell" to her face, not simply write the words in the salutation of a letter.

The appellation, however, was becoming inappropriate. It might still have been appropriate for her age, but Eleanor was growing up fast in her father's absence, becoming "an independent and willful child." That is how her mother described her at this time. "Since Anna never took her into her confidence, [Eleanor] created a life of her own. [She] understood only that her home was a battlefield. . . . She looked accusingly at Anna. She blamed her mother for all her unhappiness."

It was, of course, not true. In fact, according to Blanche Wiesen Cook's view of the family dynamics, Anna deserves at least some of the credit for the relationship Eleanor had formed with her father. Believing that emotional nearness was the best thing for both of them, especially Elliott, she worked at it, encouraged it. Cook asserts that Anna "had no intention of turning her daughter away from Elliott, of betraying the unquestioning devotion Eleanor felt for her father. It might have been easier for Anna if she had. But, with enormous self-control, even as [Eleanor's] clear blue eyes gazed at her with such hatred and misunderstanding, even as they reflected her own pain and suffering, Anna said nothing." She hoped that, eventually, her husband and daughter would find enough contentment in each other to be less hostile toward her, and that with less hostility would come peace of mind, as well as fewer nagging ailments for her, ailments that persisted and were at times debilitating. Ailments for which Eleanor could find only minimal sympathy.

⬥

On numerous occasions, Elliott begged Anna for a reconciliation. She would have none of it. The time was not right. It was Eleanor and his two boys, his wife knew, with whom he really wanted to be reconciled, not her, and she would not allow his presence to torment her for the children's sake. She was not even sure that the boys longed for him, and little has been written about Elliott's relationship with them.

Anna's initial refusals angered Elliott, then brought replies that were equal parts frustration and grief.

> I have not found one person in either my wife's or my connection who encourages me . . . when I propose that the Children join their Father.

What he *did* find, he said, was that the family had united against him, conspiring in their belief that Anna, Eleanor, Ellie, and Hall belonged with Anna's mother, with whom all of them now lived. There, he continued, complaining enviously, they were

> surrounded by every thing in the way of luxury and all the advantages, both educational and otherwise to which they have become accustomed. . . . I have told my Mother-in-Law that she shall have the children until I feel I *must* have them and when that time comes she has promised to give them up to me—No matter if I am living alone on White Top [in Abingdon] or in Ceylon.

The effect of her father's exile on Eleanor was greater loneliness than she had known before. To combat it, she spent more time on her tree limb, sometimes without a book. When on the ground, she often kept quietly to herself, sometimes imagining that Elliott was accompanying her, walking with her, that they were talking privately and silently to each other. It is not as strange as it sounds. Many children who are seven, eight, or nine have imaginary friends; in Eleanor's case, it was her father.

And she did not want to be interrupted when the two of them were together. She was referring to other members of the teeming Hall household—her mother, grandmother, aunts and uncles, little Ellie and littler Hall, maids and other servants, governesses and tutors—when she complained as follows: "They always tried to talk to me and I wish to be left alone to live in a dream world in which I was the heroine and my father the hero. Into this world I retired as soon as I went to bed and as soon as I woke in the morning, and all the time I was walking or when any one bored me."

In October 1892, Anna needed surgery. Eleanor told her father and, although he did not know the reason for the operation, he wrote to Grandmother Hall, insisting that a husband's place at a time like this was at his wife's side.

He was told he was not wanted.

No, he insisted, he belonged in New York.

He should stay in Abingdon, he was told again, and it was an order; he would be notified by mail of the results of the procedure. Elliott did not understand how his family could believe that such coldhearted exclusion would rehabilitate him. If anything, it made him thirstier.

Several days later, he received a letter. The operation, whatever the reason for it, was successful. But Anna's good health was always a tenuous thing, more so under the present circumstances than ever before. As it turned out, she would barely outlive her period of recuperation.

However, both she and her mother, with Theodore's assent, had already conceded the point that, for Eleanor's sake, Elliott must be allowed the occasional visit with her. They laid down the conditions. Elliott was not allowed to spend more than a day or two at a time with his daughter, despite having to make the journey of 581 miles each way. He was not allowed to see her without first being given approval of the activities he had planned for them. Sometimes, he was actually chaperoned by another family member, or told that the two of them were to report in partway through the day. As for warning him not to drink in Eleanor's presence, not a word was uttered. It was understood that, if he stopped again at the Knickerbocker Club or any of the other watering holes he once frequented, he would never see his daughter again. Nothing, no treatment that he had yet endured, was more effective in keeping Elliott sober. For short periods of time, at least.

"Though he was so little with us," Eleanor wrote of her attitude when Elliott's appearances drew near, "my father dominated all this period of my life. Subconsciously I must have been waiting always for his visits. They were irregular, and he rarely sent word before he arrived, but never was I in the house, even in my room two long flights of stairs above the entrance door, that I did not hear his voice the minute he entered the front door. Walking down stairs was far too slow. I slid down the banisters and usually catapulted into his arms before his hat was hung up." One can only imagine what Anna thought when she watched her normally sullen child become so suddenly animated.

Elliott and Eleanor seldom had much time together, and so they passed the majority of it in their favorite activity: mapping out a future that neither of them fully believed would come. "They would spend the day walking around Central Park, spinning out fantasies of the ideal life they would have together when he finally got a house of his own and was able to bring her and her brother, Hall, to live with him."

Another visit, however, not nearly so dreamy, offered yet another reminder of the donkey ride near Sorrento.

On the way to Central Park, along Madison Avenue, a streetcar frightened Mohawk, her father's high-spirited hunter. When the horse shied, her father's hat flew off, and when it was retrieved, Elliott looked at his daughter and asked, "You weren't afraid, were you, little Nell?" She was but did not want to disappoint him by admitting it. When they reached the park and joined the procession of carriages and horses, her father said teasingly, "If I were to say 'hoop-la' to Mohawk he would try to jump them all." Eleanor prayed he would not. Yet despite her "abject terror," she later wrote, "those drives were the high point of my existence."

Elliott might have stopped for a few drinks that day before calling on his daughter. Getting up his nerve no less than quenching his thirst. Or he might just have been exhibiting his normal recklessness, exacerbated by his declining mental state. Eleanor might or might not have known that he had imbibed before his visit. Regardless, she was not about to tattle on him, especially since his behavior with her was usually above reproach.

⬧

BACK IN ABINGDON AFTER THIS or another of his New York treks, Elliott found himself on the verge of the greatest misfortune of his life so far. Slightly more than a year and a half later, there would come another. He barely had a chance of saving himself even before these two occurrences. Afterward, it was just a matter of time.

DAUGHTER

1936–62

A<small>S A LITTLE GIRL,</small> E<small>LEANOR</small> wrote to keep herself company as much as to express herself. She read her poems to her mother, but seldom; her mother never asked to hear them. Other than that, she was too timid to impose her thoughts on others.

That was then. Now her shyness was overwhelmed by exuberance. Her voice boomed, ideas forming at so fast a rate that they exceeded the available forums: a press conference here, the occasional speech there, a magazine article, or a meeting with her husband and his advisers about matters of national or international import—these were simply not enough anymore. She needed more reach, more expansiveness for the serious matters on her mind these days—and even for her musings, which might have been far less serious but were equally appealing to her, deserving of her time and ability. She simply could not keep herself *to* herself any longer.

Fortunately, many awaited to offer her opportunities.

Monte Bourjaily was the top executive of the United Feature Syndicate, and had been an admirer of the First Lady even before her assumption of the title. As Eleanor wrote about their first meeting, "He said he felt sure that if I would write a daily column in the form of a diary it would be of great interest to the people of the United States, who were curious about the way anyone who lived in the White House passed their time, day by day." Eleanor could not resist. In January 1936, she signed a five-year contract to produce a column that would appear in newspapers six times a week, from Sunday through Friday. It would be called "My Day."

She could not wait to get to work.

"I dictate it directly to [my secretary] Miss Thompson," Eleanor said, explaining how she turned out her pieces, "who takes it on the typewriter; then I correct it and she makes a final copy and sends it off by wire." The result was one of the most popular columns in the history of American journalism. Eleanor would write it from 1936 to 1962—twenty-six years, six times a week, no days off except Saturday!—and failing to meet her deadline only *once*. It was a remarkable feat, regardless of the length of her columns (and hers were shorter than most others in American papers) or their literary or intellectual merit. It is even more remarkable when one takes into account the fact that the author was fifty-two years old when she began her new assignment, seventy-eight when she ceased. The number of pieces she produced was in excess of eight thousand! It was a full-time job all by itself, but only one of several full-time jobs she took on.

Given that her columns were to be, in effect, diary entries, she had license to write whatever she wanted. Her first essay could not have begun in a more homey fashion: "I wonder if anyone else glories in cold and snow without an open fire within and the luxury of a tray of food all by one's self in one's room." Her last entry, which ran on September 14, 1962, was of an entirely different nature. "I often wonder, as I note how nervous we seem to be about Communist build-up in our world, why our country does not use new initiative to think out fresh approaches to the uncommitted people all over the world."

The latter column was more typical of "My Day," which expounded not just on the Communist buildup but on other significant issues of her days: the end of the Depression; the beginning, waging, and end of World War II; the beginning and waging of the Cold War; soaring food costs; the role of women in broadcasting, both radio and television; and, most poignantly, writing courageously through her sorrow, Harry Truman's sudden ascendancy to the Oval Office.

> Never before has a sudden change of presidents come about during a war. Yet, from the time that Mr. Truman . . . walked into my sitting room and I told them of my husband's death, everything has moved in orderly fashion. There was consternation and grief but, at the same time, courage and confidence in the ability of this country and its people to back new leaders and to carry through the objectives to which the people have pledged themselves.
>
> That this attitude established itself so quickly is a tribute to President Truman, to the members of the Cabinet, and to the Congress. But above all, it is a tribute to the people as a whole and it reaffirms our confidence in the future.

She wrote about relations with the Third World, the Yale Plan on Alcoholism, migratory farmworkers, the Berlin Blockade, and a "world government" to regulate the use of atomic power.

> I can quite understand why men like Prof. Einstein feel that a world government would answer the problem, but any of us who have worked in the United Nations realize that we will have to learn to crawl before we learn to walk. If the great nations find it so hard to agree on the minor points at issue today, how do any of these hopeful people think that a world government could be made to work? People have to want to get on together and to do away with force, but so far there are many throughout the world who have not advanced to the point of really wanting to do this.

And she wrote about such issues as the Taft-Hartley Act, Jimmy Hoffa and the Teamsters, the John Birch Society, military aid to the Arab states, and the Soviet launching of astronaut Yuri Gagarin into earth orbit.

> It is certainly almost breathtaking to think that a man flew into space and was gone 108 minutes circling the earth and during the trip talked to the ground by radio. . . .
>
> The Soviets, naturally, have great pride in being first to achieve scientific advances which some of us look upon as more or less incomprehensible developments but which we feel sure will eventually have more meaning to us all.

There were even times, although not many, when she opened doors to her private life that were normally kept under lock and key.

I was usually shy and frightened because I lived an entirely lonely life, with few children of my own age nearby. I had no ear for music and therefore danced extremely badly! My father sang well, loved music and had a real sense of rhythm. My mother played the piano and danced well. Something was certainly left out of me—at least at that early age—and what little appreciation of music I since have acquired has been acquired with toil and effort and was certainly not a gift of the gods!

Eleanor's "My Day" was not written in a formal manner, which was to be expected since the writing had started out as dictation. But that the First Lady of the United States was so informal, communicating to her readers as casually as if she were speaking to them, gave her columns the feeling of a conversation with an interesting, effusive, and well-informed friend. She chatted, rather than pontificating. She was there with those who wanted her company, in their homes, just a flip of the page away. Her column made her unique among presidential wives, although, as will be seen, there were a good many Americans who did not care for it, did not want her gibbering away at them—disdained her, in fact. They would not invite her into their domiciles under any circumstances.

❖

As TAXING AS "MY DAY" might have seemed, Eleanor wanted still more outlets for herself. There was Chiang Kai-shek to address and the Spanish Civil War, the new Social Security Administration and Mahatma Gandhi, *Brown v. the [Topeka] Board of Education*, and Fidel Castro. Eleanor's natural intelligence, the childhood in which she spent so many lonely hours devouring books, and her newly gained entrance to the nerve center of international events—all of these combined and combusted within her, compelling her to think more, to write more, to speak more.

She crammed as many of her interests as she could into her column, but when the North American Newspaper Alliance offered her a contract to do one piece a month, $750 for five hundred words, she could not say yes fast enough. She was instructed to write "as one woman to another, of your problems as the woman of the household," albeit hers was certainly no ordinary household.

Redbook, McCall's, the *North American Review, Current History,* and *Success* were among the magazines that asked her to contribute, and she did, energetically. For *Redbook,* she wrote "Women Must Learn to Play the Game As Men Do." For *Cosmopolitan,* a different magazine in those days from what it later became, she wrote a short-lived column. For *McCall's,* she assented to a monthly question-and-answer page for a time. She even wrote the captions—although, admittedly, they were longer than usual captions, more like short essays—for a photo spread on the Depression in *Look.* The following appeared beneath a picture of a bread line in Chicago.

> In 1933, I think we were a people who had given way to panic. Some people were facing starvation; they were justified in their fears. Others, facing a situation not nearly so serious, were nonetheless filled with misgivings because they could not see a serene future ahead. Until this period of panic, we had as a nation been remarkably free from any constant national fears, even though we participated in two wars within my memory.

Also in 1933, her first year in the White House, she somehow found time to return to the *Women's Democratic News* with a monthly effort called "Passing Thoughts of Mrs. Franklin D. Roosevelt." But most of her thoughts were enduring, not passing, and that is what attracted S. J. Woolf of the *New York Times Magazine*. When he finished interviewing her for a lengthy profile, he called Eleanor "the strongest argument that could be presented against those who hold that by entering politics a woman is bound to lose her womanliness and her charm."

She also turned out volumes of memoirs, several of them sources for this book. Most notably: *This I Remember, This Is My Story*, and *The Autobiography of Eleanor Roosevelt*.

She was not only the most literarily prolific First Lady the United States has ever had; she was one of the most prolific of all authors of her era. To be fair, though, it is worth repeating that most of her writings began in spoken form, dictated and then transcribed by her secretary, after which Eleanor made final edits. It is an easier way to proceed than starting from scratch on paper and turning out draft after draft. And she was certainly not as polished as many a full-time author. But she was herself on paper, the same person that she was with friends or at a public event, and most readers were engaged, commending her earnestness while enjoying a glimpse at her rarified position.

❖

In 1934, her interest in the role of women in radio increased greatly when she became one of the first. She accepted an offer from Johns Manville, the insulation and roofing corporation, to do a six-minute program for which she was paid $3,000, a figure that many of today's radio "personalities" would envy. Again, as was the case with her previous journalistic endeavors, most, if not all, of the money went to charity.

Later, she appeared on other programs. Among them: "Current Events," part of the Pan-American Coffee Bureau Series, which aired during the first two years of US participation in World War II; *The Eleanor and Anna Roosevelt Show*, Anna being her daughter, broadcast on ABC; and other offerings on the NBC network and WNBC, the network's station in New York.

Her move to television was a natural one. Her first position before a studio camera was as host of a Sunday afternoon program whose format might be summarized as "tea with Mrs. Roosevelt." She presided over a silver urn, sitting on a couch with her guest, as if in her living room. It was a gracious, almost old-world setting, and the star was by this time an old hand at putting people at their ease. And while both Churchill and [Soviet politician Andrei] Vyshinsky declined her invitations to join her for televised tea, Albert Einstein, who stubbornly avoided radio and television appearances, made an exception for Mrs. Roosevelt.

Another of her TV programs, of a consistently more substantive nature, was *Prospects of Mankind*, on PBS. And there were others: substantive and lighthearted, formal and casual—all of this from the former wallflower.

Despite such a volume of work in radio and television, her producers often found it difficult to find sponsors, even after her years as First Lady had ended. Her first few attempts at television failed to attract so much as a single advertisement. She was, after all, a controversial figure, and the majority of American businesses thought it safer not to be associated with her for that reason, despite the audience she could attract. Whereupon her agent, Thomas L. Stix, was approached with a proposal he never expected. He was asked whether Eleanor would be willing to do—of all things—a margarine commercial!

It was a chore for which she would be well paid, but Stix

was hesitant. She would come in for a lot of criticism on the grounds that it was undignified, he cautioned her, but if it were successful she would no longer be "poison" to sponsors. She thought it over and the next day she told him, "I'll do it. For that amount of money I can save 6,000 lives," thinking of the number of CARE packages the approximately $35,000 fee would purchase. She did the commercial and the protests poured in. "The mail was evenly divided," she said. "One half was sad because I had damaged my reputation. The other half was happy because I had damaged my reputation."

But it worked. Americans bought so much Good Luck margarine that if cows had had the sense to fear unemployment, they might well have done so.

In addition to her previous association with Johns Manville, such disparate entities as "Selby shoes, a mattress company, even food and beverage concerns paid for her broadcasts" in the future. Occasionally she even found herself with a waiting list of prospective sponsors. And more than occasionally there were outbursts against the high salaries she was paid, as well as continuing opposition to her being paid at all.

Which meant that Eleanor had to keep on explaining. "The money I earned from all of my radio work and some of my writing during the years I was in the White House," she said to critics, "I felt should be used not simply for charity donations but primarily to help people help themselves. Because that is also the philosophy of the [American] Friends [Service Committee], I chose them to handle the money for me."

❖

ELEANOR'S VOCAL CORDS SEEMED NEVER to tire. Thus, Louis Howe's gruff advice: "Get out and talk," he told her, and with that, the First Lady, seemingly with time to kill, took to the lecture circuit.

In 1936, a month-long tour began in Pennsylvania and ended in Michigan. "On 8 November in Philadelphia, she addressed an audience of two thousand at Temple University, where she made a rousing speech on the need for democratic action and community activism." Another lecture tour, earlier in 1936 and ranging farther geographically than the later one, was called "Ways of Peace," and like every other word she uttered in a public forum that year, its purpose was to return her husband to the White House for a second term. Her speeches went well, she wrote to him, but the experiences had been wearing ones. "It would be easy to be a lecturer or the wife of the President but both, Oh! My." And a columnist, a radio commentator, a television hostess . . .

In non-election years, however, most of her lectures were made on behalf of her own ideas and philanthropic concerns, not her husband's platform. And she seemed to have more ideas about more subjects than could ever be quantified. Thus, writing her speeches was probably the most demanding of all her means of expression.

Today's stars of the lecture circuit have three or four stock addresses, general in content, that they deliver over and over, choosing the one most appropriate for their audience. They add a few lines to refer to a particular item in the news, and to the specific interests of their listeners, perhaps poking fun at a few prominent members of the audience; essentially, though, they are like standup comedians, delivering only material that has been tested and proven on previous occasions.

But, for the most part, Eleanor's talks were different, full of detail and related to the most current of current events. As a result, and with assistance, she usually produced a new speech for each audience. Sometimes, the demands proved so great that her talks were largely improvised, but no less lacking in substance for their not having been written down. She knew her subjects even without the aid of a script.

When she became a private citizen again after more than a dozen years in the White House, she accepted a speaking engagement in Saint Petersburg, Florida. But no sooner had her appearance been announced than a bomb threat was phoned in. "Isn't it ironical," Eleanor said, "that in the Communist countries I have visited there has never been so much as an unkind *word*?"

Assuming that the caller was one of the many she encountered who opposed her support for Negro causes, and who did not really have the nerve to wreak violence, she said she would go ahead with the speech anyhow.

Those who had initially planned to attend also went ahead anyhow. But once the auditorium had filled and Eleanor was introduced, a security official of some sort stepped to the podium and announced that the auditorium was to be vacated immediately. It is not clear why the program was allowed to start and then so suddenly stopped, but Eleanor was furious. And furthermore, she was unwilling to comply. Her audience might have been herded outside, but she would not budge. Remaining on stage for as long as it took the venue to be searched for an incendiary device, she was even calm enough to sit and doze. It was an admirable display of fortitude on her part.

But there was another display, even more admirable: "[Eleanor] was touched by the courage of a little woman, possibly of her own age, who lingered on in the front row, protesting, 'If I'm going to be blown up, I can't think of any better company to be blown up with.'"

No bomb was found. The speech went on as scheduled, although considerably later.

❖

As a seventy-five-year-old widow—still writing "My Day" six days a week, remember—she became a visiting lecturer at Brandeis University. Offered the honorific "professor," she turned it down, explaining that, since she had not even attended college, she did not deserve to be addressed so grandly. A year later, still at Brandeis, she refused to have a car pick her up at the Boston airport and bring her back to campus. As she had done from time to time as First Lady, she took public transportation. She wanted no special treatment. She had never thought of herself as a Swell and was not about to start now.

FATHER

1892-94

O N October 9, 1892, with his daughter's eighth birthday only two days away, Elliott sat at the desk in his rented rooms in Virginia and poured out the longing he felt about missing the occasion. It was one thing not to spend Christmas with Eleanor; that was *everyone's* holiday. But the anniversary of her birth belonged to her and her alone. Well, her and her father. But in 1892, Elliott would miss it for the first time.

> My darling little Daughter,
> Many happy returns of this birthday[,] little Nell. I
> am thinking of you always and I wish for my Baby Girl

the greatest of Joy and the most perfect happiness in her sweet young life.

Because Father is not with you is not because he doesn't love you tenderly and dearly. And maybe soon I'll come back all well and strong and we will have such good times together, like we used to have. I have to tell all the little children here often about you and all that I remember of you when you were a little bit of a girl and you used to call yourself Father's little "Golden Hair"— and how you used to come into my dressing room and dress me in the morning and frighten me by saying I'd be late for breakfast. . . . Some day you must meet little Lillian and little Emily [young girls he met in Abingdon] and they will be glad to know you in person; they say they know your photograph so well.

Now I must stop writing[,] dearest little Nell, do take care of yourself and little Brothers, Ellie and Brudie, and kiss them for me.

Love dear Mother for me and be very gentle and good to her 'specially now that she is not feeling well. Goodbye[.] my own little Daughter.

God bless you. . . .

Your devoted Father,

Elliott Roosevelt

At least part of the reason Anna was not feeling good, one might conclude, was that "her frail health [had been] broken by two years of humiliation" nurtured by her husband. But late in November another factor emerged: she contracted diphtheria. Elliott immediately made plans to go to her, but before he could leave Abingdon he received a telegram. "DO NOT COME." Three words, capital letters, just that. The message was not signed, but Elliott was certain that Grandmother Hall wrote it on Anna's instructions. Anna knew what was going to happen to her. She did not want the man she had so mistakenly loved to see it.

As his wife continued to fail, Elliott wrote frantic letters to Grandmother Hall. "It is too awful to me to feel I have forfeited the right to be in my proper place. . . . Oh the misery of my Sin! . . . I am so relieved though to know that you are in charge. . . . Is my wife very ill[,] Mrs. Hall? *Two* trained nurses has such a terrifying sound. . . . If I should be wanted, in mercy forgive and remember that I am a husband and a Father and your son by adoption—though I have failed in many things. . . . I have a *right* in the sight of God to be by my wife's side in case she should wish me. . . . Do please *trust* me."

But Anna, who for some reason had demanded his presence when Hall was born, did not want Elliott with her now any more than she did for her earlier surgery. And her mother did *not* trust him. In fact, she believed, with some justice, that Elliott had ruined her daughter's life, causing an already delicate woman such stress and apprehension that she was more susceptible than she would otherwise have been to the disease that was now sapping her of life. She would never forgive him, and would tolerate his future visits, as she had tolerated those in the past, for Eleanor's sake only.

On December 3, Anna lost consciousness. Just as she sensed that the end was coming for her, so, somehow, did Elliott, and he reacted in the way that came most naturally to him, blanketing his mind with more and more lethal varieties of alcohol. It has been reported that, by 1894, he was "consuming up to six bottles of anisette, green mint [raw] brandy, or champagne prior to noon."

On the evening of December 7, well after noon, when he had had time to anesthetize himself even more, Elliott was dining and drinking with friends just outside of Abingdon. He was enjoying the company, and they were enjoying his. But he had arrived at the restaurant having had too much to drink, some of his companions thought, and was drinking all the more as he ate. Somehow, he was still able to talk coherently but just barely, and more and more words were being slurred together. The group was just about to rise from the table to exit when a messenger arrived with another telegram for Elliott. He opened it reluctantly, knowing the contents. His wife, his still beloved wife, his one and only, his dearest, Anna Rebecca Ludlow Hall, had died earlier that day. Without bothering to explain, Elliott dashed out of the restaurant and into his carriage, racing through four miles of muddy road to the railroad station. He arrived just in time to catch the overnight train to New York. He jumped aboard and fell in and out of sleep in the most drunken of stupors as he rattled northward through the darkness.

⋄

THE EXPRESSIONS OF GRIEF FOR Anna's death came from near and far and farther. The *New York Times* struck a familiar chord in its obituary.

> She was one of the most beautiful and popular women in New York society. She was Miss Anna Ludlow Hall, the oldest daughter of Mrs. Valentine G. Hall, who has been identified with the social life of this city for many years.
>
> It was Mrs. Hall who originated the "dancing classes" and at Mrs. Parson's class Miss Anna made her debut. She shortly afterward married Elliott Roosevelt, the brother of Theodore Roosevelt.
>
> The Elliott Roosevelts were members for years of the riding and tennis set on Long Island. Mrs. Roosevelt was

also fond of the drama, and she founded the Amateur
Comedy Club, in which her brother Valentine G. Hall,
Miss Elsie de Wolfe, the Misses Lawrence, and other well-
known amateurs made histrionic successes.

A little later, the *Times* got around to Elliott, referring to him merely
as an "invalid," and providing no more information other than that he
had been living in the "South." No reason was given. But he was in New
York now, and appeared uninvited and unwanted at the funeral home
where his estranged spouse lay. Without acknowledging any of the other
mourners, many of them family, he stared for the last time into the face
of the woman he had once courted so assiduously. It was centered on a
satiny pillow in such a way as to make her appearance flawless, almost
otherworldly in its perfection. It was too much for him. "Elliott wept at
the sight of his wife in her coffin, her slender young body still lovely in
a pale pink silk wrapper with white lace at her throat."

The other Roosevelts let him cry, no one asking him to leave, for
fear of a scene. Besides, Elliott left on his own after a few minutes,
again ignoring those assembled, and wasted no time. Within minutes he was seated in the nearest tavern. He "drank immoderately,
sang bawdy songs, and was quickly ushered out of town." It was a
pitiable performance.

Eleanor did not see it. Grandmother Hall kept her away from the
funeral home, and Eleanor seemed pleased with the arrangement.
She did not know her father was back in town and, although saddened by her mother's passing, had no desire to join the chorus that
sang hosannas to her. As Joseph Lash tells us chillingly,

Eleanor's account of her mother's death, written almost
forty-five years later, did not dwell on the loss of her
mother but on the return of her father. "Death meant

nothing to me, and one fact wiped out everything else—my father was back and I would see him very soon." . . . Later she realized, she wrote, "what a tragedy of utter defeat" her mother's death meant to her father. "No hope now of ever wiping out the sorrowful years he had brought upon my mother—and she had left her mother as guardian for her children. My grandmother did not feel she could trust my father to take care of us. He had no wife, no children, no hope.

This passage, as I am quoting it, is followed by another paragraph worth calling to the reader's attention. But it is also worthwhile to stop here to reflect on the last sentence that Eleanor wrote above: ". . . no wife, no children, no hope." It was as depressing a picture of a man's existence as could possibly be presented in so few words. The first two, inevitably, would ensure the last.

Continuing:

[Eleanor] wept for her father, not for her mother. Yet that engaging man's capacity for love and devotion was fatally flawed: it was totally self-centered, without steadiness or altruism. He made large promises, was full of warmth, charm, and affection, but there was no follow-through, no constancy, little on which his family could build.

What Joseph Lash concludes is reasonable, even accurate, as far as it goes. But it does not go far enough. It does not take into account Eleanor's opinion of her father and the crucial role he played in her life and development.

To include this information in Lash's portrait of Elliott is to present a diptych, with a different rendering of the man in each of the two hinged frames. This volume certainly respects Lash, has in fact relied on his facts and portrayals in many cases, but my primary interest is on the other side of the diptych—the good Elliott, Eleanor's Elliott. He might have produced "little on which his family could build," as Lash wrote, but more than any other human being he laid the groundwork upon which Eleanor would so magnificently stride one day, becoming, against all odds except those established by her father, the most influential and admired woman of the twentieth century.

⋄

AFTER HER MOTHER'S DEATH, AND according to the wishes expressed in her will, Eleanor returned to live with Grandmother Hall in the zany but welcoming household previously described. Elliott's first visit there as a widower was an important one for both father and daughter, although confusing in one important aspect. It is Eleanor who tells the story.

> He sat in a big chair. He was dressed all in black, looking very sad. He held out his arms and gathered me to him. In a little while he began to talk, to explain to me that my mother was gone, that she had been all the world to him, and now he only had my brothers and myself, that my brothers were very young, and that he and I must keep close together. Some day I would make a home for him again, we would travel together and do many things which he painted as interesting and pleasant, to be looked forward to in the future together.
>
> Somehow it was always he and I. I did not understand whether my brothers were to be our children or whether

he felt that they would be at school and college and later independent.

There started that day a feeling which never left me—that he and I were very close together, and some day would have a life of our own together. He told me to write to him often, to be a good girl, not to give any trouble, to study hard, to grow up into a woman he could be proud of, and he would come to see me whenever it was possible.

When he left, I was all alone to keep our secret of mutual understanding and to adjust myself to my new existence.

Elliott's emotional imbalance is unmistakable in this passage, at least to an adult. By itself, it surely seems to reinforce the notion that he was using Eleanor as a balm for his miseries, taking advantage of her, playing snake oil salesman to a little girl in need of a nostrum. Provided lovingly, but a nostrum nonetheless.

But to accept this interpretation of his black attire, sad countenance, and confusingly rendered image of the future, is to ignore the fact that Elliott had been enraptured with his daughter all his life, that he had found her a "miracle" on first sight, when his mother's impression of her was as a wrinkled old woman. Yes, Elliott was unbalanced even then, but, somehow, he was also capable of being a good father, a blessed father, the only light in a child's tunnel of darkness. And perhaps the only light in his own tunnel, despite its being much longer than Little Nell's. She gave him his one chance to redeem himself.

He might have been melodramatic when he first visited his motherless daughter in her new home, but his love and sincerity, and their effect on the recipient, shine through.

❖

BEFORE ANNA'S DEATH, ELLIOTT HAD a dog for a roommate in Mrs. Mary Branch Campbell's rooms. Returning to his Abingdon residence after visiting Eleanor, he added two puppies to the household. A family now of four, the best that Elliott could do for company. "They are both in the armchair beside me," he wrote to his daughter about the pups, "and the old dog is curled up at my feet in the rug dreaming, I suppose of all the rabbits he did not catch today."

The young dogs amused Elliott with their playfulness, perhaps bringing him more contentment than he had yet known in his exile. But not by much and not for long. In fact, his relative ease lasted less than six months. Then, in May 1893, both of his sons came down with scarlet fever. Hall soon recovered, and was sent to stay with his sister at Tivoli. But Elliott's namesake gradually worsened, and his troubled father shared his fears with Nell.

> Darling little Daughter
>
> I write you only a line to thank yoy [*sic*] for your letter received today and to let you know that little Ellie is very, very ill and may go to join dear Mother in Heaven. There is just a little chance that he may not die but the Coctors [*sic*] all fear that he will.
>
> Dear little Daughter[,] you are Father's love and joy. Give my devoted regards to Uncle Ned and Aunt Maggie [members of the Hall Tivoli household] and tell them what an awful fear we have.
>
> Your fond
> Father
> New York
> May 24, 1893

Eleanor responded, revealing her own awful fear, but by the time her letter arrived, it was too late. Elliott Roosevelt Jr. had died on May 25, the first step in eliminating the accursed name from the family. In his sister's opinion, he "was simply too good for this world, and he never seemed to thrive after my mother's death."

Once again, Eleanor was kept away from a scene of family mourning, and not incidentally to prevent Elliott from seeing her. There was nothing for him to do but take pen to paper again.

My own little Nell:

We bury little Ellie tomorrow up at Tivoli by mother's side. He is happy in Heaven with her now so you must not grieve or sorrow. And you will have to be doubly a good Daughter to your Father and good sister to own [*sic*] little Brudie boy [a nickname for Hall] who is left to us. I cannot write more because I am not feeling very well and my heart is too full. But I wished you to know you were never out of my thoughts and prayers for one instant all the time.

I put some flowers in your name as I knew you would like me to do. With abiding and most tender devotion and love I am always

Your affectionate Father

Elliott Roosevelt

May 26, 1893

55 West 33rd Street

Other than Eleanor, only one member of the Roosevelt family seems to have sympathized with Elliott for his loss, or at least set her sympathy to paper, however briefly. His sister Corinne, who had once admired him even more than Theodore, sent a telegram that he received on May 27. "My thoughts and sympathy are with you constantly," she said, but that was the entirety of her message, so short as to be perfunctory, duty more than sincerity. But condolence more than silence.

⊷◈⊶

EVEN THROUGH HIS OWN BEREAVEMENT, Elliott worried about his daughter, who at this point, was only nine years old. There had already been too much sadness in her life, and now her brother had died only fours months before his fourth birthday. In an attempt to lighten her spirits, as well as to soften Grandmother Hall for requests he would soon make to spend more time with Eleanor, he had made arrangements to send a special present to her.

Monday

My darling little Nell:

I am so glad you wrote Father such a sweet note on Saturday. I received it today and it has comforted me a great deal to know my little daughter was well and happy.

Ask Aunt Maggie to tell you what a sad day today was for all of us. I do not want to write it to you though I would tell you if your dear golden head was on my breast, my dear, loved little Nell. But do not be sad[,] my Pretty, remember that Mother is with Ellie and Aunt Gracie now.

I send Morris, my groom, on with your poney [*sic*] and cart [on] tomorrow afternoon's boat so that he will deliver him to you on Wednesday morning with Fathers tender love to his sweet daughter. You must get Aunt

Maggie's coachman to teach you how to drive him. He is perfectly gentle and only needs reasonable handling for you to drive him alone. Tell Aunt Maggie this. . . . I wich [*sic*] I could be with you to teach you how to drive myself, but that cannot be. Thank Aunt Maggie for asking me to come on after the 22nd and say that I am writing her.

With a heart full of love,

Everfondly, your Father

Eleanor told her father she was confident that Ellie would be "safe in heaven," and further wrote that "Our Lord wants Ellie boy with him now, we must be happy." As for the pony, despite having already been prepared for its eventual arrival, she was thrilled nonetheless. She did not feel, however, that this was an appropriate time for gushing, and reacted to the news with restrained gratitude.

⇤◇⇥

IN AN UNDATED LETTER WRITTEN with both Anna's and Ellie's deaths in mind, his syntax muddled and his handwriting increasingly illegible, Elliott sums up what he hopes the future will bring for them. He tells Eleanor that out "of joy and sorrow, my little darling, I long so for this for with it—comes our perfect love." In the meantime, imperfect love, confined to the epistolary and the rare visits, would have to do.

⇤◇⇥

IT WAS THE FALL OF 1893, and Elliott, racked by loneliness in Abingdon despite the continued friendliness and sympathy of his neighbors, decided that his exile had lasted long enough—Theodore and the rest of the Roosevelts be damned! He returned to New York, this time intending to stay. He immediately resumed his relationship with Mrs. Evans, and snuck off occasionally to see Mrs. Sherman, who still seems not to have known she was sharing her paramour with another woman, one who shared not just her man but her ignorance. Renting a house for Mrs. Evans and himself, he used the name Maxwell Eliot.

It was a poor choice of alias, but none would have hidden him better. Elliott's movements were being carefully monitored at the time, although it is not certain whether the Roosevelts were doing it themselves or had hired professionals. Regardless, his older brother knew about Elliott's return to New York shortly after he arrived, and he saw to it that the rest of the family was immediately notified.

But none of them did anything. None of them seemed to care. They were worn out by having had to deal with Elliott; they could no longer rouse themselves to take actions that the criminal in their family—as some of them thought of him—would try to thwart, perhaps bringing more unwanted publicity. He lived, according to Theodore, "like some stricken, hunted creature." It may also be true that at least a few members of the family thought Elliott was in such bad shape that he would not be around to plague them much longer.

One night in May of the following year, "he spent the night in a police lockup, too drunk to tell his cabbie where he lived." The family was not surprised. "His behavior had become so outrageous that his sisters and his brother Theodore began receiving anonymous letters concerning Elliott's activities." Did they all come from the same person? Or, if from different persons, just how many people were there who knew about the humiliation Elliott was bringing to the Roosevelt name?

Theodore could only sigh in sorrow. "He can't be helped," he wrote to Bamie. "He must simply be let go his own gait . . . Poor fellow! If only he could have died instead of Anna."

It is a fair guess that only one Roosevelt would have taken issue with Theodore's lament.

⊲◇⊳

A MONTH AFTER HER FATHER'S night in jail, about which she was not informed, and a year after she had delightedly received the pony from him, Eleanor was still riding the animal, still exhilarated by the experience, which had become an important part of her routine at Tivoli.

> June 14th, 1894
>
> Dear Father:
> I hope you are well. I am very well and so is every one else. . . . I rode my pony to-day for the first time this summer. I did not go very far but to morrow I am going for a long ride with Uncle Valley wont it be fun. I wish you were up here to ride with me. Give my love to the puppies and every one else that you know. Madelein [a friend of Eleanor's, name properly spelled Madeline], Brudie and I often drive with my pony.
> With a great deal of love I am your little daughter
> Nell

But the letter was sent to Abingdon, not New York. It is doubtful that Elliott ever saw it. And the gift of the pony never altered Grandmother Hall's edict that Elliott could spend no more time with his daughter than he had been doing previously. It was not enough, not nearly enough. He might have been back in New York, but his exile from Eleanor seemed permanent.

DAUGHTER

1948–59

I N HER LAST YEARS AS a dynamic public presence, Eleanor continued to seek resolutions to the most vexing of global issues. She also continued to write, to lecture, and, most of all, to matter.

When her husband no longer occupied the White House she could have faded into a kind of public insignificance, as had been the fate of other presidential wives. But not this one. It had been a long time since insignificance afflicted Eleanor Roosevelt, and now that she was a different person she would not allow it to happen again. As the colleague (rather than the conjugal companion) of the late chief executive, and a woman who had influenced numerous and varied pieces of legislation on her own, she was seen by many in the worlds of public affairs and journalism as a repository of the knowledge, acumen, and connections at the highest levels of governance.

But the acknowledgment of her power, and the dedication with which she wielded it, came well before widowhood did. On the occasion of her fifty-fourth birthday, with her husband more than halfway through his second term, the *New York Times* celebrated Eleanor in two editorials, commenting in one of them that she was "not in the tradition of the wives of former Presidents. But she is so patently . . . unpretentious in all she says and does, so ebulliently a part of every activity she undertakes, so good-humored even in the face of criticism, that she remains today one of the most popular women who ever lived in the White House. At 54 she could command a landslide of votes as Mrs. America."

She had opined on international issues for the *Women's Democratic News*, and gone on from there to write articles and columns on foreign affairs for numerous other publications, as well as speaking on such topics at the most prestigious forums. But she probably made her first indelible impression on the world stage three years after her husband's death, when she was named chairman of the United Nations Commission on Human Rights, which opened its hearings modestly enough in the library of Hunter College in the Bronx. "She kept the job when sessions were moved to Geneva [Switzerland], then back again closer to home, into temporary United Nations headquarters in Flushing, Long Island. Since she was also to be reconfirmed as an American delegate, she would be wearing two hats, as an individual and as a diplomat." But two hats was one too many. Perhaps, given all of her other duties, it was two too many. Regardless, the strain was great. It "erupted in a case of shingles, a considerable embarrassment because she was impatient of impairment to her health. A scarf around her neck concealed the rash."

In his biography of Eleanor, her son Elliott gives an idea of the scope of her duties, which could not have ranged further, and at the same time easily damaged her health.

> The unchangeable subject there was how to prepare an international bill of rights, which Mother and her fellows decided was the main task. Foremost was writing a declaration to define literally everything to which mankind has just claim—life; liberty; freedom from servitude and torture; equality before the law; the right to travel, choose a job at adequate pay, join a church, a political party or a union; to enjoy the vote, schooling, social security, rest and leisure time.
>
> The charter, assuming it could ever be completed, would be followed up as the second step by treaties, legally binding on those nations which signed them— mere resolutions of the United Nations carried no such power. The third and final step would be to develop a system for enforcing the covenants.
>
> The challenge was more intimidating than that confronting the Continental Congress, gathered in the summer steam of Philadelphia in 1776 . . .

But the Continental Congress succeeded, as did future assemblies of the Founding Fathers. The United Nations Commission on Human Rights did not. The Continental Congress was in tune with the temper of the times, representing the views of the majority. The UN Commission on Human Rights seemed in opposition to the very core of human nature, with a set of goals virtually utopian.

A few years later, though, Eleanor came closer to one of those goals, passage of the UN's Universal Declaration of Human

Rights. It was a nonbinding series of aspirations inspired by the Holocaust, "by the victims beyond tally of that Social Darwinist category Hitler introduced into the mainstream of world politics . . . Eleanor Roosevelt was among the first civilian witnesses to speak with Holocaust survivors, to tour concentration camps, to consider the needs of the future as mandated by that historical moment. And she wondered: 'When will our consciences grow so tender that we will act to prevent human misery rather than avenge it?'"

The question, of course, does not have a satisfactory answer. As for the Universal Declaration of Human Rights, it was one of the great struggles of Eleanor's life, bringing out all that was fiery and impatient in her, qualities seldom seen. "Some meetings left her dazed" by the complexity of the task.

> At others, she would remove her spectacles, which automatically deprived her of her hearing aid, and catnap for a while, relying on a friendly nudge to awaken her if a television camera peered in her direction. As Madam Chairman, she would slam down her gavel so hard it made the water pitcher jump, as when she shrilled at [Soviet representative] Dr. [Alexei] Pavlov, "We are here to devise ways of safeguarding human rights. We are *not* here to attack each other's governments, and I hope when we return on Monday the delegate of the Soviet Union will remember that." One more crash of the gavel. "Meeting *adjourned!*"

At this point, the fate of the declaration seemed uncertain at best. But Eleanor would continue to work ceaselessly on its behalf—ending up, one glorious but exhausting night, in Paris.

⌐◈⌐

W‌HEN HER OFFICIAL DUTIES WITH the United Nations ended in 1953, her unofficial duties began. For much of the next decade, by the end of which she would be seventy-six years old, she traveled around the world speaking on behalf of human rights as a private citizen. Her conscience drove her relentlessly, from the grand forum to the grass roots. In 1958, she asked touchingly:

> Where, after all, do universal human rights begin? In small places, close to home—so close and so small they cannot be seen on any maps of the world. Yet they *are* the world of individual persons; the neighborhood . . . ; the school or college . . . ; the factory, farm or office. . . . Such are the places where every man, woman and child seeks equal justice, equal opportunity, equal dignity without discrimination. Unless these rights have meaning there, they have little meaning anywhere. Without concerned citizen action to uphold them close to home, we shall look in vain for progress in the larger world.

As an ambassador sans portfolio, Eleanor represented causes of the United States or United Nations the world over, becoming in the process our country's most admired export. Her journeys were supported by various groups, most often the federal government, but regardless of the sponsoring agency, she spoke and wrote her mind, no matter whose point of view she was ostensibly representing.

To name a few, though only a few, of the places she alighted, there were the Scandinavian nations . . .

She was received at royal palaces and trade-union head-quarters. She visited industrial and agricultural cooperatives as well as housing and health projects, addressed large meetings of women, held press conferences, and spoke over national radios. "Eleanor Roosevelt has come to Stockholm," wrote the conservative *Svenska Dagbladet*. "She came and lived up to every expectation."

There was Brussels, where she made it clear that . . .

Just as she was a reassuring symbol to the labor and social-democratic movements of western Europe of the basic sanity, decency, and idealism of the United States, she also was the country's most effective ambassador to the emerging Third World.

There were Paris, Beirut, and Chile, in the latter of which . . .

she visited housing projects and health and hospital centers, toured slum areas, held a free-swinging press-conference, and so won the hearts of press and people that not even the Communists dared to criticize her.

There was Hiroshima, which she found . . .

a moving experience. . . . I walked on eggs while there. I know we were justified in dropping the bomb but you can't help feeling sorry when you see suffering. . . . It is always hard to tell people that it is the causes of war which bring about such things as Hiroshima, and that we must try to eliminate these causes because if there is another Pearl Harbor, there will be undoubtedly another Hiroshima.

Hong Kong, where . . .

she was feted and shown the sights. She was briefed on the Chinese refugee problem and given "the English point of view" on the Far Eastern question "with a heavy hand," she wrote her son John . . .

Greece, where she . . .

toured archeological diggings, visited the Acropolis at sunset, and she lunched with the king and queen. . . . She evidently did a little missionary work in the palace of the Hellenes, for she asked her son to send Her Majesty information about Berea and Antioch colleges, where work was a part of the curriculum, as well as material on the Henry Street settlement and the Alfred E. Smith low-cost houses.

And there was Yugoslavia, where she conversed with Marshall Tito, the independent Communist leader who, among other things, took Eleanor to his private vacation island in the Adriatic Sea and showed her his fleet of speedboats. "You cannot meet this man," Eleanor said, "without recognizing that he was a real mind. He is a doer and a practical person."

On a personal level, her most important destination was India, which had been such a splendid hunting ground for her father many years earlier, and perhaps the apex of his public persona. Among other cities, she stopped at Agra, and her son Elliott wrote of what her father Elliott had said about the site many years earlier, of how profound she would find the experience.

"'Little Nell,'" Elliott [the father] had told her, 'when you grow up you must go and see the Taj Mahal on a night of the full moon. There is a bench not far away, next to one of the lotus-leaf basins, where you should sit and contemplate.'

"This was such a night. She waited through the day, then, finding the same place where he had sat before she was born, she recaptured his feeling that this was the one unforgettable sight he had seen in India.

"'I will carry in my mind the beauty of it as long as I live,' she said. She had never known great tranquil joy than this."

Little Nell was no longer afraid of either strange people or strange places.

❖

For a long time, Eleanor had wanted to visit the Soviet Union. Shortly after World War II ended, and the United States and the Soviets, nominal allies, were settling into the cloak-and-dagger, hide-and-seek of the Cold War, she got her wish. She departed "to see this vast, mysterious troublesome country with her own eyes." Although she made the trip as a correspondent for a newspaper syndicate, she had conferred with government officials beforehand and been assured by Harry Hopkins, formerly one of Franklin's top advisers, that the Soviets would permit her to visit "everything you wanted to see everywhere in the country . . . although, of course, the Russian Government and the Russian people would receive you as the widow of the President and there is just no way out of that one."

It was not until a later trip to the Soviet Union in 1957, four years after Stalin's death, that she satisfied another desire, meeting the mass murderer's successor, the First Secretary of the Communist Party, Nikita Khrushchev. At first, there were no assurances that she would see him. She did her homework nonetheless, reading everything from books to newspapers, from position papers to once-classified documents. Thus, even before Khrushchev agreed to talk to her, she believed that she had learned some new and valuable lessons about the people over which he now presided.

"The most important thing she learned about the Soviet Union," according to Joseph Lash, "she summed up in the formula—Lenin and Pavlov [the Soviet physiologist known for his theory of reward and punishment that results in 'Pavlov's dogs']. As she watched thousands of Soviet citizens patiently queue up outside the tomb of Lenin—and, at that time, the tomb of Stalin as well—she realized that it was through the teachings of these two men—and chiefly that of Lenin—that the Soviet citizen saw his society and the world, and that this vision embodied relentless hostility to the West. And in a visit to a pediatrics institute in Leningrad, it dawned on her that the Pavlovian system of conditioning children embodied the methods by which the Russians as a whole were turned into a 'completely disciplined and amenable people.'"

It was not a conclusion that made Eleanor want to meet Khrushchev any the less. It did, however, make her feel a certain eeriness, confirming specifically what she had previously thought in general terms about the Soviet Union. But despite the photographs and newsreel footage she had seen of Khrushchev, her first look at him was a jolt, as he seemed terribly miscast for the role of an Orwellian despot. "In a loose-fitting suit that did nothing to disguise his paunch, the stocky, bald little man was standing outside the villa, grinning a welcome." He might have been a farmer, not a tyrant.

A tape recorder was set up on a table between Eleanor and Nikita, and the second most powerful man in the world began to talk to the most influential woman for posterity.

"I want to speak of President Franklin Roosevelt . . ." Khrushchev began. "He was a great man, a capable man who understood the interests of his own country and those of the Soviet Union. We had a common cause against Hitler, and we appreciate very much that Franklin Roosevelt understood this task." And on he went, with Eleanor, who had other things on her mind than listening to yet another encomium for her late husband, growing ever more impatient. Finally, Khrushchev stopped to catch his breath, and his companion rushed into the breach.

"Mother proceeded to business," son Elliott wrote. "Disarmament was the opening subject on the agenda. The Red Army outnumbered United States armed forces. Why was that?"

Eleanor knew that nothing substantive would come of their conversation, that the Soviets' First Secretary was not about to make any revelations, alter any policies. The point of the conversation was to satisfy her own curiosity about the Soviet leader, and, further, to establish a friendly basis for continued dialogue between Khrushchev and American officials. "Sometimes, the discussion grew sharp, but [Khrushchev] was consistently affable, revealing nothing of the boorishness displayed three years later, when he took off a shoe to pound a desk at the United Nations General Assembly in New York."

After two and a half hours, the tape recorder was turned off, and Eleanor and her few escorts joined their host, his wife, daughter, and son-in-law for a hearty Russian peasant meal. It represented more than just the image he wished to portray; the food was the truth of his upbringing, a staple of his heritage.

The two principals got along so well that they exchanged visits. The following year, when President Eisenhower invited Khrushchev to tour the United States, he agreed. But only on the condition that he be able to stop at Hyde Park. Permission was granted, and, with government assistance, Eleanor began to prepare the Big House for company.

Once she and Khrushchev greeted each other and chatted for a few minutes, grinning widely for the cameras, he told her he had something important on his mind. Then there came "a moment of the deepest solemnity and ceremony when Khrushchev, preceded by two aides carrying a large floral wreath and followed by Mrs. Roosevelt and Mrs. Khrushchev, proceeded to the Big House's rose garden and placed the wreath at FDR's graveside. It bore the inscription:

To the outstanding statesman of the United States of America—the great champion of progress and peace among peoples.

Chief of the Council of Ministers of the
Union of Soviet Socialist Republics
N. S. Khrushchev

It almost sounded as if the Soviets would support the Universal Declaration of Human Rights. Eleanor, of course, knew better.

Afterward, she offered Khrushchev and his party their choices from several tables full of food, but they did not have time for it. Nor for more conversation, a resumption of their previous bonhomie; the First Secretary was on a tight schedule. Not so tight, however, that his wife would refuse a glass of champagne. She took one and gulped, rather than sipped; Khrushchev smiled ruefully. "They call me a dictator," he said to Eleanor. "You see how little power I have? I told my wife not to drink any alcohol, and in front of me she takes champagne." Khrushchev himself took a roll, a single roll from the table of plenty, and was hurried out the cottage door, back to his limousine. "One for the road!" he called back, waving the roll at his hostess, and then he was gone.

When he returned to Manhattan, Khrushchev sent Eleanor a present, a handmade, Soviet-knitted shawl. "Tell your wife and daughter," Eleanor wrote, expressing her gratitude, that "if they are here and in need of any help in shopping, I can easily arrange to give them guidance."

⊰◈⊱

KHRUSHCHEV WAS NOT THE ONLY dignitary to call on Eleanor in the long, venerated days of her widowhood. Although part of the reason that others came to Hyde Park was to pay their respects at her husband's final resting place, they also wanted to meet the remarkable woman who had accomplished so much both with and without her legendary spouse. She happily took them on a tour of the grounds, fed them, and picked their minds for forthcoming columns, articles, and speeches. No one in the United States, man or woman, had the access that Eleanor Roosevelt had.

Mohammad Reza Pahlavi, "the young, hawk-eyed shah of Iran," who would later be overthrown by less dictatorial forces in his country, was one of her first callers. He had admired Roosevelt ever since the American president spoke to the shah about irrigating his desert nation, explaining to him how the construction of dams and consequent availability of hydroelectric power could transform "a country of sand and dust into an oasis of industry serving as a bugger to Soviet expansion in the Near East. The shah was following the course outlined for him by FDR, he explained, and Mother," wrote Elliott Roosevelt, "glowed with pleasure."

She took Haile Selassie, the emperor of Ethiopia and the so-called "Lion of Judah," on a tour of her property as part of a visit to America arranged by the State Department. He had little of interest to say to her and she was not especially impressed with him.

Jawaharlal Nehru was the first man to serve as prime minister of an independent India, and Eleanor found him "a remarkably intellectual man," one who proclaimed himself an apostle of Mahatma Gandhi. Eleanor took advantage of his thoughtfulness. When the Hyde Park sightseeing was over and he sat cross-legged on the floor in front of his hostess's chair, the first words out of her mouth were, "What do you contemplate as India's future, Mr. Nehru?" Right to the point, and a substantive one at that; so did Eleanor converse with the world leaders who sought her company. They were small-talkers no more than she.

And not long after entertaining Nehru, despite the fact that "Mother was of an age to qualify for social security," Secretary of State Dean Acheson asked her to go winging off again. She accepted the mission, and became again, as she had long been an unofficial but most eminent ambassador for the United States. Her destinations this time included England, France, Belgium, Luxembourg, Sweden, Finland, and Denmark.

It was the last trip she would make with so many stops, and she could not have been more pleased. Or more weary. But she never lost her interest in world affairs; to the contrary, she cared about them and wrote about them more than ever, and had built up a storehouse of firsthand information greater than that of any other columnist—perhaps more than any government official—in America. Her perspective was a unique one, and more often than not perceptive. She was, thus, worth reading for the rest of her life. Her writing style remained as it had always been: simple, informal. But the foundation of her commentary was deep, more sturdily based than ever. She is to be forgiven if she thought she knew more about how the world worked than President Eisenhower, a Republican for whom she did not have the highest opinion.

With few exceptions, though, her globe-hopping days were now over. It was time to live a more sedentary life, and although she continued to maintain an active lecturing schedule, she also began to settle at Val-Kill for longer periods of time than she had before. Her mind was active as ever, but her body was nearing the end of its ability to ride the whirlwind.

FATHER
1894

❖

ELLIOTT WAS IN NEW YORK in the summer of 1894, still leading his addled, adulterous life, although having settled into an apartment of his own, no longer a transient, no longer living in sin with Mrs. Evans. It seems that he continued to see her, though, as well as continuing to see Mrs. Sherman, and, most of all, continuing to dispatch expressions of longing to Grandmother Hall, pleading to visit his daughter. But that summer, he began sending letters to a new address.

Eleanor and others from Grandmother Hall's menagerie had left New York to enjoy the cooler temperatures of Bar Harbor, Maine, where the highlight of the season for her was catching six fish the first time she ever cast a line into the water. She wanted her father to know, to be proud of her, sending him a letter about her success that very night. Did he receive it? Had he made arrangements for mail to be forwarded from Abingdon to New York? It is simply not known. Eleanor signed the letter in her usual fashion: "Goodby dear dear Father I send you a great deal of love I am your little daughter, Nell."

In July, Elliott sent a note asking her to give his love to "all the dear home people and all of my good friends who have not forgotten me." He also asked whether she would like a cat; she had had an angora when she lived with her mother and father and perhaps he could provide her with another. She said yes, and eagerly awaited the little pet. Unlike the pony, the cat would never come. Perhaps her letter never reached him, either. A few weeks later, perhaps hallucinating at the time—according to his valet, hallucinations were a frequent occurrence these days—"he drove his carriage into a lamppost and was hurled onto the street."

<hr />

"I HOPE MY LITTLE GIRL is well," Elliott wrote, in what might have been his last communication with Eleanor. Or his last communication might have been an undated letter he dictated to a nurse, who not only wrote it down for him but mailed it. Regardless, he confessed that he had been "quite ill," probably because the effects of the carriage accident compounded his other woes. He closed the letter by admonishing her to *"never forget* I love you."

She wouldn't. He didn't have to ask. But something about the admonition chilled her.

<hr />

ON AUGUST 14, 1894, JAMES King Gracie and Douglas Robinson, the members of the family who lived closest to Elliott's apartment on West 102nd Street, in the northernmost, least settled, and cheapest region of Manhattan, were summoned by police officers to meet them there. Both knew the reason before they arrived. It was Elliott's valet who had found him.

> The exact circumstances of Elliott's death are unclear. Some authors state that Elliott, who had contemplated suicide as early as 1890, jumped out of the parlor window of his Manhattan apartment while others claim that, in a state of delirium, he attempted to jump from the window. All historians agree that he died in his apartment bedroom after suffering a convulsion, sleeping quietly, and awaking with a moment of rationality just prior to his death.

The convulsion might have been a seizure and it is possible that he fell victim to it while under the spell of delirium tremens, having taken a brief hiatus from his imbibing. But that is unlikely. As far as anyone knew, he was still drinking several bottles of liquor a day at the time, along with morphine and laudanum, and he was always so deeply under the influence of these mind-altering substances that his mind was very nearly altered beyond even his own powers of recognition. "The attending physician gave heart failure as the chief cause of death," we are told, "with alcoholism as the contributing reason."

When the end came, the once-dashing, now demolished Elliott Roosevelt was a mere thirty-four years old.

The obituary in the *New York Times* settled on "heart disease" as the cause of death. The *Times* stated that Elliott's passing "was unexpected, although he had been somewhat ailing for more than a year. . . .

"Mr. Roosevelt was severely afflicted by the death of his wife eighteen months ago. She was Miss Anna Hall, and was the daughter of Valentine Hall. The blow was added to by the death of a son in May, 1893. About two weeks ago Mr. Roosevelt was thrown from his carriage. The shock aggravated the trouble with his heart and hastened his death. Two children survive, Eleanor Roosevelt and Hall Roosevelt, aged respectively ten years and three years."

The *New York World*, like the *Herald* before it, was more melodramatic where Elliott was concerned. Under a headline that read "ELLIOTT ROOSEVELT DEAD . . . HE WAS ONCE KEPT IN A MADHOUSE," it wrote the following:

The curtains of No. 313 West 102nd Street are drawn.

There is a piece of black crepe on the door-knob. Few are seen to pass in and out of the house, except the undertaker and his assistants. . . . In a darkened parlor all day yesterday lay a plain black casket. Few mourners sat about it. Beneath its lid lay the body of Elliott Roosevelt. . . . To [James K. Gracie] was left the duty of breaking the news to the others. Many of them did not know that Elliott Roosevelt was in New York. Few of them had seen him for a year. At the clubs no one knew his address. Even the landlord from whom he rented his house knew him only as Mr. Elliott. Under that name he has lived there with his valet for over ten months. He sought absolute seclusion.

Many people will be pained by this news. There was a time when there were not many more popular young persons in society than Mr. and Mrs. Elliott Roosevelt.

⬥

THEODORE, STILL A STATE ASSEMBLYMAN, returned to Manhattan from his legislative duties the day after his brother died. At first, he seemed impassive. "I only need to have pleasant thoughts of Elliott now," he said, but that was as far as he could get without breaking down. His sister Corinne found him "more overcome than I have ever seen him—cried like a little child for a long time." He told Corinne that he knew how much his brother had been drinking, "But when dead the poor fellow looked very peaceful, and so like his old, generous, gallant self of fifteen years ago. The horror, and the terrible mixture of madness and grotesque, grim evil continued to the very end, and the dreadful flashes of his old sweetness, which made it all even more hopeless. I suppose he has been doomed from the beginning; the absolute contradiction of all his actions, and of all his moral even more than his mental qualities, is utterly impossible to explain."

It was probably at Theodore's insistence that no coroner's inquest was ever conducted, or at least that no record of such an occurrence was ever found. Also possible is that Theodore was responsible for the *Times*'s not emphasizing the role of alcoholism and drugs in ending his brother's life. There is no evidence that Theodore had threatened to use his power in Albany against the paper if it told the whole truth; it would not, however, have been beyond him. But the Roosevelt family's position in society might have been enough by itself to bring about the *Times*'s restraint.

⬥

BOTH OF ELLIOTT'S MISTRESSES CONTACTED the family after their lover had passed away. Mrs. Sherman wrote to Corinne, who was struck by the obvious depth of her emotions. She sent Corinne a letter immediately after Elliott died, and another a year later. "I've been sadly wondering about his children," she told their aunt, "if they are well and strong—and inherit anything of his charms." It is not known whether Corinne replied. She was, however, touched by the woman's concern.

And an odd little addendum: In 1914, a full two decades after Elliott's death, "[a] tender exchange had evidently occurred between [Corinne and Mrs. Evans]," an exchange about which I could find no additional details. But not long afterward, Corinne published a book of poetry whose title verse was dedicated to Mrs. Evans. In fact, the poem, called "One Woman to Another," was written as if Corinne were doing the speaking and her late brother's inamorata was the listener. It concludes with the two women hugging—and more.

> What! You would kiss me? Yes, I take your kiss;
> We are both women, and we both have loved!

⋖◆⋗

THERE QUICKLY AROSE THE MATTER of a burial place for Elliott, something to which no one had given any thought about a man in his midthirties. The logical site, it was suggested would be next to his wife. Theodore was indignant; it was a "hideous plan," he believed, and he promptly vetoed it. He refused even to allow his brother to be buried in the same graveyard as his wife. Instead, revealing his well-hidden sentimental side, he decided that Elliott should be interred in Brooklyn's Greenwood Cemetery, "beside those who are associated only with his sweet innocent youth."

At the funeral, Theodore noticed to his surprise that among those in attendance was "the woman," [most likely Katy Mann, not Sherman or Evans] accompanied by two of her friends. He was relieved to note that the three of them "behaved perfectly well, and their grief seemed entirely sincere." They left immediately after the obsequies, speaking to no one.

⟨◆⟩

ELEANOR FOUND OUT ABOUT HIS father's passing from afar, her aunts telling her; "but I simply refused to believe it, and while I wept long and went to bed still weeping I finally went to sleep . . ." She could not imagine a world without her father in it, nor could she conceive of a place for herself in such a world. So, she "began the next day living in my dream world as usual."

But it was not as usual, not for a while. Needing time to recover from the deepest sorrow she would ever know, and which so closely followed the deaths of her mother and brother, Eleanor dwelled more deeply in her dream world than ever before, her flight from reality more complete than had ever been possible in her books. On occasion she did not seem to be aware that others were talking to her, and certainly was not interested in what they had to say. On other, more extreme occasions, she appeared disoriented, not noticing where she was, not particularly caring. It is possible that she had spirited her mind away to somewhere sunny and remote with her father.

Her most intense period of grieving lasted as long as it did because she was not allowed what we today call "closure." As she later wrote, "My grandmother decided we children should not go to the funeral and so I had no tangible thing to make death real to me. From that time on I knew in my mind that my father was dead, and yet I lived with him more closely, probably, than I had when he was alive."

Although Eleanor would not have believed it at the time, it was fortunate that her father died when he did. Or so Theodore insisted. "By his death," Joseph Lash wrote, paraphrasing his views, "Elliott made it possible for his daughter to maintain her dream-picture of him."

But at what price? By maintaining the dream-picture, some in the family believed that, "her own sense of reality was impaired. She tended to overestimate and misjudge people those who seemed to need her . . ." And because she ignored her father's shortcomings, she got into the habit of ignoring those of others with whom she worked later in life. She would instead "become closed, withdrawn, and moody when people she cared about disappointed her."

On the other hand, Lash posits . . .

> Although idolization of her father exacted a price, it was also a source of remarkable strength. Because of her overwhelming attachment to him, she would strive to be the noble, studious, brave, loyal girl he had wanted her to be. He had chosen her in a secret compact, and this sense of being chosen never left her. When he died she took upon herself the burden of his vindication. By her life she would justify her father's faith in her, and by demonstrating strength of will and steadiness of purpose confute her mother's charges of unworthiness against both of them.

Allowing for its length, only a paragraph, it is as important an explanation as ever written about the transformation of Little Nell into Eleanor Roosevelt.

DAUGHTER

1952–62

ELEANOR SUPPORTED ADLAI STEVENSON, THE former governor of Illinois, for president in 1952, and her support was vital to his campaign. She had met Eisenhower a few times and did not dislike the man, but, as a Democrat, found herself more sympathetic to Stevenson's views. Stevenson was also, like Eleanor and her husband, of patrician background, although unlike the Roosevelts, was not able to stand down from his perch and communicate with the average American. Eleanor tried to help him bridge the divide.

But though he made the effort, however halfhearted it might have been, Stevenson realized that his perceived standoffishness was probably the biggest reason for Eisenhower's being heavily favored to succeed Truman. In fact, so troubled was Stevenson by his opponent's eventual victory that he considered not running again in 1956. He asked Eleanor for advice.

Where Stevenson was not sure, Eleanor was decisive. He had to seek the White House once more, she told him. He owed it to the party; he was the best man the Democrats had. "She urged Stevenson to don an old suit, get into a jalopy, and travel about the country talking to farmers, gas station attendants, housewives, and not leave an area 'until you can "feel" what they are feeling.'"

Since this was Eleanor Roosevelt talking, Stevenson surely listened. But just as surely, he was appalled by such counsel. Why should a man of his background engage in conversation with common laborers and women raising babies, forcing himself to ask their opinions and, worse, actually heed those opinions and consider them as a basis for policy? The next thing he knew, Eleanor would be advising him to kiss babies! He refused.

Stevenson lost his bid for the White House in 1956 by an even greater margin than he did in 1952, both popular and electoral. There is no way to calculate how many farmers, gas station attendants, and housewives refused to vote for him.

❖

In 1961, at Stevenson's suggestion, President Kennedy appointed Eleanor to be a member of the US delegation to the special session of the United Nations General Assembly. On her first return to this building in which she had spent so much time in the past, she stopped in at a meeting of the Human Rights Commission. The delegates interrupted their business the moment she appeared, to greet her with applause. Asked to say a few words, for which she was not prepared, she nonetheless told the commission that she hoped to live long enough to see the principles of the Declaration of Human Rights rise from their status of wishful thinking to one day be adopted as law.

Eleanor later accepted a position on the Tractors for Freedom Committee, one of Kennedy's attempts to atone for the disaster that was the Bay of Pigs invasion. She also served the new, young chief executive as a member of the advisory council of a new kind of organization called the Peace Corps, which was far superior to the Bay of Pigs as a basis for foreign relations. Perhaps most important, Kennedy urged Eleanor to become an unofficial adviser to him; she would always have his ear, he promised, and he was true to her word.

Among the issues Eleanor brought to Kennedy's attention in the following months were the plight of migratory farmworkers; "the subject of the president as educator"; the nascent warfare in Vietnam, which she believed should be settled by the United Nations, not American military troops; and the need for the United States to continue attempts at negotiation with Nikita Khrushchev, despite the Soviet Union's having built the Berlin Wall and ignoring an existing moratorium on the testing of nuclear weapons.

To the attorney general, the president's brother Bobby, she wrote about the civil rights movement in the South. Kennedy assured her that the administration was monitoring it carefully and doing all it could to help without, at the same time, inciting a second Civil War. More realpolitik, which was always clashing with Eleanor's idealism. The president eventually did take action, however, and Eleanor congratulated him after the Justice Department persuaded officials in Albany, Georgia, to drop charges against the Reverend Martin Luther King Jr. for leading a march through their town.

But she was getting tired, so tired. Her knack of dozing off from time to time during the day had been recharging her for many years, but her personal physician believed that her brief naps were not quite the respite they seemed. In 1960, Eleanor was felled for a time by an ailment that Dr. David Gurewitsch diagnosed as a blood disease called aplastic anemia; in its earlier stages, it could have led to her need to doze off during the day. Said another doctor, Eleanor's son-in-law James Halsted, to his wife, "You have to realize this [the anemia] will shorten her life. You will get to broken down veins and transfusions."

Eleanor was aware of the diagnosis, but she did not lessen her pace despite the urging not only of physicians but also of her daughter, Anna. "The illness would flicker and subside—infections, fevers, chills, and aches," Anna later explained. "She dealt with them by ignoring them. Doctors, children, friends told her repeatedly that by any standard she was overdoing things, but she had her own firm ideas on how she wished to live—and die."

At the age of seventy-seven, when, "in some sense, despite all her achievements, she was still Little Nell, orphan of her father's stormy passage . . . she took a battered Bible that had belonged to him and showed it to an Episcopal priest near Val-Kill to ask about getting the cover repaired.

This led to a lengthy conversation in which Eleanor described her father's failings and asked if they were such as to bar him from heaven. When the clergyman said he thought not, Eleanor was visibly pleased at the thought that she would see her father again someday. And she knew that for her, "someday" was drawing ever closer. The realization was as likely to have consoled her as to frighten her.

Early in 1962, wondering whether she would make it to the age of eighty, she was subjected to a number of tests and diagnosed with a form of tuberculosis that was destroying her bone marrow—"a disease, ironically, that physicians theorized might have lain dormant in her body since the summer of the FDR-Lucy affair, when

Eleanor had been afflicted by what she dismissed at the time as a particularly bad flu."

Dr. Gurewitsch believed that "extreme remedies" might save her life, but she refused to try them. "No, David," she told him, without asking for details of the remedy, "I want to die."

In the hospital for the final time, she watched coverage of the Cuban Missile Crisis on television, but by now she had had enough of men and their politics, their wars, so much preening and posturing, so little thought, deep thought, behind their actions. She had no advice to send to the White House. Her only advice was for the doctors and nurses in the hospital who kept trying to medicate her: Leave me alone. Let me die in peace.

But they don't do such things in hospitals. When a nurse took it upon herself to tell Eleanor that it was the Lord's decision when to take her, not the patient's, she could not have been more dismissive. "'Utter nonsense,' she said, looking at the intravenous tube in her arm, the oxygen tank, and the needle punctures in her skin. Confused and incoherent, often in a semicoma, her determination to die alone was steady and iron-willed."

She would not take pills. If clenching her teeth against a nurse's effort to force them into her mouth didn't work, she simply accepted the little tablets, secreted them between her back teeth and the inside of her cheek, then removed them and hid them under the mattress when the nurse departed. Quite a stash was found when, after her death, the mattress was turned.

⌘

On November 7, 1962, "her strong heart finally ceased to beat." Eleanor Roosevelt, who some thought would be an eternal American presence, had died. She was seventy-eight years old, but there was so much more mileage on her body than her age suggested. She was buried next to her husband at Hyde Park.

It was Adlai Stevenson who asked, on behalf of tens of millions of men and women the world over, "What other single human being has touched and transformed the existence of so many?" But it was a statement, not really a question.

TWO LEGACIES

PERHAPS THE MOST MEMORABLE OF the Simon and Garfunkel songs from the iconic movie *The Graduate* is "Mrs. Robinson." Think back on it. In all likelihood, you will recall it as a scathing commentary on the older woman who seduces the movie's title character. But is it, really? If you're old enough, you can still bring to mind some of the lyrics. For instance: "God bless you please, Mrs. Robinson. Heaven holds a place for those who pray." And: "We'd like to learn to help you learn to help yourself. Look around you, all you see are sympathetic eyes." And: "Going to the candidates' debate. Laugh about it, shout about it. When you've got to choose. Every way you look at it you lose." Is there a facetiousness to these lyrics, or is it sincerity?

And: Who, precisely, is it that would like to help Mrs. Robinson learn to help herself? Are all the eyes around her sympathetic?

Hardly. And what does a candidate's debate have to do with anything? Mrs. Robinson never went to one, never mentioned one. Finally, what about the reference to losing? Is it a comment on Mrs. Robinson, or on the quality of the candidates in the debate?

The song is *not*, despite our memories to the contrary, a scathing commentary.

The mystery is solved when you learn that the original title of the song might not have been "Mrs. Robinson." It might have been "Mrs. Roosevelt," with the lyrics originally intended as a paean to Eleanor from the composer. Paul Simon admired the former First Lady, sharing her politics, her hopes for the American future, her worldview, her long life devoted to public service. He had not completed the words for the tune when, as one story goes, Mike Nichols, who directed *The Graduate*, asked for it. And quickly. So Simon rewrote a few lines. But not all of them. The result is a classic piece of popular music that doesn't make nearly as much sense lyrically as it is supposed to, that wouldn't make any sense at all had it not been for the context of the movie in which it was heard, and the mind-set of the audience by then.

If Mike Nichols had not known of the song, or had not wanted it for *The Graduate*; if Simon and Garfunkel had recorded it as Simon might have originally intended; and if "Mrs. Roosevelt" had been a hit, as is probable given the beat, the catchiness of the melody, and the popularity of the singers—if all of this had happened, Eleanor Roosevelt would have been memorialized in a way she never would have imagined, a way that no US political figure has ever been honored. The song would have leaped to *Billboard*'s top ten. It was not to be.

Yet even without Simon's song, Eleanor has been memorialized in virtually every other way imaginable. The list is too lengthy to be presented here, but a few examples will suffice.

Thirty years before *The Graduate*'s release, Eleanor had been named the "outstanding woman of 1937" in a poll conducted by an NBC newsman named Howard Claney.

Before that, she had won the American Peace Award, established in 1923 by Edward Bok, the former editor of the *Ladies' Home Journal* and a powerful figure in publishing. His goal was to "provide a practicable means whereby the United States can take its place and do its share toward preserving world peace, while not making compulsory the participation of the U.S. in European wars if any such are, in the future, found unpreventable."

More than twenty years later, with Eleanor still alive and vital, the New York League of Business and Professional Women concluded that Eleanor should be the governor of New York, and began working toward that end. A newspaper editorialized that, instead of Franklin's running for a third term as president, which no man had ever done before, his wife should run for a first as governor. It was an opinion shared by several journalists, and more than a few Democrats. It was not an opinion shared by Eleanor, nor did she have the slightest desire to govern the state of New York.

On her fifty-fourth birthday, Eleanor was honored by the Women's National Press Club in Washington. Its annual party and awards dinner was dedicated to "Good Queen Eleanor."

The Eleanor Roosevelt monument, in New York's Riverside Park, dedicated in 1996, is believed to be the first public monument ever erected for a president's wife.

In 1999, more than three and a half decades after her death, she finished ninth in the Gallup Poll's list of Most Widely Admired People of the Twentieth Century, a century her father never saw. She was the highest-ranking woman in the poll.

Early in the present century, the *Christian Science Monitor*, in a survey conducted by the Siena Research Institute, asked "more than 300 scholars in the fields of history, American studies, and women's studies" to name the most influential American woman of the twentieth century. The winner was Eleanor Roosevelt, by this time referred to by many as the "First Lady of the World."

And to the nation's leading college newspaper, the *Harvard Crimson*, she was "The world's most respected woman." No matter that she was long deceased; Eleanor's ideas lived on, all of them threaded together by a sense of justice, demands for fairness, and respect for the dignity and worth of people of all nations and faiths.

⊰◈⊱

THE TRIBUTES WERE ONE THING. The never-ending influence of her father, even though his life had ended so long ago and so miserably, was quite another. He remained a vital presence in his daughter's life as long as she was able to take a breath. "Everything I did with my father," Eleanor wrote, well into her years, "remains in my memory today, a vivid moment not to be forgotten." Joseph Lash knew she spoke the truth. "People who lived on in the memories of those alive, [Eleanor] said, were not dead. She read and reread her father's letters, and each time it was a fresh invocation of the magic of his presence."

Earlier in her life, she had acknowledged that magic by publishing a collection of Elliott's letters. She gave him further literary recognition in her memoir, *This Is My Story*. It is dedicated

To
the memory of my father
who fired a child's imagination,
and to the few other people
who have meant the same inspiration
throughout my life

But there were no other people who meant the same inspiration. She was merely being polite to friends who had, to a far lesser degree than her beloved parent, given her friendship, encouragement, and love.

⬥

In 1927, FOR A REASON now unclear, Eleanor wrote the following in a notebook—for her eyes, and her emotional reasons, only.

> I knew a child once who adored her father. She was an ugly little thing, keenly conscious of her deficiencies, and her father, the only person who really cared for her, was away much of the time; but he never criticized her or blamed her, instead he wrote her letters and stories, telling her how he dreamed of her growing up and what they would do together in the future, but she must be truthful, loyal, brave, well-educated, or the woman he dreamed of would not be there when the wonderful day came for them to fare forth together. The child was full of fears and because of them lying was easy; she had no intellectual stimulus at that time *and yet she made herself as the years went on into a fairly good copy of the picture he had painted.*

Eleanor would far exceed her father's picture. As much as he adored his daughter and believed in her, Elliott would never have thought to create so grand a tableau as the one she actually made of her life, would never have imagined achievements so magnificent, so far-ranging. To study these achievements is to find oneself agape before an enormous work of art, a mural that portrays half a century of American and world history. As for the dreams that Elliott wanted so desperately to convert into reality for Eleanor, dreams that were dismissed at the time as wild fantasies, they are laughably modest by comparison to the life she produced with her own palette in reality.

Somehow, Eleanor's father, a man who was the shame of his family, the only worthless Roosevelt, managed to battle his way through the constant miasma of his drunkenness to erupt in sobriety, or a facsimile thereof, in one area of his life, and one only. He loved his Little Nell because she was his miracle from heaven. That he could summon the desire, the strength, the perseverance, to give voice to that love, to display it on so many occasions and to feel it always, to insist on it so adamantly that his daughter could not help but grow up to be certain of her worth, is a miracle of his own making.

To quote Arthur Miller's newly widowed Linda Loman: "Attention, attention must finally be paid to such a person."

And so this book insists.

EPILOGUE

THE GOODNIGHT KISS

The date: December 10, 1948.
The place: Paris.
The time: 3:15 A.M.
The occasion: A meeting of the United Nations General Assembly.

E LEANOR ROOSEVELT SPEAKS ON, WITH the Universal Declaration of
the United Nations having been passed:
"... We stand today at the threshold of a great event both in
the life of the United Nations and in the life of mankind. This Universal Declaration of Human Rights may well become the international Magna Carta of all men everywhere. We hope its proclamation

by the General Assembly will be an event comparable to the proclamation of the Declaration of the Rights of Man by the French people in 1789, the adoption of the Bill of Rights by the people of the United States, and the adoption of comparable declarations in other countries."

Of course, it did not happen that way. In 1988, on the fortieth anniversary of the passage of the Universal Declaration of Human Rights, Richard Gardner wrote in the *New York Times* that the document "stands to this day as the most widely recognized statement of the rights to which every person on our planet is entitled." But a widely recognized statement is not the same thing as a mandate for widely recognized actions. The Universal Declaration has not been universally recognized; what are rights in one nation can still be proscribed behavior in another.

And, one suspects, Eleanor knew this was the declaration's failing from the start. "She knew its words were not self-enforcing," Gardner said. "The real challenge, she liked to tell United Nations delegates in later years, was one of 'actually living and working in our countries for freedom and justice for each human being.' That is a challenge she readily accepted, and her example is one that inspires us today."

But, on that night in Paris, three years after the end of World War II, Eleanor would be as optimistic as she could. After all, she had worked so long and hard for the cause.

"In conclusion," she said, "I feel that I cannot do better than to repeat the call to action by Secretary [of State George] Marshall in his opening statement to this assembly. Let this third regular session of the General Assembly approve by an overwhelming majority the Declaration of Human Rights as a standard of conduct for all; and let us, as Members of the United Nations, conscious of our own shortcomings and imperfections, join our effort in good faith to live up to this high standard."

A FEW MINUTES LATER, ELEANOR started back to her hotel room within walking distance of the Arc de Triomphe, exhausted by her efforts, hoping to get a few hours sleep before her flight back to the United States. Whether she actually walked or allowed herself the luxury of a government vehicle is not known.

Back in America, she would make more speeches on behalf of the declaration, a new round of pleas for human beings to behave more sensibly, and peacefully, toward one another. So many speeches had she made already. So intransigent did human nature remain.

But before she went to bed in the blackness of that Paris morning, she opened a container of some sort: an overnight bag or carryall, perhaps a sack of some sort. In it were letters, dozens of letters, perhaps more than a hundred, their tone "tender, chivalrous, playful, and, above all, full of protestations of love." They had been sent to her by her father during his exile from the family in Abingdon, Virginia, between 1892 and 1894. From the day he died, when his daughter was but ten, until the day her own life ended, sixty-eight years later, Eleanor carried them with her everywhere she went. Near to her heart at all times, they were also near to her person.

She withdrew some of the messages from the container at that strange hour in Paris, after so much talk of human rights, and placed them next to her on the nightstand. If she had the energy, she would have picked one out of the stack at random and read it. Yet again. She had reread all of her father's letters, read them and handled them so many times that by now they were worn and torn, fragile and faded. A few were scraps around the edges, with holes beginning to form in the text and the addresses faded beyond recognition on many of the envelopes. She was proud of their appearance. It was proof that her father's sentiments had been of constant use to her. Proof of her daily reliance on them. Proof of a lifetime's love and support.

If she was too tired to have read a missive on this occasion, she would have smiled down on it and put it in the stack. Then she either returned the correspondence to its container or left it on the night-stand, to be replaced in the morning. Regardless, as she drifted into sleep, it was next to her bed, where it would be safe. And comforting.

She is said to have kissed her father's letters, the top one on the stack, every night of her life.

ACKNOWLEDGMENTS

MORE THAN ANYONE ELSE, CAROLYN Zygmont of the Westport Public Library in Westport, Connecticut, is the recipient of my gratitude for the preceding pages. She stepped in after my researcher of more than a decade retired, and did so effortlessly, dealing with my requests for information in such a manner that I could write *Someone to Watch Over Me* with relative ease (a book is never *easy* to write) and relative speed (a book is never *speedily* written). In fact, Carolyn and I have already done much of the research for my next volume, and she seems none the worse for the wear I continue to exert on her.

Perhaps more than any other volume I've written, and this is the twelfth, *Someone to Watch Over Me* has depended on letters, those to and from Eleanor Roosevelt and her father. They were produced over a brief period, only two years, with Eleanor having turned a mere ten years of age when the exchange of correspondence ended. Yet there was an uncommon number of these missives, and even the ones from which I did not quote were the key to explaining the extraordinary relationship between Elliott and his daughter. No letters, no book; it is that simple. For finding this material, I express my gratitude to the archivists at the FDR Presidential Library and Museum in Hyde Park, New York, three of them in particular: Sarah Malcolm, Kirsten Carter, and Bill Baehr.

On my visits to the Library and Museum, I was accompanied by Lorraine Battipaglia, an educator with a fine sense of precisely what kinds of material would best suit my purposes. I appreciate her efforts. And much more about her.

When Elliott and Eleanor were writing to each other, her father lived in Abingdon, Virginia, and Carol Taylor provided me with information about both the time during which Elliott was a resident and the place that it was in those days.

Marlo Sexton, at the Theodore Roosevelt Center at Dickinson State University in Dickinson, North Dakota, also informed me well; I could not have progressed satisfactorily without her suggestions.

Two biographers of Eleanor were mentioned prominently in the text, but must be mentioned again. Although I wrote a very different book from theirs, one with a much narrower focus, one that remained as much as possible in the center of the mural, I could not have written the preceding without the virtually lifelong studies of Joseph Lash and Blanche Wiesen Cook. I am a very appreciative reader of their volumes. Indispensable volumes to me.

And I am a very appreciative colleague of the people who make Pegasus Books such a creative and thoughtful publisher. At the head of the list is Jessica Case, whose edits, as always, made a book of mine better. No less am I grateful to Iris Blasi and Claiborne

Hancock. This is my third book for Pegasus, my third invigorating experience.

My new agent is Linda Konner, and she and I are off to a grand start in a relationship that I hope will continue to grow. I am a dedicated suburbanite, unable to tolerate the din and crowds of Manhattan except in short, widely-spaced doses. She is a dedicated New Yorker, a woman committed to its precincts and lifestyle. Yet, my dealings with her are consistently courteous, thoughtful, productive, and encouraging. We get along superbly. Go figure.

On the other hand, there was the woman with whom I communicated at Paul Simon's foundation, called Peregrine Inc. I found the "Mrs. Robinson"/Mrs. Roosevelt story a charming one, if not crucial to the book's main theme. It had been cited in several sources, and certainly seemed to make sense; nonetheless, I phoned the foundation to see whether I could verify the tale without doubt. No sooner did I mention my interest in the song's lyrics than the woman said, "Sorry, there's nothing I can tell you," and hung up, as if I had been asking for information on a sex scandal. Common courtesy is as uncommon as common sense.

As the years go by, the number of people to whom I am related grows smaller and smaller; hardly do I have an extended family anymore. It is actually rather a chilling thought. Most important to me among those who remain are my son, Toby, whom I seldom see and love mightily; my daughter, Cailin, whom I do see and does her best to make certain I am stylishly attired; and her husband, Martin, against whom I hope to play tennis more competitively in the summer of 2017. Just knowing they are there, wherever "there" is, makes life richer for me.

Eric Burns
Westport, CT
September 1, 2016

BIBLIOGRAPHY

❖

PRIVATE PAPERS, DOCUMENTS, AND RESOURCES

The Eleanor Roosevelt Papers Project, George Washington University, Washington, DC. (GWU)

The FDR Museum and Presidential Library, Hyde Park, New York (FDR)

In Loving Memory of Anna Hall Roosevelt. Three authors, writing anonymously. New York: privately printed, 1893.

The Joseph Lash Papers at the FDR Museum and Presidential Library, Hyde Park, New York (FDR-L)

The Theodore Roosevelt Center at Dickinson State University, Dickinson, North Dakota (TRC)

NEWSPAPERS AND JOURNALS

Children: The Magazine for Parents (CMP)

Christian Science Monitor (CSM)

Datebook (DB)
The Freeholder (TF)
Harvard Crimson (HC)
The Hudson Valley Regional Review (HVRR)
Look magazine *(Look)*
New York Herald Tribune (NYHT)
New York Herald (NYH)
New York Times (NYT)
New York World (NYW)
Poughkeepsie Eagle News (PEN)
Richmond Times-Dispatch (RT-D)
Women's Democratic News, New York State *(WDN)*

BOOKS

Beasley, Maurine H., Holly C. Shulman, Henry R. Beasley, eds. *The Eleanor Roosevelt Encyclopedia.* Westport, CT: Greenwood, 2001.

Birmingham, Stephen. *America's Secret Aristocracy.* Boston: Little, Brown, 1987.

Bradley, Harold Whitman. *The United States from 1865.* New York: Scribner, 1973.

Brands, H. W. *T.R.: The Last Romantic.* New York: Basic Books, 1997.

Burns, James MacGregor, and Susan Dunn. *The Three Roosevelts: Patrician Leaders Who Transformed America.* New York: Atlantic Monthly Press, 2001.

Churchill, Allen. *The Roosevelts: American Aristocrats.* New York: Harper & Row, 1965.

Collier, Peter, with David Horowitz. *The Roosevelts: An American Saga.* New York: Simon & Schuster, 1994.

Cook, Blanche Wiesen. *Eleanor Roosevelt, Volume One: 1884–1933.* New York: Viking, 1992.

———. *Eleanor Roosevelt, Volume Two: 1933–1938.* New York: Viking, 1999.

Dalton, Kathleen. *Theodore Roosevelt: A Strenuous Life.* New York: Knopf, 2002.

Dickens, Charles. *Hard Times.* Norwalk, CT: Easton, 1966.

———. *The Old Curiosity Shop.* Norwalk, CT: Easton, 1968.

Goodwin, Doris Kearns. *The Bully Pulpit: Theodore Roosevelt, William Howard Taft, and the Golden Age of Journalism.* New York: Simon & Schuster, 2013.

———. *No Ordinary Time: Franklin and Eleanor Roosevelt: The Home Front in World War II.* New York: Simon & Schuster, 1994.

Kaplan, Fred. *The Singular Mark Twain: A Biography.* New York: Doubleday, 2003.

Kaplan, James. *Sinatra: The Chairman*. New York: Doubleday, 2015.

Kaplan, Justin. *Mr. Clemens and Mark Twain: A Biography*. New York: Simon & Schuster, 1996.

Lash, Joseph. *Eleanor and Franklin: The Story of Their Relationship, Based on Eleanor Roosevelt's Private Papers*. New York: Norton, 1971.

———. *Eleanor: The Years Alone*. New York: Norton, 1972.

Lee, Harper. *Go Set a Watchman*. New York: Harper, 2015.

McCullough, David. *Mornings on Horseback: The Story of an Extraordinary Family, a Vanished Way of Life, and the Unique Child Who Became Theodore Roosevelt*. New York: Simon & Schuster, 1981.

Miller, Nathan. *Theodore Roosevelt: A Life*. New York: Morrow, 1992.

Morris, Edmund. *The Rise of Theodore Roosevelt*. New York: Coward, McCann & Geoghegan, 1979.

Niven, Penelope. *Thornton Wilder: A Life*. New York: Harper, 2012.

Pottker, Jan. *Sara and Eleanor: The Story of Sara Delano Roosevelt and Her Daughter-in-Law, Eleanor Roosevelt*. New York: St. Martin's, 2004.

Roosevelt, Eleanor. *The Autobiography of Eleanor Roosevelt*. New York: Harper, 1961.

———. *Empty Without You: The Intimate Letters of Eleanor Roosevelt and Lorena Hickok*. Edited by Rodger Streitmatter. New York: Free Press, 1998.

———. *My Day: Her Acclaimed Columns, 1936–1945, Volume I*. New York: Pharos, 1989.

———. *My Day: Her Acclaimed Columns, 1945–1952, Volume II: The Post-War Years*. New York: Pharos, 1990.

———. *My Day: Her Acclaimed Columns, 1953–1962, Volume III: First Lady of the World*. New York: Pharos, 1991.

———. *On My Own*. New York: Hutchinson, 1959.

———. *This Is My Story*. New York: Harper & Brothers, 1937.

———. *This I Remember*. New York: Harper, 1949.

———. *You Learn By Living: Eleven Keys for a More Fulfilling Life*. New York: Harper, 1960.

Roosevelt, Elliott. *Hunting Big Game in the Eighties: The Letters of Elliott Roosevelt, Sportsman*. Edited by Eleanor Roosevelt. New York: Scribner, 1933.

Roosevelt, Elliott, and James Brough. *Mother R: Eleanor Roosevelt's Untold Story*. New York: Putnam, 1977.

Roosevelt, Theodore. *Hunting Trips of a Ranchman & The Wilderness Hunter*. New York: Modern Library, 1996.

Rowley, Hazel. *Franklin and Eleanor: An Extraordinary Marriage*. New York: Farrar, Straus and Giroux, 2010.

Smith, Jean Edward. *FDR*. New York: Random House, 2007.

Twain, Mark. *The Gilded Age and Later Novels*. New York: Library of America, 2002.

Ward, Geoffrey C. *Before the Trumpet: Young Franklin Roosevelt, 1882–1905*. New York: Harper & Row, 1985.

———. *A First-Class Temperament: The Emergence of Franklin Roosevelt*. New York: Harper & Row, 1989.

Ward, Geoffrey C., and Ken Burns. *The Roosevelts: An Intimate History*. New York: Alfred A. Knopf, 2014.

Wharton, Edith. *The Age of Innocence*. Norwalk, CT: Easton, 1973.

White, William L. *Slaying the Dragon: The History of Addiction Treatment and Recovery in America*. Bloomington, IL: Chestnut Health Systems/Lighthouse Institute, 1998.

NOTES

PROLOGUE: HUMAN RIGHTS

xxi: "something happened," Richard Gardner, *NYT*, "Eleanor Roosevelt's
        Legacy," *NYT*, December 10, 1988, p. 27.

xxii: "Mr. President, fellow delegates," and following excerpts from address,
        Eleanor Roosevelt, "On the Adoption of the Universal Declaration of Human
        Rights," www.americanrhetoric.com/speeches/eleanorrooseveltdeclara
        tionhumanrights.htm.

xxiii: "The Russians seem to have met," quoted in "Eleanor Roosevelt's Legacy,"
        NYT.

xxiii: "Determined to press," ibid., p. 27.

PART ONE
ELLIOTT

3:      "charming, good-looking," quoted in Cook, *Volume One*, p. 23.

3:      "Oh! My darling," quoted in Lash, *Eleanor and Franklin*, p. 3.

4: "Dear old Govenor," quoted in ibid., p. 6.

4: "little Motherling," quoted in Cook, *Volume One*, p. 45.

4: "his sweet little China Dresden," quoted in ibid., p. 4.

4: "Elliott had a special claim," Lash, *Alone*, p. 173.

4: "[s]he had been his anchor," ibid., p. 45.

4: "Ellie boy," quoted in Eleanor Roosevelt, *Story*, p. 71.

4: "decidedly pretty," quoted in ibid., p. 32.

5: "dashing, outgoing," "Questions and Answers About Eleanor Roosevelt. Question: Who Were Her Parents?" GWU.

5: "As a youth," ibid., p. 4.

5: "blessedly robust," Churchill, *The Roosevelts*, p. 125.

5: "protective of his elder brother," Cook, *Volume One*, p. 4.

6: "By showing Elliott up," Dalton, *Theodore Roosevelt*, p. 55.

6: "aggressive egotism," quoted in Cook, *Volume One*, p. 32.

6: "Oh, Father," quoted in Lash, *Eleanor and Franklin*, p. 7.

7: "Has not our dear Thee," quoted in McCullough, *Horseback*, p. 238.

7: "build their dream house," quoted in ibid., p. 241.

7: "It delights me," quoted in ibid., p. 241.

7: "He had always envied the ease," Collier and Horowitz, *The Roosevelts*, pp. 68–69.

7: "to that keenest of sportsmen," Theodore Roosevelt, *Hunting Trips*, dedication page.

7: "the long competition still smoldered," ibid., p. 69.

8: "was not self-righteous," Mason White, "Elliott, the Tragic Roosevelt," *HVRR* 5, no. 1 (March 1988), p. 18.

8: "the Roosevelt he liked best," McCullough, *Horseback*, p. 237.

8: "He was one," quoted in ibid.

8: "How different people are," quoted in ibid., p. 243–44.

9: "a remarkable combination," "Elliott, the Tragic Roosevelt," *HVRR*, p. 18.

9: "one of the most popular," ibid.

9: "one of society's great gallants," Lash, *Eleanor and Franklin*, p. 23.

10: "one signed," quoted in "Questions and Answers," GWU.

10: "took me to help serve," Eleanor Roosevelt, *Autobiography*, p. 12.

10: "was also a trustee," ibid.

11: "innumerable little children in casts," Eleanor Roosevelt, *My Story*, p. 28.

11: "a steel brace," ibid.

12: "a small and ragged urchin," quoted in Cook, *Volume One*, p. 32.

12:     "He was the one," quoted in Lash, *Eleanor and Franklin*, p. 3.

13:     "Greatheart," Cook, *Volume One*, p. 46.

13:     "He was so mad with pain," quoted in Morris, *Rise of Theodore Roosevelt*, p. 94.

13:     "Oh my God my Father," quoted in ibid., p. 94.

13:     "devotion to his father," McCullough, *Horseback*, p. 183.

13:     "He was extolled," McCullough, *Horseback*, p. 185.

13:     "seemed demolished by the loss," Lash, *Eleanor and Franklin*, p. 19.

14:     "I had never caused," quoted in Morris, *Rise of Theodore Roosevelt*, p. 94.

14:     "From the beginning," Cook, *Volume One*, p. 40.

15:     "might teach our 'lovers of men,'" quoted in ibid., p. 12.

15:     "Arriving in Bombay," McCullough, *Horseback*, p. 239.

15:     "a grand prince," quoted in Lash, *Eleanor and Franklin*, p. 12.

15:     "I would not trust myself," quoted in McCullough, *Horseback*, p. 239.

15:     "all too Arabian night–like," quoted in Cook, *Volume One*, p. 41.

16:     "By George," quoted in McCullough, *Horseback*, p. 240.

16:     "all of them," Cook, *Volume One*, p. 41.

17:     "In fact, he rather swooned," ibid.

17:     "through long lines," quoted in Lash, *Eleanor and Franklin*, p. 12.

17:     "for if ever there was a man," quoted in ibid.

18:     "What a fellow that is." quoted in McCullough, *Horseback*, p. 242.

18:     "In his travels," White, *Slaying the Dragon*, p. 20.

ANNA

22:     "In the economic renaissance," Bradley, *The United States*, pp. 23–24.

23:     "the New York of the eighteen eighties," Lash, *Eleanor and Franklin*, p. 17.

24:     "a serious satirical book," Fred Kaplan, *The Singular Mark Twain*, p. 299.

24:     "*The Gilded Age* echoes," Justin Kaplan, *Mr. Clemens and Mark Twain*, pp. 161–62.

25:     "What is the secret," Stead, W. T. *The Americanization of the World*. London: Horace Markley, 1901. For citation, quote Stead, p. 381.

25:     "In that society," Eleanor Roosevelt, *Autobiography*, p. 4.

26:     "that New York Society," ibid.

26:     "one of the most beautiful," ibid., p. 3.

26:     "acclaimed as one," Lash, *Eleanor and Franklin*, p. 17.

26:     "stunning, regal," McCullough, *Horseback*, p. 248.

26:     "polo and tennis matches," "Elliott, the Tragic Roosevelt," *HVRR*, p. 22.

26:     "set the fashion in dress," Lash, *Eleanor and Franklin*, p. 21.

26:     "The proud set of the head," quoted in Lash, *Eleanor and Franklin*, p. 21.

27:     "that she lacked the stamina," "Elliott, the Tragic Roosevelt," *HVRR*, p. 22.

27:     "sit and gaze," McCullough, *Horseback*, p. 249.

28:     "Why, with beauty," www.poemhunter.com/poem/a-pretty-woman.

29:     "slightly but attractively mad," Lash, *Eleanor and Franklin*, p. 14.

29:     "so many friends," quoted in McCullough, *Horseback*, p. 248.

29:     "My life has been a gamble," quoted in ibid.

30:     "same colorless thing," quoted in "Elliott, the Tragic Roosevelt," *HVRR*, p. 26.

30:     "little fat figure," ibid.

30:     "Poor Sophie," quoted in McCullough, *Horseback*, p. 248.

30:     "Hudson River gentry," ibid.

30:     "in a household that demanded," quoted in "Questions and Answers," GWU.

30:     "out of a gothic novel," Miller, *Theodore Roosevelt*, p. 131.

30:     "religious fanaticism," ibid.

30:     "In the country," Eleanor Roosevelt, *Autobiography*, pp. 3–4.

COURTSHIP

34:     "completely helpless when faced," Lash, *Eleanor and Franklin*, p. 4.

34:     "efforts at control," Cook, *Volume One*, p. 25.

34:     "tall, slender, fair-haired," quoted in "Elliott, the Tragic Roosevelt," *HVRR*, p. 20.

35:     "the dashing, well-traveled," Lash, *Eleanor and Franklin*, p. 3.

35:     "only comfort," quoted in Cook, *Volume One*, p. 42.

35:     and, "our interests, our lives" quoted in ibid., p. 43

35:     "Elliott's reverence," quoted in ibid.

35:     "a Sweet Hearted," quoted in ibid.

36:     "taught that success," "Elliott, the Tragic Roosevelt," *HVRR*, p. 20.

36:     "The two young people," ibid.

37:     "He sent flowers," McCullough, *Horseback*, p. 249.

37:    "There were morning walks," "Elliott, the Tragic Roosevelt," *HVRR*, p. 21.

37:    "were seen at parties," McCullough, *Horseback*, p. 249.

37:    "all about one another," David McCullough, *HVRR*, p. 20.

37:    "The summer of '83," ibid.

38:    "I don't know whether," quoted in Daniel E. Spinzia, "Elliott Roosevelt, Sr.—A Spiral into Darkness: the Influences," *TF*, Fall 2007, p. 5.

38:    "gloomy," ibid., p. 20.

38:    "feared his sudden explosions," Cook, *Volume One*, p. 43.

39:    "All my love and ambition," Roosevelt, ed., *Hunting Big Game*, p. 149.

39:    "Please never keep anything from me," quoted in Cook, *Volume One*, p. 44.

39:    "I know I am blue," quoted in ibid., p. 19.

39:    "Darling Baby," FDR Library, box 68.

40:    "Womanly, in all purity," quoted in Cook, *Volume One*, p. 43.

41:    "My dear Miss Hall," FDR Library, box 68.

41:    "My dear Anna," ibid.

41:    "Dearest Anna," ibid.

MARRIAGE

43:    "one of the most brilliant social events," quoted in Lash Papers, p. 20.

43:    "One of the most brilliant weddings," *NYT*, December 2, 1883, p. 3.

44:    "were in the Catherine de Medici style," ibid.

44:    "pledged a life together," "Elliott, the Tragic Roosevelt," *HVRR*, p. 21.

44:    "Dear Lady," quoted in Lash, *Eleanor and Franklin*, p. 20.

44:    "to enter their union," "Elliott, the Tragic Roosevelt," *HVRR*, p. 21.

45:    "Their income, although comfortable," ibid., p. 22.

45:    "In the spring of 1887," ibid.

46:    "My dear Elliott," FDR Library, box 5.

47:    "Elliott partied frantically," Cook, *Volume 1*, p. 47.

47:    "Poor old Nell," quoted in ibid.

47:    "precious boy," quoted in Lash, *Eleanor and Franklin*, p. 24.

48:    "a miracle from heaven," quoted in ibid.

48:    "a more wrinkled," quoted in ibid.

48:    "I am told," quoted in Elliott Roosevelt, *Hunting Big Game*, pp. 37–38.

48:    "She is such a funny child," Burns and Dunn, *The Three Roosevelts*, p. 86.

49:    "wanted to sink through the floor," Lash, *Eleanor and Franklin*, p. 33.

49:    "with a look of kind indifference," ibid.

49:    "Always correct and generally aloof," ibid., p. 46.

50:    "for I was a solemn child," Eleanor Roosevelt, *Autobiography*, p. 5.

50:    "I loved candy and sugar," Roosevelt, *My Story*, p. 14.

51:    "I was always disgracing my mother," quoted in Lash, *Eleanor and Franklin*, p. 42

51:    "Her forty-fifth birthday," ibid., p. 43.

51:    "The first were my mother," FDR Library, box 1.

52:    "I doubt that the background," quoted in Cook, *Volume One*, p. 23.

53:    "she organized countless charity balls, ibid., p. 47.

53:    "I know now," quoted in Smith, *FDR*, p. 43.

54:    "cold virtue, severity," Lash, *Eleanor and Franklin*, p. 28.

54:    "'More care!' said the old man," Dickens, *Curiosity Shop*, p. 14.

PART TWO
NELL'S HOMELINESS

58:    "The proud set of the head," quoted in Lash, *Eleanor and Franklin*, p. 21.

58:    "Her mouth and teeth," quoted in Pottker, *Sara and Eleanor*, p. 71.

59:    "the ugly duckling," quoted in ibid.

59:    "gawky daughter," Elliott Roosevelt and Brough, *Mother R*, p. 95.

59:    "at the time," Pottker, *Sara and Eleanor*, p. 71.

59:    "Mother grew up," Elliott Roosevelt and Brough, *Mother R*, p. 95.

59:    "an ugly little thing," quoted in Collier and Horowitz, *The Roosevelts*, p. 81.

60:    "I was a poor dancer," Roosevelt, *My Story*, p. 51.

61:    "A gentle and overprotected boy," Collier and Horowitz, *The Roosevelts*, p. 81.

61:    "I am plain," quoted in Elliott Roosevelt and Brough, *Mother R*, p. 95.

61:    "and from the time," Birmingham, *America's Secret Aristocracy*, p. 126.

61:    "as a child senses those things," quoted in Goodwin, *Bully Pulpit*, p. 92.

62:    "those who mock the person," Cook, *Volume One*, pp. 2–3.

62:    "I knew I was the first girl," Roosevelt, *My Story*, p. 101.

62:    "took everything—most of all herself—," quoted in Smith, *FDR*, p. 44.

62:     "most attractive," Lash, *Eleanor and Franklin*, p. 95.

62:     "very much sought after," ibid.

63:     "usually had a tongue," Pottker, *Sara and Elizabeth*, p. 73.

63:     "Alice was strong and supple," Collier and Horowitz, *The Roosevelts*, p. 86.

64:     "little golden hair," quoted in Lash, *Eleanor and Franklin*, p. 28.

64:     "over her little girl's," ibid.

NELL'S SHYNESS

68:     "had her coupe in town," "Elliott, the Tragic Roosevelt," *HVRR*, p. 21.

68:     "a golden secure world," Lash, *Eleanor and Franklin*, p. 25.

69:     "My earliest recollections, Smith, *FDR*, p. 6.

69:     "was always devoted to me," Elliott Roosevelt and Brough, *Mother R*, pp. 36–37.

70:     "I feel sure," ibid., p. 9.

70:     "I rather imagine," ibid.

70:     "Eleanor dreaded her debut," Pottker, *Sara and Elizabeth*, p. 95.

70:     "Her memory was colored," ibid., p. 95.

70:     "I hasten to tell you," quoted in ibid., p. 95.

71:     "Eleanor Roosevelt never used," Cook, *Volume One*, p. 168.

71:     "she never missed an opportunity," Cook, *Volume One*, p. 9.

71:     "In 1922, she joined," www.npr.gov/nr/travel/presidents/eleanor_roosevelt_valkill/html

71:     "She never thought of herself," Cook, *Volume One*, p. 1.

72:     "Eleanor's capacity to lose herself," Cook, *Volume One*, p. 99.

72:     "read the Chanson de Roland," ibid.

73:     "I have to this day," *CMP*, no page.

73:     "No one tried to censor," Eleanor Roosevelt, *Autobiography*, p. 16.

74:     "Some people consider ambition," FDR-L, box 12

74:     "Of course it is easier," ibid.

74:     "To be the thing we seem," ibid.

75:     "It is very hard to do," quoted in Cook, *Volume One*, p. 98.

75:     "remembered her first days in school," Lash, p. 42

76:     "I was perfectly happy," quoted in Goodwin, *Bully Pulpit*, p. 92.

76:     "He was the one great love," quoted in Roosevelt, *Africa*, p. viii.

76:     "Father's own little Nell," quoted in Cook, *Volume One*, p. 82.

76:     "days through the Grand snow," quoted in ibid.

NELL'S FEARS

78:     "an extended tour," Cook, *Volume One*, p. 48.

78:     "helped his wife," ibid.

79:     "the accident [had] left Eleanor," ibid.

80:     "would break into tears," ibid., p. 42.

80:     "In Eleanor's later portrayals," ibid., p. 28.

81:     "was not relieved by," Cook, *Volume One*, p. 219.

81:     "I don't think you read my letters," quoted in ibid.

81:     "I hated to leave you," quoted in ibid.

82:     "'I was always afraid,'" quoted in Elliott Roosevelt and Brough, *Mother R*, p. 96.

82:     "shockingly mercurial with the daughter," Pottker, *Sara and Elizabeth*, p. 71.

82:     "I remember my father," Eleanor Roosevelt, *Autobiography*, p. 6.

83:     "I never knew you were a coward," quoted in Pottker, *Sara and Elizabeth*, p. 71.

83:     "the tone of disapproval," Eleanor Roosevelt, *Autobiography*, p. 6.

NELL'S LONELINESS

85:     "Between her parents' disappointment," Lash, *Eleanor and Franklin*, p. 24.

86:     "Eleanor's uncles," Rowley, *Franklin and Eleanor*, p. 52.

86:     "Strict and adamant," Cook, *Volume One*, pp. 93–94.

86:     "short skirts," ibid., p. 94.

86:     "a new sense of belonging," quoted in Smith, *FDR*, p. 44.

87:     "the center of attention," ibid.

87:     "benefit from a year or two," Ward, *Trumpet*, p. 49.

88:     "The three years," ibid.

88:     "The summer [of my third year]," Eleanor Roosevelt, *Autobiography*, p. 35.

89:     "one stone after another," FDR-L, box 6.

90:     "A sweet sight," quoted in Pottker, *Sara and Elizabeth*, p. 144.

90:     "She had viewed motherhood," ibid., p. 147.

90:     "I felt . . . in some way," quoted in ibid.

91:     "Although Eleanor saw no 'alienist,'" ibid.

91:     "a pregnancy at this time," ibid., p. 148.

91:     "It did not come naturally to me," Rowley, *Franklin and Eleanor*, p. 52.

92:    "ordeal to be borne," Rowley, *Franklin and Eleanor*, p. xx.

92:    "worried that her talents," Cook, *Volume Two*, p. 9

92:    "Her great friend Lorena Hickok," ibid.

92:    "My zest in life," quoted in Goodwin, *Bully Pulpit*, p. 90.

93:    "Frequently flirtatious," Cook, *Volume Two*, pp. 199–200.

NELL'S COLDNESS

96:    "She was not a saint," Cook, *Volume Two*, p. 2.

96:    "[T]hough long-suffering," ibid., pp. 2–3.

96:    "a large, distracting presence," ibid., pp. 56–57.

97:    "other incidents," ibid., p. 56.

98:    "One might argue," ibid., p. 57.

98:    "That was a sad day," ibid.

98:    "once became very annoyed," Cook, *Volume Two*, p. 16.

98:    "the White House became," Cook, *Volume Two*, p. 269.

PART THREE
FATHER, 1873–1889

107:    "mysterious problems," Churchill, *The Roosevelts*, p. 159.

107:    "Handsome Ellie," ibid.

108:    "Whatever was wrong," Cook, *Volume One*, p. 34.

108:    "experiencing fainting spells," "A Spiral into Darkness," *TF*, p. 2.

108:    "The doctors called it," Rowley, *Franklin and Eleanor*, p. 9.

108:    "He . . . began to show symptoms," Brands, *T.R.*, p. 104.

109:    "I jump involuntarily," "nearly always low," quoted in Brands, *T.R.*, p. 105.

109:    "could make more friends," quoted in Goodwin, *Bully Pulpit*, p. 42.

110:    "It came from overexcitement," quoted in Cook, *Volume One*, p. 34.

110:    "He is nervous," quoted in ibid.

110:    "I should be afraid," quoted in ibid.

110:    "haunted by nightmares," Cook, *Volume One*, p. 30.

111:    "*make* your body," quoted in McCullough, *Horseback*, p. 112.

111:    "an undiagnosed disorder," Cook, *Volume One*, p. 30.

111:    "a tumor developed," Elliott Roosevelt and Brough, *Mother R*, p. 95.

111:    "Out of the family orbit," Miller, *Theodore Roosevelt*, p. 63.

112:    "studied hard and worked late," quoted in Cook, *Volume One*, pp. 34–35.

112:    *"Private.* During my Latin lesson," FDR-L, box unknown.

114:    "Dear Father," FDR-L, box unknown.

115:    "had a good deal of experience," quoted in Cook, *Volume One*, p. 35.

115:    "as if I was ill," quoted in ibid.

115:    "to rest and restock," McCullough, *Horseback*, p. 39.

115:    "We have come back here," quoted in ibid., p. 40.

116:    "was drinking heavily," Morris, *Rise of Theodore Roosevelt*, p. 430.

116:    "There had been a complete," ibid., p. 430.

117:    "Anna wrote that [he]," "Elliott, the Tragic Roosevelt," *HVRR*, p. 23.

118:    "The birth of his first son," Cook, *Volume One*, pp. 53–54.

119:    "Anna still loved her husband," Rowley, *Franklin and Eleanor*, p. 10.

119:    "Anna's own father," Pottker, *Sara and Elizabeth*, p. 69.

120:    "His leg was broken," Roosevelt, *My Story*, p. 8.

120:    "completely broke his nerves," quoted in Cook, *Volume One*, p. 52.

121:    "Unable to find any real comfort," ibid., p. 38.

121:    "Sometimes I woke up," Roosevelt, *My Story*, pp. 15–16.

121:    "was well acquainted with," Rowley, *Franklin and Eleanor*, p. 21.

122:    "'Finally,' Eleanor's eldest grandson," quoted in Pottker, *Sara and Elizabeth*, p. 71.

122:    "began to drink," Eleanor Roosevelt, *Autobiography*, p. 6.

122:    "Like most children," Cook, *Volume One*, p. 39.

122:    "When he was not drinking," Goodwin, *Bully Pulpit*, p. 92.

123:    "It is a perfect nightmare," quoted in "A Spiral into Darkness," *TF*, p. 5.

123:    "It is all horrible," quoted in Ward, *Trumpet*, p. 45.

123:    "preferred her warm and affection father," ibid.

124:    "dominated my life," Roosevelt, *My Story*.

DAUGHTER, 1917–28

125:    "The opportunity to move," Smith, *FDR*, p. 147.

126:    "Uncle Ted," Eleanor Roosevelt, *My Story*, p. 123.

126:    "politics still meant little to me," ibid.

126:    "I have no recollection," ibid.

126:    "One afternoon at tea," ibid., p. 137.

126:    "When Eleanor and her children finally moved to Washington," quoted in Smith, *FDR*, p. 147.

127:    "I did very little war work," Roosevelt, *My Story*, p. 250.

128:    "Everyone in the canteen," ibid., p. 254.

129:    "I went to the Red Cross," ibid., p. 258.

129:    "I cannot do this," quoted in Smith, *FDR*, p. 173.

129:    "took flowers, cigarettes," Roosevelt, *My Story*, p. 256.

129:    "The sun in the window," ibid., p. 257.

130:    "I want to thank you," quoted in Lash, *Eleanor and Franklin*, pp. 218–19.

131:    "Out of these contacts," Roosevelt, *My Story*, p. 260.

132:    "If I had to go out," Eleanor Roosevelt, *Autobiography*, p. 85.

132:    "I can't say I am set up," ibid.

132:    "In New York," Roosevelt, *My Story*, p. 346.

134:    "And so, for months," Cook, *Volume One*, p. 311.

135:    "'Mrs. Roosevelt's activity,'" *NYHT*.

136:    "[N]ational health insurance," Lash, *Eleanor and Franklin*, p. 290.

137:    "I believe that the best interests," quoted in *PEN*, July 16, 1920.

137:    "well, they are more conservative," ibid.

138:    "She wrote the editorials," Lash, *Eleanor and Franklin*, p. 309.

138:    "Our Foreign Policy," quoted in Cook, *Volume One*, p. 364.

138:    "we do nothing constructive," quoted in ibid., p. 365.

138:    "we do not wish to be entangled," quoted in ibid., p. 364.

138:    "The Republican Administration," *WDN*, July 1928, p. 2.

140:    "If I wanted to be selfish," quoted in Lash, *Eleanor and Franklin*, p. 355.

FATHER, 1890-92

141:    "saw this as banishment," Lash, *Eleanor and Franklin*, p. 36.

142:    "I was not yet six years old," Eleanor Roosevelt, *Autobiography*, p. 6.

142:    "[S]he was the center," ibid., p. 7.

142:    "She took me away in disgrace," ibid.

143:    "I am sorry to say," ibid.

144:    "seriously wrong," Lash, *Eleanor and Franklin*, p. 38.

145:    "ELLIOTT ROOSEVELT DEMENTED," *NYH*, August 18, 1891.

146:    "ELLIOTT ROOSEVELT 'INSANE,'" *NYT*, August 18, 1891.

146:    "Try to remember," quoted in Cook, *Volume One*, p. 47.

147:    "You publish in your edition," *NYH*, August 18, 1891.

148:    "abominable," Lash, *Eleanor and Franklin*, p. 38.

148:    "madman," ibid.

148:    "[s]poiling for a fight," Cook, *Volume One*, p. 72.

148:   "after a week," ibid.

149:   "In certain respects," Brands, *T.R.*, p. 249.

149:   "Thank Heaven I came over," quoted in Cook, *Volume One*, p. 73.

149:   "surrendered completely," quoted in ibid.

151:   "This morning," quoted in ibid., p. 38.

151:   "was more famous," White, *Slaying the Dragon*, p. 50.

152:   "wicked and foolish," quoted in Lash, *Eleanor and Franklin*, p. 39.

152:   "*in my family*," quoted in ibid.

152:   "see me as I *am*," quoted in ibid.

152:   "As I regain my moral," quoted in Cook, *Volume One*, p. 76.

DAUGHTER, 1932–36

153:   "most momentous decision," Cook, *Volume Two*, p. 23.

154:   "many shortcomings," Roosevelt, *Africa*, p. viii.

154:   "was the one great love," ibid.

154:   "Although it was not," Cook, *Volume Two*, p. 24.

155:   "most extraordinary tribute," ibid.

155:   "When you come," quoted in ibid.

155:   "There was no heat," quoted in ibid.

156:   "After all, this is the richest," quoted in ibid.

156:   "we will have to pay," quoted in ibid., p. 11.

156:   "end the worldwide depression," ibid., p. 11.

157:   "With her activist team," ibid., p. 12.

158:   "complex," Cook, *Volume One*, p. 374.

158:   "ER had hoped," ibid., p. 347.

158:   "she now believed that," ibid., p. 374.

159:   "Eleanor, on the other hand," ibid., p. 346.

160:   "great majority of the working women," quoted in Lash, *Eleanor and Franklin*, pp. 309–10.

160:   "The battle for the 48-hour law," ibid., p. 310.

161:   "Although it did not last," Beasley, et.al., *Encyclopedia*, p. 44.

161:   "But Eleanor, darling," quoted in Lash, *Eleanor and Franklin*, p. 346.

162:   "Franklin was the politician," ibid., p. 348.

162:   "She is not doing the President," quoted in Smith, *FDR*, pp. 402–03.

162:   "Some of Roosevelt's closest advisers," Lash, *Eleanor and Franklin*, p. 346.

163:   "Roosevelt receptions and parties," ibid., p. 376.

163:    "'a Washington cave dweller,'" ibid., p. 376

163:    "delighted to know," quoted in ibid., p. 357.

163:    "the most influential woman," Rowley, *Franklin and Eleanor*, p. 219.

163:    "became the most outspoken first lady," ibid., p. xiv.

164:    "the wisdom of the serpent," quoted in ibid., p. 219.

164:    "as much as her husband," Lash, *Eleanor and Franklin*, pp. 377–78.

165:    "He was a showman," ibid., p. 344.

166:    "she could entertain," www.nps.gov/nr/travel/presidents/eleanor_ Roosevelt_valkill.html.

166:    "where I used to find myself," quoted in ibid.

166:    "They hoped to train," ibid.

FATHER, 1891

169:    "a maniac morally," "a flagrant man-swine," quoted in Ward, *Trumpet*. p. 275.

170:    "not large-souled enough," quoted in "Elliott, the Tragic Roosevelt," *HVRR*, p. 24.

171:    "no longer denied sleeping," Morris, *Rise of Theodore Roosevelt*, p. 439.

171:    "realized that if [Katy Mann's] claim was true," Brands, *T.R.*, p. 247.

171:    "hideous revelation hangs over me," quoted in ibid.

172:    "to help raise her child," quoted in Cook, *Volume One*, p. 60.

172:    "if she can make out at all," quoted in ibid.

173:    "If you and I were alone," quoted in Morris, *Rise of Theodore Roosevelt*, p. 439.

174:    "expert in likenesses," quoted in Miller, *Theodore Roosevelt*, p; 217.

174:    "Rooseveltian features," quoted in Collier and Horowitz, *The Roosevelts*, p. 282.

174:    "he believed [alcoholism]," Morris, *Rise of Theodore Roosevelt*, p. 430.

174:    "little short of criminal," quoted in ibid., p. 275.

175:    "[w]hatever settlement was reached," Cook, *Volume One*, p. 65n.

176:    "He drank like a fish," McCullough, *Horseback*, p. 247.

176:    "rhapsodies of an idyllic time," Cook, *Volume Two*, p. 64.

177:    "He and Anna walked," ibid.

179:    "'Oh, my dear father," Dickens, *Hard Times*, p. 37.

DAUGHTER, 1920s–1950s

181:    "was forever attracted to people," Cook, *Volume One*, p. 4.

181: "felt understood and loved," ibid., p. 39.

182: "I became a much more ardent citizen," Roosevelt, *My Story*, p. 297.

182: "What housewife can detect," quoted in Cook, *Volume Two*, p. 64.

182: "became the most influential," ibid.

183: "Luckily, I went," Roosevelt, *My Story*, p. 109.

183: "It had never occurred," ibid.

184: "I explained that I had had," ibid., p. 324.

185: "Throughout the 1930s," ibid., p. 69.

185: "Long before her husband," Cook, *Volume One*, p. 17.

185: "When, as wife of the assistant secretary," Cook, *Volume Two*, p. 317.

185: "[t]he Jew party appalling," ibid.

186: "tinged with a vague sense," ibid.

186: "He thought her gracious," ibid., p. 318.

187: "ER was disturbed," ibid., p. 285.

187: "old lady Roosevelt," Lee, *Watchman*, p. 110.

187: "[h]er views changed slowly," Cook, *Volume One*, p. 6.

188: "was among the first to see," ibid., pp. 16–17.

188: "I was told this morning," quoted in Cook, *Volume Two*, p. 349.

188: "Alas as I was reading," quoted in ibid.

189: "offensive to many of your readers," quoted in ibid.

189: "I am terribly sorry," quoted in ibid.

189: "The colored race has the gift," Roosevelt, *Story*, pp. 295–96.

189: "about as aggressive," quoted in Lash, *Alone*, p. 258.

190: "that President Eisenhower," ibid., p. 259.

FATHER, 1892–93

191: "the most sympathetic," Brands, *T.R.*, p. 258.

191: "went voluntarily into exile," Miller, *Theodore Roosevelt*, p. 218.

192: "One evening, drunk and naked," "Elliott, the Tragic Roosevelt," *HVRR*, p. 25.

192: "Dear little Nell," *FDR-L*, box 68.

192: "Dear little Nel," *FDR-L*, box 5.

193: "a sprawling old Virginia village," *RT-D*, Wilson, Goodridge.

194: "My little Darling Daughter," *FDR-L*, box 8.

194: "My darling little Nell," ibid.

194: "Please write to me soon," ibid.

196: "lived for Elliott's letters," Miller, *Theodore Roosevelt*, p. 219.

196:   "A child stood at a window," quoted by Goodwin, *Bully Pulpit*, p. 93.

197:   "The Robinson properties," Lash, *Eleanor and Franklin*, p. 39.

198:   "a very stiff and formal," *RT-D*, p. 2.

199:   "He dropped into homes," Lash, *Eleanor and Franklin*, pp. 39–40.

200:   "This letter from Elliott," quoted in ibid., p. 40.

200:   "a lovely old lady," "A Spiral into Darkness," *TF*, p. 7.

200:   "to drive with him," ibid., p. 8.

201:   "an independent and willful child," Cook, *Volume One*, p. 71.

202:   "had no intention of turning," ibid., pp. 71–2.

202:   "I have not found one," quoted in ibid., p. 83.

203:   "more time on her tree limb," ibid., p. 85.

205:   "Though he was so little with us," Eleanor Roosevelt, *My Story*, pp. 29–30.

205:   "They would spend the day," Collier and Horowitz, *The Roosevelts*, p. 87.

205:   "On the way to Central Park," Lash, *Eleanor and Franklin*, p. 51.

DAUGHTER, 1936-62

208:   "He said he felt sure," Eleanor Roosevelt, *My Story*, p. 177.

208:   "I dictate it directly," ibid., p. 178.

209:   "I wonder if anyone," Eleanor Roosevelt, *My Day, Volume I*, p. 3.

209:   "I often wonder," Eleanor Roosevelt, *My Day, Volume III*, p. 318.

209:   "Never before has a sudden change," Eleanor Roosevelt, *My Day, Volume I*, p. 396.

210:   "I can quite understand," Eleanor Roosevelt, *My Day, Volume II*. pp. 129–30.

210:   "It is certainly almost breathtaking," Eleanor Roosevelt, *My Day, Volume III*, p. 275.

211:   "I was usually shy," Eleanor Roosevelt, *My Day, Volume II*, p. 170.

212:   "as one woman to another," quoted in Lash, *Eleanor and Franklin*, p. 373.

212:   "In 1933 I Think We Were a People," *Look*, May 23, 1939, p. 6.

213:   "the strongest argument," quoted in *New York Times Magazine*, p. 312.

214:   "tea with Mrs. Roosevelt," Lash, *Alone*, p. 184.

214:   "It was a chore for which," ibid., p. 304.

215:   "Selby shoes, a mattress company," Cook, *Volume Two*, p. 202.

215:   "The money I earned," Eleanor Roosevelt, *Remember*, p. 14.

216:   "On 8 November in Philadelphia," Cook, *Volume Two*, p. 388.

216:   "It would be easy," quoted in ibid., p. 389.

217:   "Isn't it ironical," quoted in Elliott Roosevelt and Brough, *Mother R*, p. 250.

FATHER, 1892–94

219:   "My darling little Daughter," FDR-L, box 8.

220:   "her frail health [had been] broken," Morris, *Rise of Theodore Roosevelt*, p. 456.

220:   "DO NOT COME," quoted in ibid.

221:   "It is too awful," quoted in Cook, *Volume One*, p. 77.

221:   "consuming up to six bottles," "A Spiral into Darkness," *TF*, p. 6.

222:   "She was one of the most beautiful," *NYT*, December 9, 1892, p. 5.

223:   "Elliott wept at the sight," *Loving Memory*, p. 25.

223:   "drank immoderately, sang bawdy songs," Smith, *FDR*, p. 43.

223:   "Eleanor's account of her mother's death," Lash, *Eleanor and Franklin*, p. 44.

225:   "He sat in a big chair," Eleanor Roosevelt, *My Story*, p. 20.

227:   "They are both in the armchair," quoted in ibid., pp. 25–26.

227:   "Darling little Daughter," FDR-L, box 1.

228:   "was simply too good," Eleanor Roosevelt, *My Story*, p. 32.

228:   "My own little Nell," FDR-L, box 1.

229:   "My thoughts and sympathy," FDR-L, box 6.

229:   "My darling little Nell," FDR-L, box 1.

230:   "safe in heaven," quoted in Cook, *Volume One*, p. 84.

230:   "Our Lord wants Ellie boy," ibid.

230:   "of joy and sorrow," FDR-L, box 6.

231:   "like some stricken, hunted creature," quoted in McCullough, *Horseback*, p. 369.

231:   "he spent the night," Smith, *FDR*, p. 43.

231:   "He can't be helped," quoted in ibid.

232:   "Dear Father," FDR-L, box 6

DAUGHTER, 1948–59

234:   "not in the tradition," *NYT*, October 13, 1948.

234:   "She kept the job," Elliott Roosevelt and Brough, *Mother R*, pp. 90–91.

234:   "erupted in a case," ibid., p. 91.

235:   "The unchangeable subject there," ibid., p. 91–92.

236:   "by the victims beyond tally," Cook, *Volume One*, p. 17.

236:   "Some meetings left her dazed," Elliott Roosevelt and Brough, *Mother R*, p. 142.

237:   "Where, after all," quoted in Cook, *Volume One*, p. 18.

238:   "She was received," Lash, *Alone*, p. 192.

238:   "Just as she was a reassuring symbol," ibid., p. 194.

238:   "She visited industrial and agricultural cooperatives," ibid., p. 205.

238:   "a moving experience," quoted in ibid., p. 225.

239:   "she was feted," ibid., pp. 229–30.

239:   "toured archeological diggings," ibid., p. 231.

239:   "You cannot meet this man," quoted in ibid., p. 232.

240:   "'Little Nell,'" Elliott [the father] had told her," Elliott Roosevelt and Brough, p. 192.

240:   "to see this vast," Lash, *Alone*, p. 32.

240:   "everything you wanted to see," quoted in ibid., p. 33.

241:   "The most important thing she learned," ibid., pp. 269–70.

241:   "In a loose-fitting suit," Elliott Roosevelt and Brough, *Mother R*, p. 246.

242:   ". . . I want to speak of President Franklin Roosevelt," quoted in ibid., p. 246.

242:   "Mother proceeded to business," ibid.

242:   "Sometimes, the discussion grew sharp," ibid., p. 246.

243:   "a moment of the deepest solemnity," Lash, *Alone*, p. 272.

243:   "They call me a dictator," quoted in Elliott Roosevelt and Brough, *Mother R*, p. 249.

244:   "One for the road!" quoted in ibid., p. 249.

244:   "Tell your wife and daughter," FDR-L, box 48.

244:   "the young, hawk-eyed shah," Elliott Roosevelt and Brough, *Mother R*, p. 173.

244:   "a country of sand," ibid.

245:   "What do you contemplate?" quoted in ibid., p. 174.

245:   "Mother was of an age," ibid., p. 176.

FATHER, 1894

248:   "Goodby dear dear Father," quoted in Lash, *Eleanor and Franklin*, p. 55.

248:   "all the dear home people," quoted in "Elliott, the Tragic Roosevelt," *HVRR*, p. 27.

248: "he drove his carriage," Rowley, *Franklin and Eleanor*, p. 11.

248: "I hope my little girl," quoted in ibid., p. 14.

248: "quite ill," quoted in ibid.

248: "*never forget* I love you," quoted in Cook, *Volume One*, p. 88.

249: "The exact circumstances," "A Spiral into Darkness," *TF*, p. 6.

249: "heart disease," *NYT*, August 16, 1894, p. 4.

249: "was unexpected, although he had been somewhat ailing," ibid.

250: "The curtains of No. 313 West 102nd Street," *NYW*, August 16, 1894.

251: "I only need to have," quoted in Lash, *Eleanor and Franklin*, p. 56.

251: "more overcome than I have ever seen him," quoted in Cook, *Volume One*, pp. 88–89.

252: "I've been sadly wondering," quoted in ibid., p. 90.

252: "[a] tender exchange," ibid.

252: "What! You would kiss me?" quoted in ibid.

252: "hideous plan," quoted in Morris, *Rise of Theodore Roosevelt*, p. 474.

252: "beside those who are associated," quoted in ibid.

252: "the woman," quoted in ibid.

253: "behaved perfectly well," quoted in ibid.

253: "but I simply refused," Eleanor Roosevelt, *Autobiography*, p. 13.

253: "began the next day," ibid.

253: "My grandmother decided," quoted in Lash, *Eleanor and Franklin*, p. 57.

253: "By his death," ibid.

254: "her own sense of reality," ibid.

254: "become closed, withdrawn," ibid, p. 58.

254: "Although idolization of her father," ibid.

DAUGHTER, 1952-62

256: "She urged Stevenson," Lash, *Alone*, p. 242.

257: "the subject of the president," ibid., p. 318.

258: "You have to realize," quoted in ibid., p. 322.

258: "The illness would flicker," ibid.

258: "in some sense," Collier and Horowitz, *The Roosevelts*, p. 469.

258: "a disease, ironically," ibid.

259: "extreme remedies," ibid.

259: "No, David, I want to die," quoted in ibid.

259: "Utter nonsense," quoted in Lash, *Alone*, p. 331.

259: "looking at the intravenous tube," ibid.

259: "her strong heart," ibid., p. 332.

260: "What other single human being," *NYT*, November 7, 2012, "50 Years After Her Life, Eleanor Roosevelt's Admirers Will Celebrate Her Life," by David W. Dunlap.

TWO LEGACIES

263: "outstanding woman of 1937," quoted in Cook, *Volume Two*, p. 484.

263: "provide a practicable means," quoted in Cook, *Volume One*, p. 342.

263: "more than 300 scholars," quoted in search.proquest.com/ christianscienc-emonitor.pintviewfile?acc.

264: "People who lived on," Lash, *Eleanor and Franklin*, p. 46.

265: "I knew a child once," quoted in ibid., p. 46.

266: "Attention, attention," Arthur Miller, *Death of A Salesman*, p. 112.

EPILOGUE: THE GOODNIGHT KISS

267: "We stand today," Roosevelt, Eleanor, "On the Adoption of the Universal Declaration of Human Rights," www.americanrhetoric.com/speeches/eleanorrooseveltdeclarationhumanrights.htm.

268: "stands to this day," "Eleanor Roosevelt's Legacy," *NYT*, p. 27.

268: "She knew its words," ibid.

INDEX

ERIC BURNS is a former correspondent for NBC News and the TODAY Show. For ten years he was the host of the top-rated "Fox News Watch," and he has won an Emmy for media criticism. He is the author of *The Golden Lad: The Haunting Story of Quentin and Theodore Roosevelt, 1920: The Year that Made the Decade Roar*, a *Kirkus Reviews* "Best Book of the Year," *Infamous Scribblers, The Spirits of America*, and *The Smoke of the Gods*, and the latter two were named "Best of the Best" by the American Library Association. Eric lives in Westport, Connecticut.